Presidential Saints and Sinners

Presidential Saints and Sinners

Thomas A. Bailey

THE FREE PRESS
A Division of Macmillan Publishing Co., Inc.
NEW YORK

Collier Macmillan Publishers
LONDON

THE FREE PRESS
A Division of Macmillan Publishing Co., Inc.
866 Third Avenue, New York, N.Y.   10022

Collier Macmillan Canada, Ltd.

Library of Congress Catalog Number: 81-67159

Printed in the United States of America

Printing number

2 3 4 5 6 7 8 9 10

Library of Congress Cataloging in Publication Data

Bailey, Thomas Andrew
    Presidential saints and sinners.

    Bibliography: p.
    Includes index.
    1. Presidents—United States. 2. Political ethics.
I. Title.
E176.1.B173   973'.09'92   81-67159
ISBN 0-02-901330-5   AACR2

Contents

Preface

My interest in the White House goes back to my eighth birthday, when my mother presented me with a book for juveniles titled *Lives of Our Presidents* (1903) which I still cherish. Hardbound, it contains 254 printed pages and sold new for 45 cents. In mature years I have touched upon the presidents in a number of general works on American history, particularly foreign affairs. I deal with them more intimately in a book titled *Presidential Greatness*, which was published in 1966. I then concluded that the game of categorizing the chief executives precisely as Great, Near Great, Average, Below Average, or Failure is about as meaningful as comparing horses with cows, pears with oranges, or apple pie with pizza. All the presidents have had their strong points and their weak points, and no two incumbents were ever confronted with precisely the same problems in exactly the same manner. Comparing unlikes may be fun as a parlor game, but it is not intellectually satisfying.

My second book on the presidents was titled *The Pugnacious Presidents: White House Warriors on Parade* (1980). I was chiefly concerned with foreign affairs, a lifelong interest, and more particularly how the presidents reacted to assaults on American lives and property abroad, including involvement in foreign wars. Two of the presidents who were most pugnacious in their private lives,

Andrew Jackson and Theodore Roosevelt, were lucky enough not to embroil their nation in a major foreign conflict, but some of their less bellicose predecessors and successors did. These others were unfortunate enough to be residing in the White House when major foreign conflicts were raging into which the United States was eventually sucked.

The present book deals primarily with presidential integrity, which is here regarded as including such virtues as soundness of moral principles, honesty, uprightness, trustworthiness, truthfulness, and an avoidance of deviousness or calculated deception. Where relevant, some passing attention is given to an incumbent's adulterous misconduct, partly because there are those who believe that a man who will break his marriage vows may the more easily break his inaugural oath. That oath reads, "I do solemnly swear (or affirm) that I will faithfully execute the office of the President of the United States, and will to the best of my ability preserve, protect and defend the Constitution of the United States."

It is something of a truism that only great men can err greatly. A President in public life, unlike a citizen in private life, holds a position from which he can affect, for weal or woe, the lives of the great mass of people resident in the United States. Unfortunately for him, he is inevitably blamed, often unfairly, for the shortcomings of the subordinates whom he has appointed, but on whom he could not possibly ride herd at all times.

I was prompted to write this present book partly because the many supporters of former President Richard Nixon have loudly claimed that whatever he had done wrong, his predecessors had also done.Hence the movement to impeach him was condemned as "all politics." This excuse is only partially valid, and what is recorded here should do something to end the argument, while shedding a flood of light on the other presidents.

For a critical reading of all or part of the present manuscript I am indebted to Captain Paul B. Ryan, my collaborator in preparing *The Lusitania Disaster* (1975) and *Hitler vs. Roosevelt* (1979), and also to my esteemed colleague, Professor Don E. Fehrenbacher.

THOMAS A. BAILEY
History Department
Stanford University, California

Presidential Saints and Sinners

CHAPTER 1

George Washington
1789–1797

I hope I shall always possess firmness and virtue enough to maintain (what I consider the most enviable of all titles) the character of an honest man.

George Washington,
August 28, 1788

George Washington towered like a giant among the founding fathers. In commanding the American army before and during the War of Independence, he risked his reputation, his fortune, and his life. As the leading rebel, the incarnation of the patriot cause, he almost literally thrust his head into the hangman's noose. Without his inspirational influence and steadfastness, the cause that he led could hardly have triumphed.

Washington returned to the quiet of his beloved Mount Vernon after the war, but was deeply disturbed by a rash of localized outbursts that the weak national government, then under the Articles of Confederation, was powerless to control. Most alarming of all was an uprising of impoverished farmers in Massachusetts, many of them war veterans, headed by Captain Daniel Shays. This rebellion was finally quelled by the state authorities with considerable difficulty. "Good God!" wrote Washington in private regarding these disorders, "who, besides a Tory, could have foreseen, or a Briton have predicted them?"

The impotent government under the Articles of Confederation plainly needed strengthening. Washington was among those respected leaders who had a large hand in assembling in Philadelphia a constitutional convention to hammer out a new charter—actually to substitute a brand new constitution for the scorned Articles of Confederation. Washington was quickly chosen presiding officer, and although he did not join in the learned debates, his august presence was necessary to keep the delegates from flying at one another's throats. He who had commanded the Continental armies commanded respect, and his personality did much to cool off the heated arguments. The final charter that emerged did not please him in all respects, but he gave it his indispensable support because he regarded it as the best constitution obtainable in those contentious times.

The document endorsed by Washington was a conservative compact designed to avert anarchy and to preserve the precious gains for democracy growing out of the relatively recent revolutionary war. Put bluntly, the system of checks and balances devised at the constitutional convention in Philadelphia was designed in part to keep the lower classes under restraints, while permitting a reasonable degree of democratic control.

When the framing fathers at Philadelphia created the powerful office of the presidency, they suffered grave misgivings as to the wisdom of conferring such awesome authority on a mere mortal. The colonials had rid themselves of one objectionable king, and there seemed little point in subjecting themselves to a homegrown autocrat disguised as a President.

The answer to this problem was obviously General George Washington. Indeed, a number of the delegates reluctantly consented to the creation of a constitutional presidency in the hope and expectation that the Savior of His Country would consent to serve. He had heeded the call to military duty in 1775; he would heed the call to civilian duty in 1788. He had served without pay as commander in chief, although keeping a detailed expense account for reimbursement. At times he had exercised virtual dictatorial powers, and when peace came he had spurned all suggestions that he become a monarch. What he really wanted was the peace and quiet of his beloved Mount Vernon.

When the constitution of 1787 went out to the thirteen states for ratification, many solid citizens were disturbed, not to say appalled, by the lodgment of so much power in the hands of a mortal man. The most satisfying answer to these doubts was the response that Washington would consent to serve, and he was indisputably a leader who had amply demonstrated his trustworthiness. Even so, ratification of the new constitution was achieved by a disturbingly narrow margin, and with two states, Rhode Island and North Carolina, refusing to join the union until literally coerced into acceptance by the powerful new central government in 1789–1790.

Washington neither sought nor wanted the presidency, and in this respect was evidently unique in American experience. He was also unique in that he was twice elected unanimously by the Electoral College, in both instances contrary to his innermost desires and wishes. But his sense of duty was compelling, as it had been during his eight controversial years as commander of the American rebel armies. After finally accepting his unanimous election, he wrote privately, "My movements to the chair of government will be accompanied by feelings not unlike those of a culprit, who is going to the place of his execution." He fully realized that he was "embarking" his good name "on this voyage."

Before traveling to New York, the temporary capital, to take the inaugural oath, Washington was forced to borrow money to meet personal obligations and to pay his official traveling expenses. Although reputed to be one of the richest men in the new nation, he was in fact "land poor" in the sense that a large portion of his wealth was invested in non-liquid acreage, much of it speculative. He flatly declined a presidential salary, as he had refused pay as the commanding general during the War of Independence. In both cases he submitted detailed expense accounts for reimbursement. When he was President the Congress voted him the inadequate sum of $25,000, which was used for expense money. Washington was an aristocrat who believed that proper respect for his high office required him to keep up appearances in public. The transition from a monarchy to a republic was not easy, and as he rode by in the presidential coach a citizen was heard to cry, "God bless your reign."

Probably no president was ever more scrupulously honest than George Washington. As he wrote to James Madison in 1785, "It is an old adage, that honesty is the best policy. This applies to public as well as private life, to States as well as individuals." Yet cynics have noted that the schemer who chooses honesty simply because it is the most profitable policy is not completely honest.

Washington's choice of the straight and narrow path of righteousness was easier as the result of special circumstances. Because the office came to him unsought, he did not have to make campaign promises or raise "dirty" money. In 1789, when Washington first took the inaugural oath, political parties as we know them today did not exist. There had been loyalists (Tories) and rebels (Whigs) during the revolutionary war, but these factions were virtually silenced when the war was won. During the fight over the ratification of the Constitution, from 1787 to 1788, there had been two opposing camps, pro-Constitution centralists and anti-Constitution states-righters. With ratification completed, these former adversaries naturally joined other groups. Not until 1792–1793, several years after Washington's inauguration, did two full-fledged parties emerge: the Hamiltonian Federalists and the Jeffersonian Republicans, also called Democratic-Republicans.

Never having sought the presidential office, Washington was in a better position than his successors to avoid passing out jobs as rewards for political support. His primary purpose was to put into federal office only those who were in sympathy with the centralizing objectives of the new Constitution. As Washington wrote to Timothy Pickering on September 27, 1793, "I shall not, whilst I have the honor to administer the government, bring a man into any office of consequence knowingly, whose political tenets are adverse to the measures, which the general government are pursuing; for this, in my opinion, would be a sort of political suicide."

Pursuant to the first President's policy, a considerable number of men who had sat in the Philadelphia constitutional convention or in the state ratifying conventions moved to the national capital to take federal offices and to help launch the new government. Verily the Ark of the Covenant was in the house of friends.

It is difficult to find anything wrong, in ethics or in politics, with Washington's decision to work with men who were sympathetic with his general objectives. He unwittingly made one mistake when he chose Jefferson as his secretary of state, for the talented Virginian had been the American minister to France during the fight over ratifying the Constitution, and his strong support of states' rights was not well known. Alexander Hamilton, appointed Secretary of the Treasury, had been present at the Philadelphia constitutional convention and was conspicuously favorable to a powerful central government. The result was a series of verbal clashes between Jefferson and Hamilton in Washington's three-man cabinet, with the President himself acting as a kind of moderator or referee.

Secretary Hamilton, in his spectacularly successful efforts to revive the public credit, managed to persuade Congress to assume the revolutionary debts of the states, incurred in the common cause, and also to redeem depreciated federal securities at par. Although Congress passed this legislation on Hamilton's recommendation, the stench of scandal accompanied this financial transaction. As fate would have it, some holders of the semiworthless obligations sat in the Congress that approved the "funding" or redemption of the national debt at par.

Greedy speculators soon mounted fast horses and clattered into the rural areas, where the news of funding at par had not penetrated, and bought up the despised government obligations at depreciated prices. Some of the victims were even veterans who had fought the British in the recent War of Independence. But Hamilton was willing to accept scandal as the price to pay for establishing a sound national credit. Probably the holders of depreciated securities in Congress were happy that this promotion of the public interest coincided with promoting their own personal interests. Even so, the scandalous situation was created by Hamilton and Congress, not by President Washington.

Allegations of a much larger scandal were spelled out sensationally and at great length in 1913 in Charles A. Beard's *An Economic Interpretation of the Constitution of the United States.* He argued that the founding fathers who framed the constitution in 1787 were overwhelmingly men of prominence and wealth who owned real estate, businesses, or depreciated securities. If the nation's economy got back on a sound footing under a new charter, they were bound to gain financially.

This is a classic case of the irregularity known in recent times as a "conflict of interest," which has spawned legislation requiring many officeholders to disclose the sources and amount of their wealth. In a related area, for many years judges have felt under a heavy obligation to disqualify themselves from acting on cases in which they were personally or financially involved.

Does it make sense to suggest that George Washington chaired the constitutional convention of 1787 because he wanted to line his own pockets? Here was the man, perhaps the richest in the nation, who had served his country during the War of Independence without pay, and who later refused to accept a salary as president, an office that he did not want.

The basic facts are crystal clear. The nation was in desperate shape in 1787, and the time had come for the ablest leaders to sink their differences and pool their talents in a convention. If all men of wealth and position had disqualified themselves because of a conflict of interest, there probably would have been no convention, or if there had been one of laboring men, it probably would have broken up in confusion, as it almost did anyhow. The crisis called for all good men to come to the aid of their country, and these men did, even the wealthy ones.

After a long and bitter struggle, the Constitution was barely ratified by the necessary two-thirds of the states, and without the approval of Rhode Island and North Carolina. What would have been the fate of a constitution hammered out by a convention of blacksmiths and shopkeepers? Some critics of the founding fathers have also seen something scandalous in the fact that many members of the constitutional convention or the state ratifying conventions moved on to the nation's capital to accept offices under the new federal government.

What was wrong with this? Washington had taken on a solemn obligation to make the new government work, and he was not going to enlist on the new ship of state a crew of potential wreckers. The course that he insisted on taking was consonant with the oath he had just taken to uphold the new and untried Constitution of the United States.

Unaware of Thomas Jefferson's devotion to states' rights, Washington miscalculated when he named his fellow Virginian Secretary of State. This maverick cabinet member served the president for nearly four years, during whch he engaged in heated debates with the strongly nationalistic Alexander Hamilton. In fact, the head-on collision between these two gifted leaders resulted in the crystallizing of the nation's political parties in 1792–1793. They were the Federalists of Alexander Hamilton, who favored a powerful central or federal government, and the Democratic-Republicans of Thomas Jefferson, who advocated greater respect for states' rights and the common people. President Washington, born an aristocrat, found himself increasingly drawn to the Hamiltonian Federalists, and as a result began to be showered by the brickbats of Jeffersonian Democratic-Republicans. He wrote to Jefferson on July 6, 1796, "I was not a party man myself, and the first wish of my heart was, if parties did exist, to reconcile them."

Secretary of the Treasury Hamilton seems to have been a scrupulously honest man as far as his personal financial dealings were concerned. But he further brought the smirch of scandal to the Washington administration while administering the Treasury Department. He appointed to second place in this department an intimate friend but a notorious speculator, William Duer. The appointee lasted only six months and then resigned, but the Treasury under Hamilton failed to press him for some $200,000 owed the government. The defaulting Duer went on to precipitate the first financial panic in the history of New York, and he died in a debtor's prison.

Meanwhile, on July 14, 1789, about ten weeks after Washington's inauguration, the maddened masses of Paris had risen in revolt and stormed the frowning Bastille. The French revolution, which many Americans hailed as the second chapter of their own glorious uprising, had now burst forth, and in America the love-frenzy for France began to run its course. France had been the valued ally during the War of Independence, and President Washington was not unfriendly to the revolution, at least not in its earlier phases. But he was sickened by the bloodstained excesses of the guillotine, as were other conservative Federalists. Yet the Jeffersonian Republicans, speaking for the poorer classes, rejoiced over the downfall of the French aristocracy.

Early in 1793 revolutionary France declared war on monarchical Great Britain and Holland, and lasting peace was not to come to Europe until the battle of Waterloo in 1815. President Washington was faced with a critical ethical decision: France had fought side by side with the Americans in the War of Independence against Great Britain, and the Jeffersonian Republicans, speaking for the masses, clamored for repayment of the debt to Lafayette. But Washington realized fully that a weak and faction-rent American republic was in no condition to plunge into another war, even to help an old friend. He therefore issued a proclamation of neutrality, dated April 22, 1793, in which he declared that America would remain aloof during the Anglo-French hostilities.

The pro-French Jeffersonians were enraged by what they

regarded as this dishonorable act. They charged that Washington
had proved treacherously unfaithful to an old ally, and so it
seemed on the surface. The Treaty of Alliance of 1778 specifically
stipulated that in any future war the United States would "forever" assist France in the defense of her French West Indies.
Washington must have felt that strict neutrality was not the most
honorable course, but he was prepared to sacrifice a degree of
national honor to what he conceived to be the best interests of the
adolescent United States.

Fortunately for Washington's sterling reputation, the Paris
government never asked its American ally to involve itself in the
great Anglo-French War. The United States then was totally without a navy, and hence in no position to help defend the French
West Indies. But the Americans were able to use their considerable merchant marine to supply foodstuffs to these islands, and
in this hazardous way keep them from being starved out. So the
formal demand for assistance was never made by the Paris government.

It is traditional to blame the president for the misdeeds of
major appointees, including members of the cabinet. Yet this
practice is not altogether fair, because the chief executive cannot
possibly watch every move of every member of his official family,
even a small one, as was Washington's tiny group. Two scandals
surfaced regarding prominent cabinet members, one during
Washington's lifetime, and the other more than a century later.

First was the alleged misconduct of Edmund Randolph, the
Virginia statesman who succeeded Thomas Jefferson as secretary
of state. On the basis of rather flimsy evidence, it is supposed that
Randolph offered to foment civil strife in America in return for
a bribe by the French minister. When called onto the carpet by
President Washington under humiliating circumstances, Randolph resigned. He then wrote a lengthy vindication in which he
attacked the President's devious handling of the problem. As
could be expected, the French Minister in question denied that
anything improper had taken place. It is possible that Washington
overreacted so as to combat any possible accusation of dishonorable conduct directed at his administration.

The second major cabinet scandal, involving Secretary of the
Treasury Hamilton, proved much more serious but was not fully
revealed until the principals were all dead. In the spring of 1794
relations with England had neared the breaking point, largely as

a result of British seizures of American ships supplying the French West Indies with foodstuffs and other necessities. Federalist John Jay was chosen by President Washington to journey to London and there secure concessions from Great Britain regarding the disputes at issue. The United States, lacking a navy, held low cards in this diplomatic game, but there were rumors that President Washington would join with Sweden and Denmark in a "new armed neutrality," and thus wring concessions from Britain regarding neutral rights.

The proposed coalition was so weak that President Washington, after cabinet discussions, decided not to join it. But the pro-British Secretary Hamilton feared that this bluff might be used by negotiator John Jay anyhow, with a consequent ruinous war. He therefore committed the gross indiscretion of secretly informing the British Minister in America that the threat of the new armed neutrality was meaningless. Thus the only ace that Jay held—and it was a weak one—was rendered ineffective by the treacherously underhanded doings of Hamilton, who was clandestinely designated by the British intelligence operatives as "Agent Number 7."

Jay finally concluded a treaty late in 1794, but it proved to be the most unpopular of his career and of President Washington's eight years in high office. Yet it is noteworthy that Great Britain, only eleven years after the War of Independence, should have condescended to make any kind of treaty with her ungrateful and rebellious offspring. Jay's treaty did refer the questions of damages for recent seizures of American shipping and other disputes to arbitration, yet nothing was said about future seizures. In addition, the United States agreed to arrangements that were contrary to at least the spirit of the nation's treaty commitments of 1778 with France. Henceforth American foodstuffs destined for French ports might be seized by British warships, if paid for, and French property on American ships might also be confiscated.

The pro-French following of Thomas Jefferson—the Democratic-Republicans—was outraged by this alleged betrayal of a friend and ally. The American negotiator of the treaty with England was widely burned or guillotined in effigy as "that damned arch-traitor, Sir John Jay."

As a man of unstained honor, President Washington was sorely troubled by Jay's treaty. He fully recognized that common gratitude, if not the precise terminology of a treaty engagement, was involved. A nation, like an individual, was expected to conduct itself in such a way as not to discriminate against a valued friend, France, in favor of an ancient foe, Great Britain. The French, in fact, made no secret of their extreme displeasure.

Yet rejection of Jay's unsatisfactory treaty would almost certainly end in a renewal of America's war with England, a conflict that had formally ended only eleven years earlier. War with Britain probably would bring Hamilton's towering financial structure down in ruins, for much of its support depended on customs duties from British imports. In short, favoritism for France would jeopardize the new republic and run counter to President Washington's presidential oath to "preserve, protect and defend the Constitution of the United States."

When these two concepts of honor collided, President Washington, after painful deliberation, chose the one that favored his own country, of which he was often declared to be the father. His great influence narrowly got Jay's treaty through the Senate, and then he pushed the appropriation bill, also narrowly, through the House. But he paid a price among the more outspoken Jeffersonian Republicans. "Damn George Washington!" was the impassioned toast of John Randolph of Virginia. Even Jefferson expressed himself so intemperately as to write in a private letter to Philip Mazzei (April 24, 1796) that was soon made public, "Curse on his [Washington's] virtues; they have undone the country." Jefferson then went on to bracket Washington with those persons "who have had their heads shorn by the harlot England."

Before this letter was published, President Washington wrote to Jefferson (July 6, 1796) complaining of the lengths to which partisans would go while the government was attempting to establish "a national character of our own." Seeking to make the United States independent of all nations, the President was being "accused of being the enemy of one nation [France] and subject to the influence of another [England]." He had not dreamed that "every act of my administration would be tortured, and the grossest and most insidious misrepresentations of them be made, by giving one side only of a subject, and that too in such exaggerated and indecent terms as could scarcely be applied to a Nero, a notorious defaulter, or even to a common pickpocket." Republics are indeed notoriously ungrateful.

Washington probably could have had a third term, if he had wanted it. But he was weary and resentful of partisan abuse; he wanted nothing so much as to return to a long-deferred retirement at Mount Vernon. In his famous farewell address he deplored the dangers of excessive partisanship (of which he had been a victim), and warned against "permanent" alliances with foreign nations, (in reference to the treaty of 1778 with France), excessive emotional attachment to any foreign country (France and Britain), and foreign intermeddling.

Washington's departure from the presidential office evoked some bitter blasts from the editors of journals supported by Jeffersonian Republicans. These critics rejoiced over the end of the "reign" of the Stepfather of His Country. But as partisan passions cooled, Washington was universally recognized as a man of sterling integrity. Thomas Jefferson, who had known him well, wrote in a letter of January 2, 1814, about eighteen years later: "His integrity was most pure, his justice the most inflexible I have ever known, no motives of interest or consanguinity, of friendships or hate, being able to bias his decision. He was, indeed, in every sense of the word, a wise, a good, and a great man."

When Washington died in 1799, Congress adopted the resolution proposed by Colonel Henry Lee: "A citizen, first in war, first in peace, and first in the hearts of his countrymen." Alexander Hamilton who knew him well, wrote in a letter to Tobias Lear on January 2, 1800, two weeks after Washington's death, "If virtue can secure happiness in another world, he is happy."

CHAPTER 2

John Adams
1797–1801

I pray Heaven to bestow the best of blessings on this house [White House] and all who shall hereinafter inhabit it. May none but honest and wise men ever rule under this roof.

John Adams, letter to wife,
November 2, 1800

A crusty son of Massachusetts, sometimes referred to as "a chip off old Plymouth Rock," young John Adams was graduated from Harvard College. Suppressing inclinations to be a minister of the gospel, he turned to the profession of law, at a time when lawyers were widely regarded as unnecessary troublemakers. He became a profile in courage, particularly when he undertook to defend against charges of murder the British soldiers accused of shooting colonials in the so-called Boston Massacre of March 1770. In the teeth of public anger, he defended the captain and six soldiers, and although two were convicted of manslaughter, each of the twain was branded on one hand and released.

As the revolt against Britain gathered momentum, Adams served in the Continental Congress in 1774 and 1775, and there he proposed the name of George Washington as commander in chief of the colonial armies. More than that, Adams was one of the committee of five that drafted the Declaration of Independence in 1776. In 1778 he served as an envoy to Paris, where he took a disapproving view of aging Benjamin Franklin's dalliance, or attempted dalliance, with the French ladies. In 1782 he signed, with Franklin and two colleagues, the epochal treaty of peace with Great Britain, ratified in 1783.

While the peace negotiations in Paris were continuing, Adams journeyed to the Netherlands, where in 1782 he somehow managed to extract from the Dutch a favorable treaty of peace and commerce. He also performed the near miracle of securing a substantial loan from the ordinarily tight-fisted Dutch financiers.

After the peace treaty with Britain was signed in 1782, Adams served as the first United States minister in London, where he found the diplomatic atmosphere distinctly frosty. He would be frozen out of conferences with dead silence, for the British were not ready to kill the fatted calf for their rebellious offspring. As Adams wrote to John Jay late in 1785, "I am like to be as insignificant here as you can imagine." This cold-shoulder treatment went hard with Adams, who was vain and who suffered much of his life from the feeling that he was not being properly appreciated. In any event, he ranks high among all the presidents in the richness of his diplomatic experience before coming to high office.

Federalist John Adams and the Jeffersonian Republicans crossed political swords in the 1790s, so it is interesting to note Jefferson's early appraisal of the dour New Englander in the 1780s. In 1783 the Virginian wrote to James Madison concerning John Adams, "His vanity is a lineament in his character which had entirely escaped me. . . . He has a sound head on substantial points, and I think he has integrity." Four years later Jefferson again wrote to Madison saying, "He is vain, irritable, and a bad calculator of the force and probable effect of the motives which govern men. This is all the ill which can possibly be said of him."

In 1789 John Adams was named vice president, as a second fiddle to George Washington. The principal duty of the lesser official was the ghoulish one of being at hand in the event of the president's demise. The unappreciated John Adams took a bitter view of this hollow "honor," which he felt was not at all commensurate with his experience and achievements in public life. As he wrote his highly perceptive wife, Abigail, "My country has in its wisdom contrived for me the most insignificant office that ever the invention of man contrived or his imagination conceived."

Although operating jealously in the shadow of the towering Washington, John Adams served usefully throughout his eight years as vice president. As presiding officer of the Senate, he was able to exercise his tie-breaking powers on twenty separate votes —a unique experience. He habitually acted in support of Federalist legislation, for he came to the presidency as a stalwart Federalist. This stance is not surprising, for the Federalists were the party of the aristocrats, and Adams was certainly an intellectual aristocrat. The Federalists were naturally pro-British and anti-French, and Adams had come to dislike the French intensely during his days as a diplomat in Paris. On one occasion he haughtily told the French foreign minister, "The United States of America are a great and powerful people, whatever European statesmen may think of them."

John Adams succeeded Washington in 1797, after having won election over the Republican Thomas Jefferson by the narrow margin of three votes in the Electoral College. On Adams's doorstep lay a nasty break in relations with France, prompted largely by the anti-French Jay's treaty with Britain. So in mid-1797 Adams went so far as to send three commissioners to Paris, including the future chief justice, John Marshall, in the hope of settling differences by negotiation.

The trio of Americans was met by shadowy go-betweens from the French foreign minister, and these agents presented outrageous demands that would have to be met by the United States before serious negotiations could begin with the Paris Foreign Office. In addition to apologies for a recent message by Adams to Congress, the Americans would have to present a "gift" (bribe) of about $250,000 in American money and also contribute a loan of about $10 million, essentially a second bribe. The three envoys had neither this kind of money nor the instructions to expend it. Gravely affronted, they broke off the discussions in a huff, following which two of them returned to America as heroic upholders of the nation's honor.

The insulted envoys were greeted in America as conquering heroes. The slogan of the hour became "Millions for defense, but not one cent for tribute." Ironically, at this very time the United

States, lacking a navy, was sending barrels of American dollars to the Barbary pirates of North Africa as "protection money," or ransom for hostages.

Anti-French Federalist that he was, President Adams over-reacted to this affront to American honor. The French Foreign Office, with which bribes were commonplace, had not wanted to offend the Americans, and certainly it did not welcome war with the United States while already fully engaged with Great Britain. President Washington's Federalist policy, as inherited by Adams, was to avoid alliances and conflicts with Europe at all cost while the nation was still too young and weak to risk getting involved.

Yielding to his anti-French and pro-British bias, President Adams actually fed the flames of war. For perhaps the only time in his public life he savored the heady wine of real popularity, as crowds sang "Hail Columbia" and "Adams and Liberty." Mistakenly concluding that the three American envoys had been rejected, he urged Congress to pass such warlike measures as would provide protection for American seafaring interests. He would not give diplomacy another try, but would prepare for the hostilities that in his mistaken view France was trying to provoke with the United States. At this point he evidently wanted a formal declaration of war, but feared that the pro-French Republicans in Congress could muster enough votes to defeat it. In short, he was playing politics with the nation's honor, but like Alexander Hamilton he thought it wiser to permit France to declare hostilities first.

The pro-French Republicans in Congress could not believe that the three American envoys had been treated as rumored. They used their votes in the House of Representatives to pass a resolution requesting copies of the official dispatches that had been sent home to the United States. The anti-French Adams willingly complied, tactfully using the letters X, Y, and Z to conceal the real names of the three French go-betweens. The Francophobe Federalists were delighted by what they read; the pro-French Republicans were dismayed.

Here again Adams was playing politics with the nation's security. If he genuinely wanted peace, he could have refused to provide the documents on the grounds of executive privilege or confidentiality. President Washington had already done so in connection with the negotiation of Jay's treaty. But Adams was quite willing to expose the French and arouse the country further. He finally got his undeclared war, which lasted two and one-half years, from 1798 to 1800.

Under Adams's bellicose leadership, Congress created the Navy Department in April 1798. The next month it clothed the President with authority to order commanders of American warships to seize all French-armed vessels attacking American merchant ships. At about the same time Congress authorized Adams to raise an army of 10,000 men for three years (actually only partially assembled), and also the Marine Corps.

The undeclared war with France, though lasting more than two years, was confined chiefly to the waters of the West Indies. The small and improvised U.S. Navy, supported by privateers, captured about eighty armed French vessels, some of them after slam-bang naval duels.

Meanwhile the French Foreign Minister, Talleyrand, had been bestirring himself. He had not wanted war with the United States—the one with Britain was enough—and now he was the laughingstock of Europe after having been outsmarted by the three country bumpkins from America. He therefore made it known through various unofficial channels that he was prepared to negotiate respectfully with new envoys sent by the United States.

The ordinarily stubborn John Adams now began to feel the need to reverse himself. His Puritan conscience and common sense alike probably told him that there was no point in continuing to fight a war when peace was possible through quiet negotiations. Yet a prolonging of hostilities would bolster his newfound popularity, strengthen his own Federalist party, further confound the Jeffersonian Republican party, and presumably insure Adams's reelection in 1800.

What evidently turned Adams around was a fuller understanding of the ambitions of that master schemer, Alexander Hamilton, who had manipulated the official Cabinet from the outside. A frustrated Napoleon, Hamilton had managed to get himself appointed temporary active commander of the projected army of 10,000 men. He was dreaming heady dreams of conquest, in collaboration with the British navy, and he had his eye on such prizes as the Spanish-held Floridas, Louisiana, and perhaps areas as far distant as South America. Faced with such a self-seeking rival, Adams was clearly under a heavy moral obligation to put the welfare of his country above party, even above his own prospects for reelection.

Without consulting his disloyal cabinet, heavily under the influence of the pro-British Hamilton, Adams in the midst of the undeclared war with France, astounded the Federalists of his own party. On February 18, 1799, he submitted to the Senate the nomination of William Vans Murray, then in Holland, as the new envoy to France. The angered Federalists interposed dangerous delays, but finally consented to enlarge the one minister chosen to a trio of envoys.

After further delays, and with great difficulty, the new American agents managed to negotiate in France the Convention of 1800. As modified by the Senate, the French formally released the United States from the two treaties of 1778, including the Treaty of Alliance. For their part, the Americans agreed to pay their own citizens some $20 million (never fully paid) for the French spoliations of American commerce in recent years.

If President Adams's sound judgment deserted him when he launched his prolonged Federalist war against France, it failed him again when he declined to veto and then supported the Alien and Sedition Acts of July 1798. The first of these measures, spawned by the anti-French furor, was designed to suppress the numerous alien agitators. The second was aimed at stifling intemperate free speech directed at public officials. One offender was sentenced to four months in jail for publishing an attack on President Adams's "unbounded thirst for ridiculous pomp, foolish adulation, and selfish avarice." This sedition act was plainly unconstitutional, and such iron-toothed tactics all had a relatively short life. They elicited bitter criticism from the Jeffersonian Republicans, and probably contributed substantially to Adams's political downfall.

In the presidential election of 1800, Adams failed of re-election when he polled only 65 electoral votes to 73 for Thomas Jefferson, a relatively slight margin. Adams himself believed, or came to believe, that he lost out because he alienated the Hamilton wing of the party and other voters by courageously nominating a last-chance envoy to bring about peace with France.

Fifteen years after leaving the presidency, Adams wrote privately, obviously after mature reflection: "I will defend my missions to France, as long as I have an eye to direct my hand, or a finger to hold my pen. They were the most disinterested and meritorious actions of my life. I reflect upon them with so much satisfaction, that I desire no other inscription over my gravestone than: 'Here lies John Adams, who took upon himself the responsibility of the peace with France in the year 1800.' "

This proposed epitaph was never used. The heirs of Adams may have concluded that although the two missions sent to France were meritorious enough, the undeclared war with France that he had supported was totally unnecessary and largely inconclusive. It was waged under a staunch anti-French Federalist, who in so doing brought discomfiture to the rival Jeffersonian Republicans.

The blunt truth is that in courageously sending the second mission to France, Adams, though basically a man of integrity, was moved in large part by politics and jealousy of Hamilton. That Adams finally foresook the path of partisanship to pursue the national interest is commendable. But this complete and belated conversion to the proper course could not completely offset more than two years of wrongheaded bitterness and bloodshed.

Several other of Adams's alleged ethical lapses warrant comment. The federal judiciary was so overburdened that the President, himself a lawyer, backed the passing by Congress of the much-needed Judiciary Act of 1801. True partisan and legalist that he was, Adams appointed only Federalists to the newly created judicial offices. Such an act seems like pure politics, but Adams did what George Washington probably would have done: he put this judicial addition to the delicate fabric of government in the hands of those most sympathetic with it.

The Jeffersonian Federalists, whose leader had defeated Adams at the polls in 1800, raised the cry of "midnight judges." Adams was supposed to have stayed up until midnight of his last day in office signing the commissions of the sixteen newly created jurists. Actually, he continued signing until nine o'clock of the last day, at which time he signed only three of the commissions in question. Then he took off for his home in Massachusetts, without deigning to meet and greet his successor, as became customary. As the saying goes, there are no good losers, only good actors.

More questionable were some notorious cases of nepotism, a conflict of interest that most presidents have sought to avoid. President Adams was aware of this pitfall, but pressures converged on him to nominate a son-in-law, William S. Smith, as adjutant general of the nondescript army being slowly raised to fight France. This questionable nomination failed to secure Senate confirmation, much to Adams's chagrin, so he named his rejected son-in-law to be lieutenant colonel commandant. This appointment was finally confirmed.

Adams also nominated another son-in-law, Joshua Johnson, as superintendent of the Stamp Office. The Senate divided equally, so Vice President Jefferson cast the deciding vote in the nominee's favor. President Adams was greatly embarrassed by both of these cases, neither of which involved blood relatives. But he failed to see the reasonableness of excluding a man from office, when that man's comrades were ambassadors or generals, "merely because he married my daughter."

President Adams also came under some fire for appointing his gifted son, the thirty-year-old John Quincy Adams, as minister plenipotentiary to Prussia in 1797. The younger Adams, destined to become President, had received unprecedented training in European diplomacy as a youth, and had been appointed minister to the Netherlands in 1794 and to Portugal in 1796. He later became one of the most skilled and successful diplomatists in the nation's history. If this be nepotism, perhaps we should have more of it. Nepotism becomes intolerably objectionable when used as a haven for incompetents and crooks.

CHAPTER 3

Thomas Jefferson
1801–1809

Every honest man will suppose honest acts to flow from honest principles, and the
rogues may rail without intermission.

Thomas Jefferson,
letter to Benjamin Rush,
December 20, 1801

Integrity in a president is generally associated with a consistent application of principles as enunciated before, as well as after, assuming his high office. A rigid application of this test results in less than the highest marks for Thomas Jefferson.

Why was he prone to inconsistency, and why is he the boon of high school debaters, quotable, as he seems to be, on either side of almost every public question? One explanation is that he was a closet philosopher, churning over theories in private, and then often indiscreetly recording his thoughts in letters sent to his numerous correspondents. After the Massachusetts debtors of 1786 had risen in revolt under Daniel Shays and had been dispersed by the state authorities, Jefferson wrote to James Madison

(January 30, 1787): "I hold it, that a little rebellion now and then is a good thing, and as necessary in the political world as storms in the physical."

Such radical thoughts, coming from the revolutionist who had drafted the Declaration of Independence in 1776, do not seem utterly irresponsible to a later generation. But in 1807–1809, when Jefferson was President, he had on his hands an even larger revolt in New England against his harsh embargo. He tried desperately to enforce it by constitutional means, but failed, even after he had induced Congress to pass the inquisitorial and tyrannical Enforcement Act of 1809. Federalists cursed "Mad Tom" Jefferson and thought more kindly of King George III.

There was in fact more than one Jefferson. First came the private citizen, then the revolutionist, then the Secretary of State under Washington, then the organizer and leader of the Jeffersonian Republican party, and then the President, with all of that office's crushing responsibilities. Ralph Waldo Emerson wrote in 1841, "A foolish consistency is the hobgoblin of little minds, adored by little statesmen and philosophers and divines." By this standard Jefferson did not have a little mind, and it changed as his offices and other conditions changed. The scene usually looks considerably different from the top.

So it was that Jefferson, the partisan Republican, helped to start the iniquitous spoils system. Several years before the two-party system crystallized, President Washington had wisely "packed" the new federal offices with nascent Federalists who sympathized with the new and uncertain conservative regime. Jefferson likewise chose for public office some supporters of his anti-Federalist philosophy, but he did not resort to a wholesale eviction of Federalist incumbents. He actually gave much thought to the vexatious patronage problem, for he soon discovered that there were more office-hungry Republicans than there were offices. As he wrote in a private letter (July 12, 1801), this problem of finding jobs for competent and honest aspirants brought him much anxiety. Vacancies caused "by death are few; by resignation, none." This sage observation has been shortened to read, "Few die and none resign."

A so-called clean sweep of office holders under the "spoils system" did not come until the era of Andrew Jackson, when the victims were much more numerous though the percentage of removals was approximately what it had been under Jefferson.

But Jackson was much less concerned with the applicants' honesty and fitness than Jefferson.

In a sense, John Adams himself had introduced the Jacksonian spoils system. He had appointed only Federalists to the sixteen judicial vacancies ("midnight judges") created by the "deathbed" Judiciary Act of February 13, 1801. Under Jefferson's leadership, Congress repealed this offensive legislation, and thus swept away sixteen benches from under the designated jurists, even though the judges were needed to handle mounting litigation.

Jefferson, as vice president and champion of free speech, had taken a strong stand against the drastic Federalist Alien and Sedition Laws, as well as the relentless prosecutions (persecutions?) under them. As president, he allowed the Alien and Sedition Laws to expire quietly as a result of their time limitation, and he pardoned all those convicted under a sedition act, which he regarded as unconstitutional. A Jeffersonian Congress generously restored the various fines imposed, with accumulated interest.

Jefferson, though a lifelong champion of free speech, actively favored the impeachment and removal of federal judges who were too free with their speech, especially when they delivered partisan Federalist harangues in the guise of instructions to a jury. Especially noteworthy was Jefferson's prosecution of Mr. Justice Chase of the Supreme Court. Although a truly distinguished legalist, this judge became increasingly high-handed and probably deranged. In addressing a grand jury in Baltimore, he assailed the recent repeal of the Judiciary Act of 1801 and predicted the deterioration of "our Republican Constitution . . . into a mobocracy." For such blatant exhibitions of partisanhip and "bad temper," he was haled before the Senate on impeachment charges. But because he was not indictable for a specific crime, only indiscreet remarks and offensive behavior, the Senate acquitted him by a narrow vote of 19 to 15. Jefferson, although a supposed champion of free speech, was deeply disappointed.

In the arena of foreign affairs, Jefferson had gained rich experience as minister to France and later as Secretary of State under President George Washington. Ironically, he again found himself in conflict with some of his most cherished principles, but he courageously rose above them and acted in what he conceived to be, and what probably was, the national interest.

In 1801 the blackmailing Pasha of Tripoli, dissatisfied with his share of tribute money from the United States, declared war. Jefferson had been a man of peace, especially where France and America had been involved, and once wrote privately, "peace is our passion." Inheriting a small navy from President Adams, Jefferson was obligated to uphold the interests and honor of the United States off the coast of North Africa by fighting back against the Barbary pirates. The subsequent clash, featured by several spectacular operations on sea and land, ended four years later in 1805. The peace treaty terminated all annual payments of blackmail to Tripoli but provided $60,000 in ransom money for about 100 captured American sailors.

The magnificent Louisiana purchase meanwhile had fallen into Jefferson's lap in 1803. The oft-told story is that the Spanish-owned territory of Louisiana, drained by the mighty Mississippi River, was secretly ceded to France in 1802. Spain was weak and growing weaker, and the westward surging American settlers seemed certain to spill over into Louisiana in due time. But the prospective occupation of this vast area by Napoleon, the foremost military genius of his age, foreshadowed prolonged and bloody conflict. Greatly alarmed, President Jefferson wrote to Minister Livingston in Paris that from the moment of the French take over "we must marry ourselves to the British fleet and nation."

This was an extraordinary flip-flop. Jefferson had long been an outspoken friend of France and a lifelong foe of Great Britain. He was also conspicuously on record, especially in his inaugural address of 1801, as having favored "honest friendship with all nations, entangling alliances with none." Yet he finally dispatched James Monroe to Paris as a special envoy, there to join Minister Livingston, with instructions to offer as much as $10 million for New Orleans, at the mouth of the Mississippi, and as much to the east in West Florida as could be obtained. If France seemed about to close the Mississippi River to American shipping or "to meditate hostilities," the two envoys were to enter upon negotiations for an alliance with England. So wrote the hater of England, the old friend of France, the foe of alliances, and the opponent of further national indebtedness.

To the amazement of the two American envoys, Napoleon refused to haggle about a relatively small area east of the Mississippi River. Out of a clear sky he proposed dumping the vast Louisiana wilderness into the laps of the Americans, for approximately $10 million—surely the greatest and grandest real estate bargain in history. Among various motives, Napoleon was about to reopen war with Great Britain, and he did not relish the prospect of handing the British navy a present of this trans-Mississippi wilderness. The two dumbfounded American envoys had enough wit left to ignore their instructions, accept Napoleon's breathtaking offer, and send the signed treaties home.

President Jefferson, now a tangle of inconsistencies, again found himself caught in the web of a dilemma. As a foe of the Federalist Hamilton, he had long been a strict constructionist of the Constitution. In arguing against Hamilton's powerful Bank of the United States, he had in effect maintained that if the Constitution did not specifically authorize such a financial institution, then the proposal was unconstitutional. The founding fathers clearly had not authorized the president to acquire by treaty vast new expanses of territory and incorporate in the Union the Spanish, French, and Indian inhabitants, much like cattle in the field, and without due regard for their rights.

Jefferson toyed with the idea of amending the Constitution, but this clumsy process might take many months, during which a capricious Napoleon could withdraw his astounding offer. The acquisition of the Louisiana territory was so overwhelmingly in the national interest that Jefferson finally asked Congress to overlook metaphysical subtleties and pay for the purchase. The members did, with little dissent, except from a few diehard Federalists, who inconsistently objected to Jefferson's belated conversion to Hamilton's loose construction of the Constitution. Much later the Supreme Court inferentially upheld the Louisiana Purchase as sanctioned under the president's treaty-making powers.

Jefferson, the Republican with newly adopted Federalist principles, thus added a huge $10 million to the Hamiltonian debt, which he had resisted while Secretary of State under President Washington. In doing so, he has been branded by at least one historian as "a receiver of stolen goods" or "an accomplice of the greatest highwayman of the age." In turning over Louisiana to the United States, Napoleon violated a promise to Spain not to do so; he did not carry out his part of the retrocession agreement; he ignored the existing constitution of France; and he sold a vast territory that he did not actually possess. The formal French takeover came some months later and lasted only twenty days.

The transfer treaties thus approved by the United States did not specifically include West Florida, although Presidents Jefferson and Madison, both aware of this deficiency, tried to stretch the extent of the purchase that far to the east. Some would call such grasping tactics unethical; others would say that these two presidents were simply trying to make the best of a good bargain —all in the national interest. Jefferson was not a Yankee trader, yet he was not averse at times to some sharp Yankee bargaining.

At first Jefferson tried the quiet channels of diplomacy, and when they did not gain his ends he resorted to bluster. To Congress he hinted at the necessity of raising 300,000 soldiers for both offense and defense against Spain. This obvious attempt to cow Spain into yielding West Florida failed, as did Jefferson's confidential call to Congress for $2 million to facilitate the negotiations. But these moves did betray his unseemly eagerness to twist Spain's arm by devious but unsuccessful tactics.

Although Jefferson was a fellow Virginian and a lawyer, he cherished no abiding love for his famous cousin, Justice John Marshall, whom President Adams had elevated to the Supreme Court in the dying weeks of his administration. As chief justice, Marshall proved to be a persistent thorn in the flesh of Jefferson, initially for his decision in the case of *Marbury* v. *Madison* (1803). William Marbury had been a justice of the peace and also one of John Adams's so-called midnight appointments. But Marbury's formal commission was not issued to him, so he sued Secretary of State Madison for its delivery. The Marshall court held that Marbury had a right to his commission (a blow at the Jeffersonian Republicans) but that the Supreme Court had no power to issue a writ requiring its delivery to Marbury (a temporary victory for the Jeffersonian Republicans). The Marshall court also ruled that the writ could not be lawfully issued because the power to do so had not been specifically granted by the Constitution, even though stipulated in the Judiciary Act passed by Congress in 1789. The practice of judicial review was thus established, that is, the enormous power of these learned jurists on the Supreme Court to invalidate Congressional legislation that they regard as violating the Constitution.

President Jefferson was greatly displeased with Chief Justice Marshall, and this feeling also manifested itself during and after the famous trial of the infamous Aaron Burr in 1807. After killing Alexander Hamilton in a duel that Hamilton had provoked, Burr engaged in schemes and plots that apparently envisaged the creation of a small army of westerners that would tear away a substantial part of Mexico and join it with a part of the southwestern United States.

Jefferson had formed a highly unfavorable impression of Burr, who had served as Vice President under him, and the President had an active hand behind the scenes in the relentless prosecution of the conspirator. The defendant was tried for treason in the circuit court at Richmond, Virginia, in 1807. Jefferson's rigorous action against Burr does not square with his earlier condemnation of Federalist prosecutions under the Alien and Sedition Acts. Burr had notoriously been up to no good, but the stipulation in the Constitution regarding treason was crystal clear: "No person shall be convicted of treason unless on the testimony of two witnesses to the same overt act, or on confession in open court." (Article III, Section 3)

Two witnesses could not be rounded up, and Burr did not confess. The Marshall court therefore judged him not guilty, much to the chagrin of Jefferson, who wrote sourly of the legal "twistifications" of the learned justice in the *Marbury* and *Burr* cases. Jefferson's inconsistency showed itself again, quite in contrast to his criticisms of convictions of free spirits by Federalist judges in the days of John Adams and the Alien and Sedition Acts.

While a member of Washington's cabinet, Jefferson had played a leading role in crystallizing the Federalist-Republican two-party system. He had opposed Hamilton in demanding a strict construction rather than a loose interpretation of the Constitution, in favoring friendship with France rather than Britain, in minimizing the national debt, and in other ways squinting toward states' rights rather than a potent central government. Repeatedly Jefferson was forced to reverse himself in response to the iron hand of necessity, and in some respects the Republican Jefferson became more Federalist than the Hamiltonian Federalists. Critics charged with obvious exaggeration that Jefferson destroyed the Federalist party by catching it in bathing and stealing all of its clothes.

Memorable though Jefferson's major achievements as President were, his name has been indelibly besmirched by a vindictive journalist, one James Callender. In 1802 this scandal-monger charged in a newspaper, the *Richmond Recorder,* that the President had been sexually involved with at least two women. Allegedly one of them, his slave girl by the name of Sally Hemings, bore him several mulatto offspring, who were kept on as slaves at Monticello under the white father's lash. Jefferson's political enemies seized on this juicy morsel with high glee, and it has been revived in recent years by writers of historical fiction, but not by the ablest historians. These learned scholars appear to be in agreement that the supposed blot on Jefferson's character is neither proved nor provable.

CHAPTER 4

James Madison
1809–1817

*When numbers of men act in a body, respect for character is often lost, just in
proportion as it is necessary to control what is not right.*

James Madison, speech,
December 2, 1829

James Madison, a Virginia Republican like Jefferson, trod in the
footsteps of his illustrious predecessor. A small man physically,
he was a giant intellectually, notably as a political theorist. Conspicuously present at the constitutional convention of 1787 in
Philadelphia, he contributed so significantly to the resulting document that he legitimately acquired the sobriquet, "Father of the
Constitution."

President Madison's most conspicuous fall from grace as a
man of integrity involved that portion of West Florida that lay
between New Orleans on the west and the main body of the
peninsula on the east. Like Jefferson, who also knew better, Madison greedily claimed that this area was plainly included in the
Louisiana Purchase, even though convincing evidence to support
this claim has never turned up.

Footloose American settlers had moved into West Florida, where they detested the presence of their Spanish overlords. The dissidents finally rose in revolt in 1810, encouraged if not actually assisted by the administration in Washington. President Madison responded with a proclamation annexing West Florida, generously including about 100 miles more territory than the rebels themselves claimed. His conscience must have troubled him, for he stooped so low as to falsify the dates on certain important documents, obviously in an attempt to throw subsequent investigators, including historians, off the scent. In short, Madison resorted to a species of fraud.

The Spanish government protested bitterly against what it understandably regarded as connivance at theft, but its hands were too busy fighting Napoleon to take effective action. The British minister in Washington assailed the grab of West Florida as an act "contrary to every principle of public justice, faith, and national honor."

British and Spanish wrath was further aroused by President Madison's grab for a substantial part of East Florida, south of the Georgia border. He evidently hoped to engineer a coup similar to that of 1810 in West Florida, working again through "American insurgents," led in this instance by a semi-literate former governor of Georgia, George Mathews.

The so-called rebels penetrated East Florida with an armed force that reached the gates of St. Augustine early in 1812. But by this time Madison's grasping tactics were so thoroughly exposed that he was forced to disavow Mathews, and the captured territory was returned to Spain. Feeling betrayed, Governor Mathews vowed to "blow them all up," but fortunately for the President's good name this discredited agent died suddenly. The Spaniards and British again expressed their displeasure with the covetous and land-hungry Yankee.

Several years later, in the midst of Britain's War of 1812 with America, the influential *Times* of London cried out that "Mr. Madison's dirty, swindling manoeuvres in respect to Louisiana and the Floridas remain to be punished." This important journal favored continuing the war until the double-dealing Yankees had been soundly thrashed and humbled.

After Jefferson had failed in his attempt to force Great Britain to respect America's maritime rights through an embargo, President Madison sent a message to Congress that dumped the issue of waging or not waging war squarely into the lap of that body. He took this action about a week after the congressional caucus of Jeffersonian Republicans had nominated President Madison to succeed himself. This charge has often been made that the war message was the price that Madison paid for his renomination, but in more recent years historians have shown this accusation to be unfounded. If true, such a political deal would have shown that Madison did put his own personal interests ahead of those of the nation.

The philosophical Madison was not a bellicose man. Not surprisingly, the country was wretchedly prepared for war, and the proposed invasion of Canada failed miserably, actually slipping into reverse gear. The incompetence of Secretary of War Armstrong was in itself a scandal, but not one that reflected unduly on the President. The tiny American navy, though winning a number of single-ship actions, at length was virtually wiped off the high seas. The capital of Washington was invaded and the White House itself was put to the torch, as Madison himself narrowly escaped capture by the British invaders.

In the closing year of the war, with Napoleon exiled and British veterans released for service in America, the redcoats launched a powerful invasion of upper New York but were repulsed at Plattsburg. The British peace negotiators at Ghent were at last persuaded to end the fruitless fighting on the basis of no territorial gains or losses—*status quo ante bellum*. The epochal Treaty of Ghent was signed on Christmas Eve, December 24, 1814.

Meanwhile an army of some 7,500 British veterans had invaded the southern part of the United States and unwisely launched a frontal attack at New Orleans on prepared positions manned by General Andrew Jackson's nondescript militiamen and other defenders. The losses to the invaders were staggering, and they were forced to withdraw. Ironically, this great victory for American arms came fifteen days *after* the peace treaty had been signed.

News of Jackson's smashing triumph at New Orleans first reached Washington by horse, and preceded by seven days the seaborne treaty of Ghent. Many Americans received the erroneous impression that they had first beaten Britain to her knees, and that in the hour of Jackson's triumph the British negotiators at Ghent had hastened to sign a treaty of peace—any peace.

To the victors a victory is always sweeter than a defeat, and the Americans broke loose with frenzied rejoicing. The slogan in the early days of the war had been, "On to Canada." After the triumph at New Orleans and the Treaty of Ghent, the common boast ironically became, "Not one inch of territory ceded or lost." All the considerable territory seized by the British was restored. For their part, the Americans had captured none of consequence from Britain to restore.

On February 18, 1815, some six weeks after the victory at New Orleans and shortly after the formal ratification of the Treaty of Ghent, President Madison sent a special congratulatory message to both houses of Congress. As one reads it, one wonders if the author was really referring to the War of 1812. Apparently he was indulging in deliberate untruths, or at least exaggerations, to cover up his own ineptitudes, and hence look better in the eyes of posterity, including historians. Re-election could hardly have been in his mind because he had already been chosen for a second term in 1812.

Madison told Congress: "The late war, although reluctantly declared by Congress, had become a necessary resort to assert the rights and independence of the nation. It has been waged with a success which is the natural result of the wisdom of the legislative councils, of the patriotism [disloyal New England Federalists] of the people, of the public spirit of the [runaway] militia, and of the valor of the military and naval forces of the country. Peace, at all times a blessing, is peculiarly welcome, therefore, at a period when the causes for the war have ceased to operate, when the Government has demonstrated the efficiency of its powers of defense, and when the nation can review its conduct without regret and without reproach." There is scarcely an allegation in this summation whose truthfulness is not open to challenge.

We have already observed that President Jefferson had been forced by necessity, or what he conceived to be necessity, to abandon certain Republican principles and adopt those of the Hamiltonian Federalists. Jefferson had strongly opposed Hamilton's Bank of the United States, yet Madison reversed Jefferson and other Republicans when he signed a congressional bill providing for a larger and more powerful fiscal institution. He explained that on this issue he had yielded to an overwhelming "Public Judgment, necessarily superseding individual opinions."

Jefferson had been no friend of manufacturers, for he regarded farming in the open sunlight as more ennobling, and he had little sympathy for the money-grubbing merchants and traders of Federalist New England. But the Jeffersonian embargo and the Madisonian War of 1812 had created a kind of hothouse in which infant factories had sprung up. Madison further contributed to the demise of the Federalist Party when he swung behind the Hamiltonian policy of a protective wall for infant industries. He signed the new tariff act of 1816, designed to shield American manufacturers from the deluge of European manufactures dammed up by the recent war and other barriers. He also enrolled in a society for the encouragement of American manufactures, believing in the desirability of supporting within limits certain kinds of domestic articles.

It is no crime to abandon one's views to square with changing conditions, and Madison changed policies rather than his interpretation of the Constitution, to which he remained devoted. In certain areas he was consistent to the end. On March 3, 1817, the day before he left office, he vetoed a bill aimed at encouraging the construction of roads and canals. The measure also called for improving "the navigation of water courses" designed to facilitate interstate commerce among the states, as well as promoting "the common defense." In Madison's judgment, a strict Jeffersonian interpretation of the Constitution would not warrant financing commerce among the states, although there was clear sanction for controlling it. In later years this rigid interpretation relaxed under the hot sun of increased commerce and a crying need for better communication and transportation. Or, as the old saying goes, "circumstances alter cases."

CHAPTER 5

James Monroe
1817–1825

National Honor is a national property of the highest value.

James Monroe, first inaugural
address, March 4, 1817

Probably no other American President has served his country in so many different and important capacities before coming to the highest office as James Monroe of Virginia. At age eighteen he dropped out of the College of William and Mary to fight the British in the War of Independence, from 1776 to 1778. At Trenton he was gravely wounded and also promoted to the rank of captain for bravery under fire. From 1780 to 1786 he was successively military commissioner for Virginia, a member of the Virginia legislature, a member of Governor Jefferson's council, a member of the Virginia House of Delegates, a member of the Continental Congress, a student of law in the office of Thomas Jefferson, a member of the Virginia assembly, and a delegate to the Virginia state constitutional convention.

Following the establishment of the new government under President Washington in 1789, Monroe was elected to the United

States Senate from Virginia, served as minister plenipotentiary to France (where he got into hot water), held office as governor of Virginia for about four years, was sent by President Jefferson to France in 1803 as minister plenipotentiary, there to assist the regular minister, Robert R. Livingston, with the delicate negotiations for the purchase of Louisiana.

Crowned with Louisiana laurels, Monroe became minister plenipotentiary to England, and in 1804 headed a diplomatic mission to Spain, from which he returned to London, there to negotiate a treaty jointly with William Pinkney in 1806. It was pigeonholed by President Jefferson, who was particularly displeased by the failure of his agents to secure a clear-cut renunciation of impressment.

Returning to the United States in 1808, Monroe became a member of the Virginia assembly in 1810 and governor of Virginia in 1811. He served President Madison as Secretary of State from 1811 to 1817, and at critical times in 1814 and 1815 simultaneously held the portfolio of Secretary of War. He breathed new life into the demoralized war effort against Britain, and in 1817 was elevated to the presidency of the United States.

No person would be chosen for so many high positions if he did not have a reputation for integrity, and this Monroe certainly possessed. Thomas Jefferson, who knew Monroe well as a student in his law office, wrote of his younger colleague in 1786, "He is a man whose soul might be turned wrong side outwards, without discovering [revealing] a blemish to the world." In 1819 Jefferson thus characterized Madison and Monroe: "I have had, and still have, such entire confidence in the late and present Presidents, that I willingly put both soul and body into their pockets." Yet we should remember that Jefferson in private letters was prone to exaggerate.

Monroe's record was not completely flawless. As regards his first mission to France in 1794–1796, he was ardently pro-French at a time when President Washington had proclaimed neutrality in the existing war between Britain and France. Monroe was so indiscreet as to make a flaming pro-French speech to the entire Paris Convention, after which he received the fraternal kiss on both cheeks. He also assured the French that John Jay, then representing the United States in London, would not conclude a treaty favorable to Britain and unfavorable to France. When the Jay treaty turned out to be precisely the opposite of what Monroe

had promised, his usefulness completely ended, and he was per-
emptorily recalled by the United States government. Upon returning to America, Monroe published a spirited vindication of
his mission. It revealed not only wounded pride but also political
ambition and burning partisanship.

As for Monroe's claim, and that of his partisans, to joint
credit for the Louisiana Purchase, we should note that the French
had put out their first feeler to Minister Livingston on the subject
the day before Monroe reached Paris. The probabilities are that
Napoleon would have sold what he did when he did if Monroe
had never put in an appearance. The two American envoys carried no instructions whatever to buy Louisiana, but they must be
credited with both good sense and courage in rising above their
instructions (which envoys are supposed never to do), and grasping this tremendous bargain from the capricious Napoleon while
it was still available.

Monroe's mission to London in 1805–1806 is not the brightest star in his diplomatic career. He was supposed to join with
Minister William Pinkney in negotiating a new treaty in which the
British would formally renounce their objectionable yet necessary
practice of impressing seamen into the Royal Navy. Instead of a
renunciation, the best that Monroe and Pinkney could squeeze
out of the negotiations was a rather vague declaration that in the
future the British would try to avoid injuring American citizens.

After service as a member of the Virginia assembly and as
governor of Virginia from 1810 to 1811, Monroe became President Madison's Secretary of State. After Secretary of War John
Armstrong had badly botched operations against the British in
the War of 1812, Secretary of State Monroe took on the additional burdens of the Secretary of War. He managed to invigorate
prosecution of the War of 1812, and deserves some credit for
ending the conflict on a high note with victories at Plattsburg and
New Orleans.

While both Secretary of State and Secretary of War, Monroe
became involved to some extent in the devious attempt of the
federal government to seize West Florida from Spain with a vol-
unteer army of American "patriots" under the unscrupulous
George Mathews. When this force met with considerable resistance and much unfavorable publicity, Secretary of War (and of
State) Monroe was forced to disavow these unneighborly activities. The best that can be said for Monroe's ethics is that he was

obviously acting under instructions from President Madison, that Congress had secretly authorized some such activity in East Florida, and that the clearing out of such a nest of lawless characters was in the national interest, though not so clearly in the interest of Spain.

Capitalizing on Monroe's commendable record as both secretary of state and secretary of war, the congressional Republican caucus nominated the stately Virginian for the presidency by a rather close margin. The dying Federalist party officially named no candidate, and Monroe triumphed in the Electoral College in 1816 by a lopsided margin. So pervasive was the "Era of Good Feelings" of Monroe's first administration that by 1820 the incumbent was re-elected by a vote of 231 to 1—a record eclipsed in American presidential history only by George Washington's two unanimous endorsements by the Electoral College.

James Monroe, the courtly Virginian, was the last of the "Virginia dynasty," which consisted of Washington, Jefferson, Madison, and Monroe. He had devoted most of his mature life to politics, or to use a more complimentary word, public service. He lacked the brilliance of his patron, Thomas Jefferson, and the philosophical depth of his chief, James Madison, but despite a few minor slips here and there, he was regarded as a man of the purest integrity, combined with devotion to the principles of Jeffersonian Republicanism.

Illustrative of his devotion to Jeffersonian principles, Monroe advised Congress that a constitutional amendment would be required before federal money could be appropriated for internal improvements within the states. When Congress defied him in 1822 and passed a bill for the repair of the interstate Cumberland Road, Monroe vetoed it. As Martin Van Buren, a later President, wrote in his *Autobiography,* "Mr. Monroe's character was that of an honest man, with fair, but not very marked capacities, who through life, performed every duty that devolved upon him with scrupulous fidelity."

The Era of Good Feelings, though promoted by Monroe, seemed not so much his creation as a natural product of the new atmosphere. The miserable little War of 1812 had ended with Jackson's exhilarating victory, peace had come, partisanship was ending with the demise of the Federalist party, industry was expanding, and the nation was on the move. Monroe traveled extensively to show himself to the people. The response was most enheartening, despite some stiffness and formality on the part of the new leader. As the last president to adopt the knee breeches and buckles of the earlier era, he came to be known as the Last of the Cocked Hats.

As for the spoils of office, Monroe suffered little or no criticism. The heads of officeholders did not really roll until the roaring days of Andrew Jackson, about a dozen years later. One obvious reason was that the old Federalist party had virtually faded out of existence, and a partisan distribution of offices is difficult unless there are parties.

The nation's designs on Florida led in 1818 to a dispute between President Monroe and Andrew Jackson as to which one was a liar. General Jackson, with an armed force in Georgia, had orders to move to the troubled area north of Spanish Florida, where he was authorized, if necessary, to pursue hostile Indians across the boundary line. But he was to respect all posts under the flag of Spain. In hot pursuit, the headstrong general burst into Florida, where he seized two towns under the Spanish banner, thereby disrupting peaceful negotiations. Jackson later insisted that he had earlier written the President and had received authorization to plunge ahead. Monroe flatly denied having taken any such step. It is probable, though not provable, that Monroe did not respond at all, thereby leaving the impression that silence gave consent. It is also possible that the request for such authorization, even if made by Jackson, never arrived at its destination. Probably we shall never discover which one of these men, one a President and the other a future President, lied.

Monroe is best known to fame as the coauthor of the Monroe Doctrine, which he embodied as a blunt warning to the European powers in his annual message to Congress of 1823. Certain features of it were the work of Secretary of State John Quincy Adams, but Monroe insisted on giving the dictum to the world as a presidential message, rather than in conventional diplomatic notes. For such housetop diplomacy he was willing to risk a barrage of foreign abuse.

The familiar background of the famed Monroe Doctrine may be sketched briefly. Following the Napoleonic upheaval, the great powers of Europe had joined in what was popularly known as the Holy Alliance, and were thought to be preparing to restore the revolted or revolting Spanish-American colonies to Spain. Americans, themselves pathbreaking revolutionists, sympathized with

the efforts of the Spanish-American rebels to establish sister de-
mocracies. It was also evident that if the great powers intervened,
they could easily secure strategic lodgments menacing the United
States. So it was that Monroe publicly warned the European powers to keep their hands off, and inferentially indicated that the
armed forces of the United States would fight these monarchs if
they attempted to come. At the same time Monroe promised, as a
self-imposed concession, that the United States would not intervene in the internal disturbances of Europe, with the current
Greek war for independence in view. In short, Monroe's warning
boiled down to: "You keep out and we'll stay out." Americans are
prone to overlook or forget the self-denying part of the dictum.

The Monroe Doctrine was greeted by a nationwide outburst
of patriotic applause, a further manifestation of the Era of Good
Feelings. The European monarchs, for their part, were vastly
annoyed by the upstart Monroe, especially since they had no specific plans for intervening. They were tired of Yankee bluster,
and no doubt toyed with the idea of teaching the objectionable
Americans a harsh lesson.

The blunt truth is that Monroe was staging a colossal bluff.
At the time Monroe sent his memorable message to Congress the
United States had only one modest-sized warship on active duty
in the entire Atlantic Ocean. The powers of Europe could not
hope to invade the revolted republics of Spanish-America in the
teeth of the British navy, which was not on their side. The Spanish-American revolutionists had thrown open their commerce to
British merchants, who were not about to permit the British navy
to close them. All this was evident to President Monroe, who in
effect was saying, "You powers of Europe, stay out—or the British navy will get you."

The Monroe Doctrine of 1823 enjoyed a warm but brief
burst of applause, and then was quietly forgotten until briefly
resurrected by President Polk in 1845. It lives today and is occa-
sionally invoked by an American public that is ignorant of its
background, or of its self-restricting feature. By invading Europe
in World War I and World War II, the United States flouted the
presumed promise to stay out of trans-Atlantic affairs. Compara-
tively, the few infractions of the Monroe Doctrine by Europeans
over the years have been as nothing compared with American
interventions.

As earlier noted, James Monroe spent most of his adult life

as a public servant on the public payroll. He was often in financial difficulties, partly because of tardy or only partial reimbursement by a frugal government. In 1826 Congress voted him the sum of $30,000 in settlement of persistent claims. Evidently the congressmen were persuaded that his affairs were free of fraud.

Lacking a pension, Monroe was finally forced to sell his Virginia farm and move to New York City, where he resided with his daughter and her husband. Appropriately, he died on the Fourth of July, 1831, six years after leaving office.

CHAPTER 6

John Quincy Adams
1825–1829

The first of qualities for a great statesman is to be honest.

John Quincy Adams,
January 22, 1809

As the son of the coldly reserved President John Adams, John Quincy Adams has been described as a chip off the old family glacier. His own presidency was a disappointment; it did not measure up to his earlier successes, sometimes brilliant, in statecraft. Certainly his previous experience in public life had been rich and rewarding. At age eleven, in 1778, he had accompanied his father on the critical mission to France. In succeeding years he had filled a number of important diplomatic or quasi-diplomatic positions, including successively the posts of minister to Portugal, Prussia, Russia, and England. He shone brilliantly as Secretary of State from 1817 to 1825, when he negotiated the acquisition of East Florida and collaborated with President Monroe in drafting the doctrine that bears Monroe's name. He had also sat in the Senate of the United States from Massachusetts from 1803 to 1808. There he learned something about the seamy game of politics.

When Adams ran for the presidency in 1824 the old Federalist party was virtually dead, leaving the dominant Democratic-Republicans to splinter into factions and fight bitterly among themselves. Four candidates were in the final running. General Andrew Jackson of Tennessee came out ahead in the electoral vote, and also scored a plurality of the popular vote. But he did not have a clear majority in the Electoral College, and under the Constitution, the House of Representatives, voting by states, was authorized to select the winner among the top three candidates. Henry Clay of Kentucky—destined to be a perennial loser—was the fourth man and thus eliminated. As fate would have it, he was also the influential speaker of the House of Representatives and in a strong position to throw his considerable weight, as he did, behind the winner, John Quincy Adams.

What lay behind the decision of Kentuckian Henry Clay? He distrusted Andrew Jackson as a brawler from Tennessee; indeed the West was not big enough for these two ambitious men. William H. Crawford, in third place, had already suffered a paralytic stroke. This situation left only John Quincy Adams, for whom Clay had no great liking personally, but whose goals as president were generally compatible with his own. The irony of subsequent events is that in any event Clay probably preferred Adams for president.

But Clay, endlessly ambitious for the presidency, evidently was not averse to making a deal to win the post of secretary of state in the new administration. This exalted position was regarded as a surefire runway to the presidency, for Presidents Jefferson, Madison, and Monroe had all been secretaries of state. Accordingly, a go-between for Clay informed Adams privately that the Kentuckian might be induced to support the frosty New Englander if Clay could be assured of "a prominent share in the administration."

Three weeks later Clay was closeted with John Quincy Adams for a long evening of confidential conversation. They could hardly have spent all this time talking about the price of codfish in New England. At all events, Speaker Clay subsequently threw his weight behind Adams in the House of Representatives, and the upright New Englander was officially named President. With what appears to have been undue haste, Adams waited only three days before formally offering Henry Clay the coveted secretaryship of state, which was promptly accepted. A wait of three weeks would have raised fewer eyebrows.

The frustrated Jacksonians, who had gleaned a strong plurality of the popular vote, let fly an outcry of "corrupt bargain" and they kept up their clamor until Jackson won a clear-cut victory four years later. Their rage was enhanced by Adams's refusal to entertain overtures from them while Clay was feathering his own nest.

The circumstantial evidence is strong that Adams struck some kind of bargain with Clay for support in the House of Representatives. But the deal, if there had been one, was not necessarily corrupt, though clandestine. Such was politics, with tactics that cause the word "dirty" to be applied to movement of the political machinery. Politicians habitually repay favors with favors of their own; in short, "you scratch my back, and I'll scratch yours." Adams had sat in the Senate of the United States for five years, and he was not exactly a babe in the woods.

The supposition is warranted that Adams gained the presidential chair by some kind of secret understanding, but there is no evidence that money changed hands.

Samuel Flagg Bemis, Adams's ablest biographer, admits that the straitlaced Puritan "let his conscience slip," but goes on to say that this bargain, from an ethical standpoint, was "the least questionable of several deals" that Adams made to secure the presidency. But the political battle cry of "bargain and corruption" was raised in 1824 and kept up by the Jacksonites until their "Old Hero" gained the White House in 1828. This campaign was probably the longest and noisiest one charging political corruption in the history of the American presidency.

By one way of reckoning, the "corrupt bargain" was not wicked at all, as Adams and many of his successors could have argued. As a high-ranking public servant, Adams was bound by conscience and the Constitution to act in the national interest, which in this instance coincided with his own personal desires. Adams greatly distrusted Jackson, the unrestrained and hot-tempered wild man from Tennessee, whose election seemingly could mean disaster for his country. Then why not, in both the national interest and his own personal interest, make a private deal with Clay? In later years many of Adams's successors have struck political bargains of some sort behind the scenes, in what could also be called the national interest. What made the Adams-Clay transaction so objectionable was that it seemed to thwart the popular will, as expressed in Jackson's strong plurality of the popular vote at a time when the uncouth New Democracy was on the upsurge.

As if to do penance for an under-the-table deal, President Adams sternly halted the tide of political spoilsmanship by refusing to throw pro-Jackson men out of office to make room for Adamsites. He removed only twelve incumbents from the public payroll during his four years of incumbency, a devotion to principle that accounts in large part for his failure to be re-elected in 1828.

Nearly four years later, in the bitter Adams-Jackson campaign of 1828, the followers of "Old Hickory" leveled vicious charges of corruption against President Adams. He was accused of having received enormous sums of public money during a career in public life that stretched over some thirty years, especially as a diplomat in foreign countries. This monetary figure was arrived at by adding together his well-earned salaries, plus his expense money. Adams was specifically charged with having bought a billiard table with public funds and having installed this gambling furniture in the Presidential Palace, as the White House was then called. Actually, the President had bought the billiard table with his own money. In vain did Adams's followers insist that all his salaries had been honestly earned. His defenders also pointed out that of $25,000 appropriated for the refurbishing of the White House, only $6,000 had been spent.

Adams was urged to present his own case to a meeting of Pennsylvania Germans and speak to them in their own language, with which he had some familiarity. He refused to do so on the grounds that a chief magistrate would demean himself and his office by huckstering on his own behalf. He even declined to restrain disloyal federal officers from attacking him publicly while they were promoting the candidacy of Andrew Jackson.

The Jacksonites, but not Jackson, were not content with accusing Adams of having acquired gaming tables and gambling furniture for the White House. They sank even lower. They accused him of having procured a servant girl, while minister to Russia, for the lust of the Russian Czar. This preposterous charge branded the stern Puritan as a pimp.

Like Jackson and many another future president, Adams had no control over the extravagances of his followers, who were not at all backward about replying in kind. One anti-Jackson newspaper charged that the candidate's mother had been a common prostitute brought to America by British soldiers. Afterwards, she allegedly married a mulatto, named Jack, by whom she had several children, one of whom was Jackson, or Jack's son.

Critics of Jackson further accused Old Hickory of having been an adulterer, and technically they were correct. Rachel Jackson had divorced her husband and married Andrew Jackson, thinking that her final decree had been granted. About two years later the couple learned to their dismay that the earlier bond of matrimony had not been cut, and they made haste to rectify their having "lived in sin." Technically a bigamist, Rachel Jackson lived long enough to see her husband elected president, but she never became First Lady of the Land.

Backers of Adams in 1828 also distributed "coffin handbills," shaped like a coffin, and detailing in lurid fashion Jackson's having ordered the hanging of six mutinous militiamen—all in strict line of duty. Despite such unpleasant reminders of the past, Old Hickory won by 178 electoral votes to 82, although the popular count was closer, 647,286 to 508,064. Neither the victor nor the vanquished could be held responsible for the excesses of their opponents, yet the outcome did not reflect favorably on either side. Professor Edward Channing of Harvard concluded in 1921, "On the whole, possibly it was more honorable to have been defeated in 1828 than to have been elected."

John Quincy Adams's four years in office came to be regarded as generally a failure. Among his most serious drawbacks were the shadow of the "corrupt bargain," the strong drift away from post-1812 nationalism, and the crystallizing of new party alignments, particularly around the issue of slavery.

Yet Adams's basic integrity appeared to good advantage in his treatment of the Cherokee Indians of Georgia. These aborigines were about to be evicted from their ancient hunting grounds by land-hungry white men. Adams intervened on behalf of the friendless natives, but was thwarted by the governor of Georgia, who threatened to resist federal authority with armed force. The defiant state won this bloodless battle, but another dark chapter was written in the disturbing growth of nullification.

The vicious Adams-Jackson campaign of 1828 found President Adams at a distinct disadvantage. It really began after the "corrupt bargain" of 1824 and never ceased until the Jacksonites had fully righted what they regarded as a grave wrong. Adams was repeatedly subject to great pressure to remove pro-Jackson office holders and replace them with Adamsites, who in turn would work for Adams's re-election. But the President resolutely resisted such a housecleaning as inconsistent with his concept of the public good. From the beginning, his removals, a mere twelve in all, evidently were confined largely to cases of incompetence and moral delinquency.

As a professional and high-minded public servant, Adams did not regard service in the national House of Representatives from Massachusetts as beneath the dignity of an ex-president. From 1831 to 1848 he served faithfully in this capacity, finally expiring in the capital building—almost literally dying in the harness. "Old Man Eloquent" finally became a popular hero as a crusader against slavery. He let a bitter and prolonged fight for a repeal of the "gag rule," which clamped a lid on all debate or action on petitions to abolish slavery. Here Adams was fighting for both free speech and free men. Because he abhorred slavery, he opposed the annexation of Texas in 1845 and the subsequent war with Mexico in 1846–1848. No one could question his integrity or morality in connection with these causes, and for the first time in his life he enjoyed personal popularity, at least among those of like mind. The taint of bargaining and corruption had receded far into the past.

CHAPTER 7

Andrew Jackson
1829–1837

If you would preserve your reputation . . . you must take a straight forward
determined course, regardless of the applause or censure of the populace.

Andrew Jackson, 1813

"Old Hickory" Jackson had many conspicuous faults, but a lack
of integrity was not among them. He was ill-educated, ill-tem-
pered, opinionated, suspicious, unbending, dictatorial ("King Andrew the First"), vindictive, and a fierce hater. But he was not
basically a dishonest man, and so sensitive was he about his honor
before becoming President that on occasion he would risk his life
before an opponent's dueling pistol.

President Jackson was a frontier aristocrat from Tennessee
who lived on a plantation of some 6,000 acres in a splendid man-
sion, The Hermitage, now a shrine near Nashville. He was swept
into office in the election of 1828 by the new manhood-suffrage
democracy, with much of its strength in the trans-Appalachian
West, from whose Tennessee Jackson hailed.

Under the leadership of Old Hickory, an uncommon man,
the common people came into their own. Jackson did not create

this tidal wave; he was the beneficiary of it. His "hickoryite" followers used tactics against President John Quincy Adams that a man of the highest principles should have been quick to disclaim. But the Adamsites conducted an equally dirty campaign, and neither Jackson nor Adams was able to exercise control over their frenzied followers. With the masses controlling the ballot box, the game of politics was pulled down to their level. He who throws dirt does not always lose ground, and the nation has yet to see the spectacle of a president-elect who declined his high office because his supporters hurled too much mud and stuffed too many ballot boxes.

Strange though it may seem, Jackson was elected as the reform candidate, the victim of the Adams-Clay "corrupt bargain" in 1824. He would right the great wrong that had been done him by the infamous Adams-Clay deal that had robbed him of the presidency. More than that, the Jacksonites would achieve reform by sweeping out the "rascals" holding office under President Adams (and then sweeping in their own rascals). This pledge was one campaign promise in American political history that was substantially kept.

Jackson's name has been traditionally and somewhat unfairly associated with the so-called spoils system, a term evidently adapted from Senator Marcy's blunt observation in 1832, "To the victor belong the spoils of the enemy." But Jackson did not invent or even introduce the spoils system. Distressing though the thought may be, President Washington had realistically and wisely appointed to high office Federalist supporters of the new Constitution who were committed to making it work. Jefferson, to a degree, was the real father of the spoils system. As a Republican he initially removed about as large a percentage of incumbent office holders as Jackson did, although far fewer in absolute terms—and with less brutality. The political decapitation of a large number of incumbents did not come until the "reign" of Andrew Jackson, and continued at a scandalous pace until partially slackened by the epochal Pendleton Civil Service Act of 1883. Actually in Jackson's first eighteen months only 919 of 10,093 officeholders were ousted, or somewhat fewer than 10 percent.

There can be no doubt that the civil service needed some kind of reform when Jackson took office. Many of the incumbents were uncivil civil servants: incompetent, indifferent, rude, lax, alcoholic, and senile. Some of these creatures looked upon their public office as a lifetime sinecure, to be handed down like a precious heirloom from father to son. A reform broom was badly needed at the time of Jackson's inauguration, even though the real clean sweeps came in later administrations.

As for the spoils of office, President Jackson used the term "rotation in office," or simply "rotation," which was his synonym for "reform." In retrospect, one is impressed with his moderation in using the headsman's axe, especially when his toll is compared with some of the housecleanings of his successors. An article of faith of Jacksonian democracy was that every patriotic citizen was as good as any other, perhaps even a little better. Government in this ox-cart age was small and uncomplicated; hence education and experience carried no great weight. No one man should be allowed to hold a lucrative office for any length of time; a turn-about was fair play, and other patriotic Americans should have a chance at the gravy trough. Besides, so the argument ran, they would be better citizens after seeing how government worked from the inside. The test would not be whether the prospect was competent in training and experience, but rather, "What have you done or what will you do for the party?" Especially pointed was the inquiry, "Can you be of help in reelecting the President?" In short, rotation in office meant that more men would experience the workings of government and hence, in theory, would become better citizens.

As the rotation system was finally perfected, the major evictions occurred when the party of the incumbent president was voted out of power. The result was a true spoils system, with the ideal of "rotation" shoved into the background. At all events, emphasis on public plunder for partisan followers did not undermine the basic integrity of the incumbent, as he was viewed by the body politic. Incumbents before Jackson had "turned the rascals out," and they were to continue to do so.

Ironically Jackson did not rotate himself out of office at the end of four years. He sought and triumphantly won a second term, for a total of eight stormy years. As the preacher once told his congregation, "Do as I tell you to do, not as I do."

One illogical burden of the presidency is that the incumbent earns little credit for the achievements of his appointees, and much discredit if they turn out to be bad apples. Jackson made one monumentally bad choice when he named Samuel Swartwout of New York, despite a strong warning from Secretary of State Van Buren, as Collector of the Port of New York—a lucrative position. Appointed in 1829, he fled to England in 1838, leaving his accounts short by $1,225,705.69. He enjoys the unenviable distinction of being the first man, but alas not the last, to embezzle more than a million dollars from the federal government. President Jackson was not privy to this thievery; his chief sin appears to have been bad judgment of character, despite emphatic warnings. Nor was he by any means the last president to be tainted by dishonest appointees. Jackson also was troubled by irregularities in some of the departments, especially the Post Office, the War and Navy Departments, and the Bureau of Indian Affairs.

President Jackson assembled a regular cabinet, but he supplemented it with informal meetings involving a group of politicians, journalists, and others, altogether about thirteen men. Critics jeered at this "Kitchen Cabinet," although it did not meet in the kitchen of the White House. Among other assets, the group enabled Jackson to keep a sensitive finger on the popular pulse. In addition, these gatherings were not unconstitutional, despite charges by the President's enemies. Actually, the cabinet is not mentioned in the Constitution, and the president is free to seek out such counselors, good or bad, as he chooses. Others have done so, including Theodore Roosevelt with his "Tennis Cabinet" and Harry Truman, who had his "Missouri Gang."

Jackson was not above permitting political animosities to warp his judgment. He adopted the policy, espoused by some of his predecessors, of not approving Congressional grants for internal improvements that lay solely within the borders of individual states. Accordingly, an appropriation for the Maysville Road in Kentucky perished before the presidential veto pen in 1830. Jackson declared in his message of disapproval that the road was "exclusively within the limits of a State" and had "no connection with any established system of improvements."

Jackson to the contrary, the Maysville Road enjoyed important interstate connections, and clearly qualified for presidential approval. Evidently the President was badly misinformed, or he could have been playing anti-Clay politics, to the discredit of the White House. Jackson and Clay hated each other, partly because the Kentuckian had allegedly robbed Jackson of the presidency in 1824 with the "corrupt bargain." The Maysville Road lay not only in Clay's Kentucky but also ranked as a pet project of Clay, who was grooming himself for election over Jackson in the forth-coming contest of 1832. If it is true, as seems probable, that Jackson vetoed the Maysville appropriation partly or primarily because of his feud with Clay, we can hardly commend him for placing personal animus above the national interest.

On May 28, 1830, the day after he vetoed the Maysville Road bill, President Jackson signed the Indian Removal Act. The Indians of what was then the lower south were suffering from the westward encroachments of acquisitive whites, and many American leaders supported the scheme of moving the aborigines beyond the Mississippi, where they presumably could pursue their ancient ways "as long as the water flows and the grass grows." President Jackson, the famous Indian fighter, had no burning dislike of peaceful red men, but he finally reached the conclusion that complete removal would best promote the future of both the white men and the red aborigines.

The forced trek west—"The Trail of Tears"—brought incredible suffering to the transplanted tribes, and much loss of life. The Indians of the Northwest resisted removal in the bloody little Black Hawk War of 1832. And despite all the solemn promises, greedy white men ultimately encroached on the new Indian lands. Yet Jackson accepted no bribes that we know of, and sincerely believed that this human uprooting was all for the best. Perhaps it was, for there might well have been worse troubles if the transfer of peoples had not taken place.

President Jackson's war on the Bank of the United States was not only perfectly legal—the big-money men to the contrary—but it resulted in one of his most spectacular victories. At New Orleans in 1815, he had only repulsed the British with bloody losses to them. In 1832, with his veto of the bill to recharter the Bank of the United States, he not only repulsed the bank but took steps that led to its being stamped out of existence. What he did was perfectly legal—and in the light of day.

The Bank of the United States was a powerful institution. A substantial portion of its stock was held by the federal government, and it was a depository for surplus funds from the treasury. First chartered in 1791, the Bank had been rechartered in 1816 for twenty years. In 1832 it had four more years of guaranteed life, but the glamorous Henry Clay, athirst for the presidency, decided to embarrass President Jackson by bringing up the Bank as a campaign issue in his quest for the highest office. The recharter bill passed Congress in due course, and President Jackson, never one to shrink from what he regarded as his duty, promptly and emphatically vetoed it. His stamp of disapproval was essentially the death warrant of the Bank of the United States.

Foes of Jackson have somehow managed to implant the impression that his veto was tainted with illegality. The fact is that the president is at perfect liberty under the Constitution to veto any bill that comes to the White House desk. And Old Hickory was not one to recoil from responsibility.

Jackson disliked monopolistic banks and hated Henry Clay, who supported the Bank. Old Hickory was from the West, where wildcat banks with depreciated currency flourished, and where burning resentment had developed against the restraining efforts of the "sound money" Bank of the United States. This powerful institution undeniably had a corrupting influence, for it freely loaned large sums of money to the members of Congress and in other ways made its influence felt. Jackson also branded the Bank of the United States unconstitutional, even though John Marshall of the Supreme Court had decreed otherwise in the famous case of *McCulloch* v. *Maryland* (1819). Old Hickory's view was that it was his privilege to interpret the Constitution as he saw it, not as John Marshall saw it.

Jackson's western prejudices, though vented legally, ultimately cost countless millions of innocent American depositors in weak banks uncounted millions of dollars. The Bank of the United States was a powerful stabilizing institution. The nation was to have no such financial colossus until the Federal Reserve system was established under President Wilson in 1913. The Federal Deposit Insurance Corporation was authorized by Congress under President Franklin Roosevelt in 1933. One of the most cherished liberties of Americans in the nineteenth century was the liberty that many citizen had, banker or barber, honest or dishonest, to set up shop, take in the depositor's money—and then go bankrupt.

High on President Jackson's hate list, along with an embittered Henry Clay, was John C. Calhoun of South Carolina. After being alienated by the Jackson administration, Calhoun became the foremost champion of states' rights and the nullification of federal laws by individual states. The crunch finally came in November 1832 when a special convention in South Carolina, con-

demning the high pro-Northern tariff laws, formally declared the
congressional acts of 1828 and 1832 "null, void, and no law."

Although a Carolinian by birth, Jackson not only reacted with
great verbal vigor but strengthened his position by some modest
military moves. Besides hating Calhoun, he felt his responsibility
as commander in chief of the armed forces. As a former general
who had sanctioned the hanging of six mutinous militia men, he
did not appreciate back talk from one of the members of the
union of states of which he was head and guardian.

As the Carolinians armed themselves, there was ugly talk of
civil war, which actually came nearly thirty years later. Ironically,
peace was largely preserved by Jackson's foe, the conciliatory
Henry Clay, who had no desire to see the President emerge with
new laurels and the scalp of South Carolina dangling from his
belt. A compromise was worked out by Clay in Congress, and on
March 2, 1833 Jackson signed the new compromise tariff bill.
Duties on imports were lowered to a level that was not completely
satisfactory to either party—but they were lowered. Thus was the
showdown to come at Fort Sumter in 1861 averted for the time
being. In fact, Jackson has been criticized for not having strangled
the serpent of secession in its cradle.

Some critics have concluded that iron-willed Old Hickory was
playing politics by first shaking his fist and then wagging his finger. Despite all his bluster, South Carolina forced a substantial
lowering of the tariff, and emerged completely unrepentant. She
could be voted the state most likely to secede in later years, as
indeed proved to be the case in 1860. But the charge of playing
politics seems unconvincing, primarily because the storm broke
several months after Jackson was triumphantly reelected for a
second and final term. Hot-tempered though he was, he could see
the folly of fighting a preventive war to avert one that might
never come anyhow.

The question has been raised, but never satisfactorily answered, as to why Jackson inconsistently went to the brink in
countering a rebellious South Carolina, although quietly acquiesc-
ing the year before misbehavior by the state of Georgia. This
neighboring state had thrice flouted the Supreme Court, most
conspicuously in 1831, by insisting on control over the resident
Cherokee Indians. Disliking the arrogant Chief Justice Marshall,
Jackson is alleged to have remarked, "John Marshall has made his
decision; now let him enforce it." The former hero general could

hardly conceive of John Marshall, clad in his black judicial robes, defending the abused Indians.

Plainly Old Hickory was not consistent in handling state defiance of the federal government. In the case of Georgia, he may have been motivated by dislike of Marshall, and by his determination to carry out his own Indian removal policy. He may also have been prompted by a desire to win the political support of Georgia and the South in his campaign for reelection. There was also the difficulty of subduing Georgia with armed force, particularly at a time when a showdown with South Carolina impended. But inconsistency in the White House is not generally regarded as a crime, even though it may be a surrender to expediency.

Jackson showed some vindictiveness in his treatment of the expiring Bank of the United States, headed by the crafty Nicholas Biddle. Suspecting that this slippery financier would use his funds unscrupulously to win support for the Bank, as he actually did, Jackson decided to withdraw all government deposits from the hated "monster bank." More accurately, he would pay out existing deposits for current use without replenishing them. When the stubborn Secretary of the Treasury would not obey orders from his commander in chief, Jackson fired him and replaced him with Roger B. Taney, who later gained both fame and infamy as chief justice on the Supreme Court.

Senator Henry Clay, Jackson's beaten rival of 1832, introduced a Senate resolution, adopted on March 28, 1834 by a vote of 26 to 20, formally censuring the President for having illegally removed the federal deposits from the Bank of the United States. An aroused Jackson entered a formal protest against the censure, which he judged to be unconstitutional. It was finally and formally expunged from the Senate journal in January 1837.

This censure was playing politics with a vengeance, for President Jackson was well within his rights when he dismissed one cabinet member and chose another more responsive to his will. As for Clay's resolution of censure, it was clearly the gratuitous intrusion of an embittered rival. Even so, there were many who believed that Jackson had acted unlawfully during his war on the Bank.

As a man of fiscal integrity, Jackson provoked a crisis with France over the nonpayment of a debt for earlier spoliations of commerce, as acknowledged by the French in a treaty concluded in 1831. The President was undiplomatically provocative, for he evidently believed that both honest nations and honest individuals should pay their just debts fully and on schedule. Jackson was correct, but tactlessly so. And he did get the money.

Jackson in actuality leaned over backward in dealing with the problem of Texas. He followed the revolution of 1836 against Mexico with great interest and sympathy, in part because his old friend Sam Houston was its leader. But Jackson held back his formal recognition of the independence of Texas until his last day in office, March 3, 1837. He thus lagged far behind the Senate, which had overwhelmingly voted for recognition some eight months earlier. He presumably did not want to stir up further an already embittered North-South controversy over slavery, and he probably wanted to avoid unnecessary unpleasantness with Mexico by premature recognition.

As presidents go, Jackson was a man of exceptional honor and integrity and he expected as much from subordinates. Most of his alleged slips from grace, especially those trumpeted by his political enemies, can be explained away with relative plausibility.

CHAPTER 8

Martin Van Buren
1837–1841

> *. . . Our government quietly but efficiently performs the sole legitimate end of political institutions, in doing the greatest good to the greatest number.*

Martin Van Buren,
inaugural address,
March 4, 1837

President Martin Van Buren, a Democrat, was the first professional politician to reach the White House. As "The Wizard of Albany," the capital of New York State, he had been the master spirit of the early political machine known as the Albany Regency. As "King Martin the First," he inherited Jackson's mantle, as well as Old Hickory's numerous and highly vocal enemies. As a result of these handicaps and others, Van Buren has been written down by early historians as a simpering sycophant—a "Little Van"— who followed furtively and dishonestly in the footsteps of the man he called his "illustrious predecessor." Actually, few of the Presidents could point to a term of four years that exhibited so few irregularities, even minor ones among subordinates for whom the chief executive had little or no direct responsibility.

Even so, probably no one-term President has ever accumulated so many pejorative nicknames, a number of them relating to his New York home at Kinderhook. Among the best known were the Kinderhook Fox, the Red Fox of Kinderhook (his hair was red), and the Wizard of Kinderhook. There can be no doubt that Van Buren was polished, urbane, courteous, suave, and captivating. But one man's charm and sophistication can easily be interpreted by critics as guile and deviousness, or even the iron hand in the velvet glove. Other nicknames were the Little Magician, the American Talleyrand, and the Machiavellian Belshazzar.

The New Testament tells us that those who take to the sword shall perish by the sword. Politics got Van Buren into the White House in 1837, and Whig politicians swept him into the discard heap with the inane Log Cabin and Hard Cider campaign of 1840. Partisan politics created a simpering dandy, renamed "Martin Van Ruin," who had never existed except in the fertile imaginations of his opponents.

Van Buren emerges as a professional who early learned that party government is essentially representative government, and that without the lubrication of democratic politics the machinery simply would not function smoothly. True democrats like Van Buren believed that the sober second-thought of the people could never be wrong. Prior to his time parties had been widely regarded as necessary evils that had to be tolerated. Van Buren reaffirmed Jeffersonian faith in the sound judgment of the masses, with strong emphasis on the role of the states within the federal system. Faithful followers would be rewarded with political offices.

President Van Buren gave the country a much better administration than he is generally given credit for. He skillfully resisted powerful pressures to become embroiled in the Canadian insurrection of 1837–1838, even though his neutral course was unpopular among countless anti-British Americans on the northern frontier. Van Buren also discontinued the policy of depositing government money in collapsible state banks, then called "pet banks," after the arrogant Bank of the United States had failed to secure a renewal of its charter. Under Van Buren's leadership the Independent Treasury system was set up by Congress in 1840. Van Buren also opposed the annexation of Texas as liable to provoke war with Mexico, as it ultimately did under President Polk in 1846. The inexorable workings of the business cycle brought the devastating panic of 1837, which many critics unfairly blamed on "Martin Van Ruin."

The Van Buren administration was free of major scandals, although unpublicized irregularities on a minor scale continued in some of the departments, as they probably always have and will. The collectorship of the Port of New York was again involved. Van Buren had strongly but unsuccessfully urged President Jackson not to appoint Samuel Swartwout, who "Swartwouted out" to England in 1838 with his accounts more than one million dollars in arrears. The result was a black mark for Van Buren, who by this time had become president.

Van Buren next appointed Jesse Hoyt to succeed Swartwout as collector of the Port of New York. Incredibly, the new appointee outdid the defaulter Swartwout in every category of crookedness except the amount actually embezzled. The Van Buren who had read Swartwout's character with amazing perception misread that of Hoyt with backfiring misperception. A large share of all revenue from customs duties flowed through the New York customhouse, which for many years continued to be a hotbed of various kinds of graft, including under-the-table payments by favored importers.

The Whigs, in their fantastic Log Cabin and Hard Cider campaign of 1840, shouted down, drank down, and lied down the luckless Van Buren, whose solid achievements were obscured by the unprecedented outburst of hoopla. Four years later, at the Democratic nominating convention in Baltimore, Van Buren led the field by more than a simple majority of the ballots cast. But he failed to reach the necessary two-thirds majority that the party now required. A man of principle to the end, Van Buren agreed to accept the lost-cause nomination of the antislavery Free Soil party in 1848. He received no electoral votes but polled 291,000 popular votes to the winner's 1,360,000. Despite certain defeat, he stood by his moral principles to the end.

CHAPTER 9

William Henry Harrison and John Tyler 1841–1845

. . . It shall be my first and highest duty to preserve unimpaired the free institutions under which we live and transmit them to those who shall succeed me in their full force and vigor.

John Tyler, inaugural address,
April 9, 1841

For Harrison, "Tippecanoe and Tyler too" had been a winning slogan in the presidential campaign of 1840. The rhyme was catching, but there the harmony just about ended. The office-hungry Whigs, headed by strong nationalist leaders like Henry Clay and Daniel Webster, had placed John Tyler on their national ticket as vice president. They hoped that this stubborn Virginian would attract votes from the South, and that Clay and Webster, as uncrowned kings, could more or less lead the elderly "Old Tippecanoe" around by the nose. But Harrison, after showing disquieting signs of independence, left his sponsors dangling when he died after only one month in office, before he had an opportunity to accomplish anything sginificant, good or bad.

Harrison's mantle then fell on Tyler, who at heart was still a states-rights Democrat in the clothing of a Southern Whig. "His Accidency" was the first man to be elevated to the White House by the death of his predecessor, and he forthwith assumed the title of president. The title of "Acting President" Tyler was not to his liking. As will be noted, he was a man of principle, and he clung tenaciously to his convictions in spite of hell or high water. In 1836, while still a member of the United States Senate, he had resigned rather than follow instructions from the legislature of Virginia to vote for a certain resolution. This state body had elected Tyler to the Senate, and he evidently felt duty bound to take this drastic and wholly unnecessary step.

Tyler's states-rights convictions continued to be such that much later, in 1861, although a former President of the United States, he served as a member of the Virginia convention that voted to break up the United States. Later in that same year he served as a delegate to the provisional Congress of the Confederate States of America, and subsequently he was elected to a seat in the Confederate House of Representatives.

The mystery is why a man of Tyler's rigid principles should have consented to accept the vice presidential nomination of the Whigs in 1840. He obviously would add strength to the illusion that the Clayites and Websterites were more favorable to Southern states' rights than they actually were. As a matter of fact, virtually no one had expected rugged Old Tippecanoe to die. Tyler, as vice president and presiding officer of the Senate, might in fact do the case of states' rights some good.

The campaign of 1840, featuring log cabins and hard cider, was the first one in which a national platform was published, in this case that of the Democrats. The Whig leaders, obviously afraid of making enemies and hence losing votes, did not publish theirs, but kept a copy safely in the pockets of men like Henry Clay, the glamorous Whig leader with burning presidential ambitions. But it was no secret that the Whigs, among other changes, strongly favored an end to the Independent Treasury System, the creation of a new Bank of the United States, and the enactment of a more highly protective tariff.

Wielding his veto pen freely, Tyler twice disapproved bills for establishing a new bank, thus sounding the death knell of the scheme. A furious caucus of Whig Congressmen formally read the stiff-backed Tyler out of the Whig party, of which he appeared to be a member in name only. "Traitor Tyler's" inherited Cabinet then resigned in a body, except for Secretary of State Webster, who was involved in delicate negotiations with Great Britain over tensions along the explosive northern border. In this area President Tyler cooperated with him commendably.

At the outset we must remember that the charges of wrongdoing leveled against the Tyler administration were trumpeted by outraged Whigs seeking to rid themselves of the obdurate Virginian. Whenever a President is faced with a hostile Congress bent on pressing impeachment charges, no matter how flimsy they may be, he must not be surprised by such harassment. They are a part of the great game of politics.

President Tyler was accused of various misdeeds by his foes in the Whig Congress, but most of these charges seem to fall into the category of nitpicking. In 1841 Tyler appointed three private citizens to investigate well-founded rumors of fraud in that den of iniquity known as the New York Custom House. The investigators were evidently being paid from funds which the president had on hand for the general welfare but which had not been specifically appropriated by Congress for sleuthing. Reasonably enough, President Tyler defended himself on the grounds that he was only honoring his constitutional oath to enforce the laws.

As Congressional interference with the presidential office increased, Tyler informed the House of Representatives that if it believed him guilty of impeachable offenses, it should impeach him so that he could defend his honor in a formal trial before the Senate of the United States. He was even attacked for having exercised his veto power, which is explicitly granted in the Constitution. The anti-impeachment members of the House finally prevailed when they voted down a motion, 127 to 83, to appoint a committee to investigate the so-called charges.

Accusations of a more serious nature were leveled against Secretary of State Daniel Webster, who enjoyed President Tyler's full support in negotiating a peaceful settlement of the Maine boundary dispute with Great Britain. The people of the Pine Tree State were loath to yield a substantial part of the land they had long claimed. Accordingly, President Tyler authorized the use of "the secret service fund," as established by Congress for activities *abroad*. But the money was to be used at *home* in Maine to persuade local editors of newspapers and members of the state legislature to support Webster's split-the-difference negotiations with Great Britain. Technically, this outlay seems like small change when compared with the misdeeds of federal agencies in modern times, including the Federal Bureau of Investigation and the Central Intelligence Agency.

Another cloud hanging over British-American relations during these anxious months was the trial of the Canadian Alexander McLeod by a New York jury in 1841. He was accused of murder following a British-Canadian raid on the American side of the Niagara River, and his hanging might have unleashed the dogs of war. Fortunately for him and the nations involved, he was acquitted when two of the principal witnesses against him did not show up and McLeod was able to establish a persuasive alibi. Secretary Webster's records reveal a transfer of $1,000 to the Attorney General of the United States at about this time. There is no proof that it was spent for bribery, although cynics may continue to speculate. If it bought peace, seldom has peace come so cheaply.

CHAPTER 10

James Knox Polk
1845–1849

. . . War exists, and, notwithstanding all our efforts to avoid it, exists by the act of Mexico herself.

James K. Polk,
war message to Congress,
May 11, 1846

The word "honesty" conjures up such concepts as truthfulness, sincerity, frankness, and freedom from deceit, fraud, or bribery. In all of these areas, Polk receives low marks; he was publicly branded by political foes as "Polk the Mendacious" or "Polk the Liar." Yet this first dark-horse president, an experienced Congressman and a former governor of Tennessee, is now esteemed as one of the more successful occupants of the White House. He added more territory to the United States than any other President, except Thomas Jefferson, who completed the Louisiana purchase. Polk succeeded by deviously provoking a war with Mexico, invading her territory, and finally inducing her, gun at head and bribe extended, to cede coveted California and the vast adjoining area stretching eastward to Texas. The Mexicans have never forgotten or forgiven their rapacious neighbor for shearing off about one half of their domain, and relations between the two nations are still partly under this cloud.

In Polk's defense, partisans say that when he stooped to questionable dealings he was clearly thinking of the national interest, not his own. So it seems in perspective, even though the quarrel over slavery in the area wrested from Mexico resulted in one of the bloodiest civil wars in history. At all events, Polk was not scheming for reelection, as many of his successors have done. At the proper time he made clear that he was not a candidate to succeed himself, and this declaration clarified and somewhat purified his motives. In any event he nearly killed himself with overwork on the job, and he died on June 15, 1849, some three months after leaving the White House.

Any assessment of Polk's integrity and that of his successors must take into consideration the published platforms of the relevant major political parties. The first such pronouncement was unveiled in 1840, and in 1844 came the first one of a winning presidential candidate, that of the Democrat Polk. Henceforth the nominees for the highest office were supposed to stand on and abide by the principles thus publicly professed. All too often the platforms have been public eyewash.

The notorious failure of presidential candidates to abide by the preachments of their party platforms, or even to carry out their own promises made during their campaigning, has led to much cynicism. American folklore tells us that the planks of political platforms, unlike those at a railroad, are constructed to get in on, not to stand on. Campaign promises often are no more than the expression of a hope, an aspiration, or an intention, invariably one with an implied predicate. Two old sayings come to mind: "Jove laughs at the promises of lovers and politicians," and "Promises and piecrusts are made to be broken." Today relatively few voters regard campaign pledges and political platforms as sacred compacts or covenants with the voters.

At the outset, Polk's inaugural address treated with slavish respect the platform on which he had run. He repeated the public declaration that America's claim to the whole of the territory of Oregon, and also Texas, was "clear and unquestionable." The fact is that the nation's title to all of the Oregon territory (and Texas) was far from being clear and unquestionable, as Polk well knew. Yet he repeated this exaggerated claim. In subsequent weeks, as a consummate bluffer in poker diplomacy, he consented, with what seemed to be reluctance, to a fair compromise on Oregon. Polk thus yielded roughly half of the territory of Oregon by establishing the boundary line of Canada along the present 49th parallel. Fortunately for the United States, he finally surrendered his extreme claim, partly because the country by this time had the war with Mexico on its hands. If forced to fight both foes at once, Polk might not have been able to defeat either.

President Polk also inherited a bitter quarrel with Mexico when Congress, by a joint resolution on December 29, 1845, admitted Texas to the union as an equal state. Mexico was still technically at war with the rebellious Texans, but had exhibited no solid evidence of a willingness or capacity to reconquer them. The Texans claimed that their southern boundary reached to the Rio Grande, rather than to the Nueces River about 150 miles north, where the line of demarcation had run during many years of Spanish-Mexican rule. Yet Polk, who knew better or should have been more fully aware of the facts, declared in his inaugural address, "The Republic of Texas was once a part of our country [and] was unwisely ceded away to a foreign power." He was referring of course to the transcontinental treaty of 1819, under which the United States received Florida from Spain, plus a delineation of the western boundary of the Louisiana Purchase. In any case the new pact with Spain specifically excluded Texas from the jurisdiction of the United States.

As far as Mexico was concerned, this so-called Texan boundary dispute was strictly one-sided. The government in Mexico City looked upon the argument as an internal matter, and not worthy of discussion with outsiders. To the Mexicans, the revolting Texans had never really established their independence, even after some nine years, and the boundary line between two administrative entities within Mexico was no legitimate concern of any other nation.

Yet the Washington government, prior to the formal annexation of Texas in 1845, had assured the Texans of protection by federal forces within the boundaries that they claimed as their own. As a preliminary step, Polk ordered General Zachary Taylor to take up a defensive position on the Texans' Nueces River, which the general reached in August 1845. Polk meanwhile attempted to make an offer to Mexico that would involve the payment of $25 million for the territory westward of Texas and including upper California. The outraged Mexicans would not even permit the special envoy from the United States to present this insulting proposition. They held fast to their soundly based historical version of the southwestern boundary of Texas.

Rebuffed on all counts, including the Texas boundary adjustment, Polk ordered General Taylor, tarrying on the Nueces River of Texas, to move south with his 3,000 or so men, and then take up a provocative position on the Rio Grande. This he succeeded in doing late in March 1846, but still there was no attack by Mexican troops on the intruders. Several entries in Polk's diary during this anxious period laid bear his purposes. He repeatedly mentions that there was no word yet of a Mexican attack, as though he hoped for one and indeed expected one, thus trumping up an excuse for asking Congress formally to declare war on Mexico.

When no clash was reported, Polk's patience finally gave way. He called a meeting of his cabinet for May 9, 1846, before which he outlined his plan to ask Congress for a declaration of war on two grounds. First was the refusal of the government in Mexico City to receive his envoy, John Slidell, who had carried Polk's last offer to buy California and the intervening territory for $25 million. The second pretext was Mexico's unwillingness or inability to pay damage claims for losses to American lives and property, amounting to about $3 million and growing out of recurrent disorders in that revolution-rent country.

Neither of these claims justified war, unless one were scrounging for excuses to provoke hostilities. The Mexicans had agreed to receive an envoy, but not one of Minister Slidell's high rank, for they had broken diplomatic relations with the United States shortly after the formal annexation of Texas in 1845. As for claims, that was an old story, and American states had already defaulted on their obligations to foreigners without bringing on an armed attack.

At this critical cabinet meeting, two of those present spoke up and said they would feel better about a war message if the Mexican forces should attack Taylor's small army first. Yet the members finally agreed that the draft of a war message should be submitted to this body for decision at the next meeting.

By one of the strangest coincidences in history, word reached Washington that very evening that Mexican troops had crossed the Rio Grande and attacked General Taylor's intruders. The

casualties included 16 Americans killed or wounded. The Mexicans had been goaded into action not only by the presence of the
invaders, but also because General Taylor had blockaded the entrance to the Rio Grande, up which Mexican troops had been
bringing supplies. Additionally, he had built a fort whose guns
threatened or would threaten the Mexican town of Matamoros
across the river. In short, Polk had succeeded completely in his
efforts to goad the Mexicans into a war that would force them to
yield the spacious territories that they refused to sell on any
terms.

Critics were reminded of the biblical story of Naboth's vineyard as recounted in the Old Testament. King Ahab coveted a
next-door vineyard owned by Naboth, whose family had held it
for generations. But Naboth would accept neither money nor a
trade, so Ahab turned the problem over to his wife, Jezebel. She
arranged to have Naboth stoned to death, after which his vineyard was taken.

What was Polk to do if he coveted territory like California
which foreign agents were reputed to be interested in grabbing
for their own country? This priceless expanse had been in the
Hispanic family for centuries, and, like Naboth, one does not sell
or barter a family heirloom. Is an American president justified,
even in the national interest, in goading its neighbor into a war so
that he can seize what otherwise is unobtainable? Polk did not go
as far as Jezebel, but his ethics were about as questionable when
he embraced the principle, "If you can't buy it, seize it."

Ulysses S. Grant, later a prominent Civil War general and
eighteenth President of the United States, was a young officer
with General Taylor's force that marched the 150 miles or so
from the Nueces River to the Rio Grande. In the memoirs that he
wrote after leaving the White House, he branded the Mexican
war that resulted from the annexation of Texas as "unholy" and
as "one of the most unjust ever waged by a stronger against a
weaker nation. It was an instance of a republic following the bad
example of European monarchies, in not considering justice in
their desire to acquire additional territory." Grant went on to
write, "The Southern rebellion was largely the outgrowth of the
Mexican War. Nations, like individuals, are punished for their
transgressions. We got our punishment in the most sanguinary
and expensive war of modern times." And Abraham Lincoln,
about a year before he became President, declared that the Mex-

ican War was unnecessary, because Mexico was "in no way molesting or menacing the United States."

Uncandid as Polk was in provoking the war, he compounded his sin by misrepresenting the facts to Congress. In his war message he declared that Mexican forces had "invaded our territory and shed American blood upon the American soil." War had come, and "notwithstanding all our efforts to avoid it, exists by the act of Mexico herself."

Polk would have been more truthful if he had said that on his orders General Taylor's troops had invaded soil to which the Mexicans had a better historic claim than the Americans, that American blood had been shed on soil that was not clearly American, and that he had made efforts to avert war by trying to purchase what he wanted. Hostilities were regarded by the Mexicans as begun by the Americans when they blockaded the Rio Grande and pointed their guns across the river at Mexico's Matamoros.

Polk continued his deviousness in subsequent messages to Congress, especially when he told that body in December 1846 that "the war has not been waged with a view to conquest." Actually, Congress declared war on May 13, 1846, and about two weeks later Colonel Stephen Kearny was ordered to occupy New Mexico and particularly California. There American intruders were preparing to take over this sun-blessed area even before the formal declaration of war.

Yet Polk wanted Mexican territory rather than a Mexican war, so he entered into a backstairs intrigue. The former dictator of Mexico, the discredited Santa Anna, was then residing in Cuba. Through secret channels he let Polk know that if the American blockading squadron would permit him to slip through, he would undertake to sell out his country. This sorry scheme backfired badly, for Santa Anna not only double-crossed Polk but also rallied the Mexicans to resist the "gringo" invader. The President's "purchased peace" netted only fierce fighting.

So anxious was Polk to secure a peace on his terms that he dispatched to Mexico the chief clerk of the State Department, Nicholas Trist. Trist accompanied the invading army under General Scott, and, as instructed, kept his eyes open for a favorable opportunity to conclude a peace. The slippery Santa Anna let it be known that if $10,000 were paid down and $1 million when peace was concluded, negotiations could be begun. General Scott paid the $10,000, but the double-dealing Santa Anna used the armistice to prepare stronger defenses for Mexico City. Polk was infuriated, not so much because bribery had been used as because it had not brought his purchased peace.

An angry President recalled Trist, who seized a fleeting opportunity to sign a treaty of peace while there was still a government in Mexico City with which to negotiate. The terms were that the United States was to receive the vast area northwest of the Rio Grande claimed by Texas, plus California and the intervening territory. The United States agreed to pay $15 million for the land and assume long-standing American claims against Mexico in the sum of $3,250,000.

The assumption of these unpaid claims is understandable, partly because they had proved uncollectible from impoverished Mexico, and many American victims were suffering in dire poverty. But the payment of $15 million for the desired land was a different problem. Polk had been willing to offer $25 million for it, but had been rebuffed and, from his viewpoint, forced to fight an expensive war. Yet the vanquished, not the victors, normally pay indemnities, especially after hostilities had been "forced" on them. Some observers have concluded that basic American generosity, plus the Anglo-Saxon spirit of fair play, dictated the terms of the peace. Other critics have even suggested that the tough-fibered Polk suffered from a guilty conscience. We may doubt that a man of his devious bent spent many sleepless nights in shame. From the outset he had sought to buy both territory and peace, and he pursued this course to the bitter end.

The Mexicans saved some face by wringing reparations from the invader. When Trist made haste to conclude a treaty with provision for an indemnity, there was a strong likelihood that there would be no government left in Mexico City to accept the terms. In this eventuality the United States would have been confronted with a costly and protracted guerrilla war—one that would cost much more than the money finally offered.

Polk, though a devout Presbyterian, appears to have been one of those individuals who kept his public morality and his private morality in separate compartments. In public life he was devious, untruthful, and grasping. One commentator believes that Polk was demonstrating his basic integrity by reacting angrily against the abortive attempt by General Scott to bribe Santa Anna into a peace. But it seems proper to conclude that the President was more concerned about the waste of the money than about the attempt at bribery itself.

In private life, and as far as feathering his own nest was concerned, Polk was either exemplary or he covered his tracks completely. About the worst that can be charged against his administration was that it set up a pro-Democratic newspaper in Washington, *The Globe,* with $35,000 advanced by the treasury. The money was repaid in due season, and Polk evidently was completely successful in insulating himself from the transaction. Certainly no publicized fuss was ever raised about his possible involvement.

CHAPTER 11

Zachary Taylor
1849–1850

I have no private purposes to accomplish, no party projects to build up, no enemies to punish—nothing to serve but my country.

Zachary Taylor, letter,
April 12, 1848

President Taylor, a babe in the woods politically, was one of the few professional soliders to reach the White House. During a lifetime with the army, he had never resided in one place long enough to vote; apparently he cast his first ballot when 62 years of age, two years before being inaugurated President.

General Taylor had served gallantly against the Indians in various campaigns, but the Mexican War made him overnight a grade-A hero. "Old Rough and Ready," as he was called because of his informal attire, extracted victory from the jaws of defeat, despite heavy odds, at the fiercely fought battle of Buena Vista, Mexico, in February 1846. Both General Taylor and General Scott, the other great war hero, were Whigs, and President Polk, a Jacksonian Democrat, feared that either or both might eventually be swept into the White House on a tidal wave of acclaim.

Polk seriously considered replacing them with inferior Democratic commanders, but in the end wisely concluded that he would be better off to win the war with Whigs than to lose it with Democrats.

President Taylor, born in Virginia and domiciled in Louisiana, owned a substantial number of slaves. Yet he was not favorable to the extension of slavery into the territory recently wrested from Mexico. In fact, he privately urged the purposeful Californians to seek admission to the Union as a non-slave state. Thus started the heated debate over what is known as the Compromise of 1850. A part of the package was the detachment from western Texas of a huge area claimed by the Lone Star State, followed by the addition of this coveted expanse to the adjacent territory of New Mexico.

The outraged Texans threatened to invade the territory in question, seize what they regarded as rightfully theirs, and thus turn it into slave territory. General-President Taylor, his military ire aroused by this mutinous talk from the rear ranks of the slave states, appeared to be ready to lead an army in person against all "damned traitors," hang the leaders, and thus "Jacksonize" Texas. At the same time he would snatch the disputed area from the blot of black slavery.

Fortunately for sectional peace, President Taylor died unexpectedly, and in the calmer atmosphere that followed his demise the epochal Compromise of 1850 was hammered out. By its terms Texas yielded all claim to the disputed westward territory for $10 million to be paid by the Washington treasury. The South was not too happy with this arrangement but at least the compromise was aboveboard and it averted the Civil War for a decade.

Taylor served only one year and four months of his four-year term, and during that time only one scandal of major dimensions broke into the open. It reflected discreditably on his administration, even though he evidently was not aware of what was going on under his nose. The affair involved a pecuniary claim of the Galphin family of Georgia, and the pejorative slogan "Galphinism" was seized upon by Democratic foes of Taylor's Whig administration to tarnish the incumbent president. This prerevolutionary claim involved the British crown. George Galphin, a Georgia trader, had declared that payments were due him from certain Creek and Cherokee Indians, and the British government had agreed to discharge this debt from the sale of lands ceded to the crown by the Indians. The payment of this obligation was fixed at the equivalent of $43,500. Yet before this sum could be paid the War of Independence intervened, and the government of the new United States inherited both the rights and obligations of the British crown. Congress finally passed an act in 1848 authorizing the payment of the amount due to the executor of the estate of George Galphin, and it was so paid.

So far so good, but then the question arose of the necessity and propriety of paying also the accumulated back interest on the original $43,500. The attorney for the Galphin heirs was George W. Crawford, who was scheduled to receive half of the award for his services. Unfortunately for his reputation, he accepted the portfolio of secretary of war in President Taylor's cabinet, and a nasty scandal developed. If the payment of interest was authorized by his colleague, the secretary of the treasury, Crawford would receive almost $100,000 instead of about $22,000. The larger figure was a princely sum, for in the early 1840s a laborer was often lucky to receive a wage of $1 for an entire day.

Secretary Crawford permitted the claim for interest to be referred to Secretary of Treasury Meredith, who passed it on to the comptroller, an honest man, who in turn disallowed it. Attorney General Reverdy Johnson, Crawford's colleague in the cabinet, next ruled that the interest must be paid. Secretary Meredith then made out an order for the Treasury to disburse $191,352.89. A small fee would go to the attorney of record, and the avaricious Secretary Crawford would pocket nearly $100,000.

The whole affair smelled to high heaven, particularly the huge interest windfall that came to Crawford. Critical newspapers had a field day. The suspicion naturally arose that two of Crawford's cooperative colleagues had had their palms greased during this outrageous raid on the Treasury. President Taylor, painfully sensitive on points of honor, was cut to the quick by this exhibition of greed and probably dishonesty within his official family. Three of the cabinet members were obviously compromised. Taylor laid plans to ask the entire body to resign and then appoint a new group of advisers. But the fierce battle over the Compromise of 1850 supervened, and then Taylor died.

Scandals at the cabinet level always besmirch to some extent the President who originally appointed its members. This regrettably was to be the fate of the ruggedly honest Taylor.

CHAPTER **12**

Millard Fillmore
1850–1853

The great law of morality ought to have a national as well as a personal and individual application.

Millard Fillmore,
first annual message,
December 2, 1850

Millard Fillmore became the fourteenth president of the United States, but only the second accidental one, upon the death of "Old Zack" Taylor. A rather colorless lawyer from New York state, he entered politics, was elected to the state legislature, and then served several terms in Congress. An unsuccessful candidate for the governorship of New York, he became controller of his state, in which capacity he earned the enmity of the abolitionists. Actually, he opposed the fanatics and disunionists of both North and South. He was placed on the Whig ticket in 1848 as vice president partly to balance the Southern slaveowner Taylor. Fillmore, a fair-minded man, had presided over the Senate as Vice President with firmness, fairness, and good humor. Favoring conciliation over conflict, he had supported and signed the five component measures of the great Compromise of 1850.

As earlier noted, the slaveowning General Taylor was prepared to force a showdown with the slaveholding Texans over the Texan claim to territory earmarked for free-soil New Mexico. Fortunately for peace, Taylor died, Fillmore became President, and then openly allied himself with the moderate Whigs like Webster and Clay, who favored conciliation and compromise with the slaveholding South. The result was the multipronged Compromise of 1850—the last great sectional compact before the Civil War erupted in 1861. Prior to its completion, Fillmore sent a special message to Congress on August 6, 1850. In it, he successfully urged that Texas be indemnified in money for yielding her claim to the western territory, and he also added a plea for the settlement of outstanding controversies. As a part of the great Compromise of 1850, Fillmore signed and tried to enforce the vexatious Fugitive Slave Law, which the Southerners demanded and the Northern abolitionists deplored.

The epochal compromise averted the Civil War for eleven years, but Fillmore, along with other moderate Whigs like Daniel Webster, were damned by the more fanatical abolitionists as apostates and traitors, worthy of being classed with Benedict Arnold or Judas Iscariot. In truth, none of these men had ever been extreme abolitionists. One result was that for many years Fillmore and his fellow moderates were damned by pro-abolitionist historians, especially by those spawned in the abolitionist centers of New England.

If Fillmore had been a traitor, his so-called treachery would have been a major sensation, but during his partial term of more than two years nothing approaching a real scandal blackened him, then or later. Some minor graft of an inevitable nature may have been undermining the burgeoning bureaus, but at least Fillmore's known record remains relatively clean.

CHAPTER 13

Franklin Pierce
1853–1857

I find that the remark, " 'Tis distance [that] lends enchantment to the view" is no less true of the political than of the natural world.

Franklin Pierce,
letter, 1832

In the decade or so before the Civil War finally erupted, each of the successive presidents was bedeviled by the problem of slavery, especially its extension into the newly acquired territories. Zachary Taylor died in office before the full fury of the storm could break, but Presidents Fillmore, Pierce, Buchanan, and Lincoln successively had to grapple with the problem. In the eyes of extreme abolitionists any person was a criminal who condoned slavery or cooperated under the Fugitive Slave Act of 1850 in catching runaways. Extremists like William Lloyd Garrison angrily refused to cooperate with sin. In their fanatical zeal the abolitionists evidently forgot that the Union was made possible by compromise, and that when compromise broke down the Union would break up, as it did for four bloodstained years.

The word "slavery" does not appear in the Constitution, certainly as a concession to growing sectional sensibilities. But partly to insure ratification by the slaveholding states, the stipulation was included that any "person held to service or labor in one state" must be "delivered upon claim of the party to whom such service or labor may be due." Congress attempted to implement this provision by the inadequate Fugitive Slave Act of 1793, which was supplanted by the severe proviso embodied in the multipronged Compromise of 1850.

Accidental President Fillmore, as earlier noted, signed the Fugitive Slave Act of 1850, for which he was condemned by the extreme abolitionists. Basically what he had tried to do was to be fair to the South and honor the Constitution under an act of Congress in which all states were represented. The Fugitive Slave Act passed the United States Senate by a vote of 27 to 12; the House by a vote of 109 to 76. The basic question was: Shall the majority rule or an abolitionist minority?

Unfortunately for the Southern slavecatchers, they ran into angry mobs in the North, as well as other obstacles. Southern leaders felt betrayed because they had reluctantly accepted the give-and-take compromises of 1850 in the belief that the shop-keeping Yankees would honor them.

The atmosphere was already poisoned when "Handsome Frank" Pierce, "the Young Hickory" from the granite hills of New Hampshire, was elected President in 1852 on the Democratic ticket. Nominated at Baltimore on the forty-ninth ballot, he was an authentic dark horse, although he had served creditably in the United States House of Representatives and the United States Senate. His chief rival at the polls, an avowed Whig, was his old commander in the Mexican War, General Winfield Scott, who lost by a substantial margin. Pierce actually received some kind of mandate when he polled more votes than his two rivals combined, thus becoming a not-too-common majority president.

President Pierce has been savagely condemned for trying to implement the sweeping Compromise of 1850, including the harsh Fugitive Slave Act. But critics usually overlook the Democratic platform, although other presidents are commended for remaining as faithful to such pronouncements as Pierce proved to be. The relevant plank declared that the Democratic party "would adhere to a faithful execution of the acts known as the compromise measures settled by the last Congress." The act for reclaiming fugitive slaves was specifically mentioned.

The abolitionists dismissed Pierce as a weak "doughface"—a

Northern man with Southern principles, who could be shaped like the raw dough in a gingerbread man. Pierce was actually trying to be true to his party's platform and execute the laws faithfully in accordance with his presidential oath. Extremist abolitionists in the North likewise condemned him for having signed the Kansas-Nebraska Act in 1854, which created a localized civil war that merged with the vastly bloodier one in 1861.

The Kansas-Nebraska Act in effect gave the two territories in question an option as to the future of salvery. Local self-rule was the very essence of democracy, but the abolitionists opposed it in this instance, obviously because they might lose. Pierce neither originated nor passed the bill, which attracted adequate majorities in both houses of Congress. He could have left the measure unsigned, in which case it might or might not have been repassed. But he signed the bill, evidently believing, as a loyal supporter of the compromise package of 1850, that the proposed Kansas-Nebraska solution was basically fair.

Probably no man could have shaped events in Kansas to the liking of both sides, and Pierce certainly was unable to do so, though he tried hard to carry out his official obligation to execute the laws. Many Southerners had assumed that the North would turn Nebraska into a free state and that the South, for its part, would be allowed to turn Kansas into a slave state. The Southerners felt betrayed when the North, particularly the Emigrant Aid Company of New England, imported well-armed abolitionists. Yet the slavery men received support from "Border Ruffians" coming over from the slave state of Missouri. President Pierce was glad to pass on this thorny problem to his successor, President Buchanan.

Two developments under Pierce require comment. One was the purchase in 1853 of the southern portions of present Arizona and New Mexico from the Mexican government, a transaction known as the Gadsden Purchase. A major purpose was to secure a satisfactory railroad route from the South to the Pacific Coast. Critics of Pierce have charged that he was working hand in glove with the Southerners to strengthen their section and thus tighten the grip of slavery. The President no doubt was more pro-Southern than the abolitionists liked, but he was also the leader of a then united nation. Obviously, what promoted the economic interests of one section in a way promoted the interests of the nation as a whole.

The antislavery people also condemned Pierce in 1854 for having been responsible for the so-called Ostend Manifesto. In effect it proclaimed to Spain, "Sell us Cuba at our price or we will seize it." His opponents alleged that Pierce was acting like an international highwayman waving a pistol.

This ugly picture is so much out of focus as to be false. The United States, especially the South, had for some years been casting covetous eyes on Cuba as fertile soil for territorial expansion and the extension of slavery. In 1854 Pierce's Secretary of State instructed the American Ministers in Britain, Spain, and France to meet secretly and prepare recommendations for the possible acquisition of Cuba. The trio met for several days at Ostend, Belgium, and then moved eastward to Aix-la-Chapelle. Their final secret dispatch to Washington recommended that the United States offer up to $110 million for all of Cuba. If this offer was refused and the dangers of a contagious slave revolt in the island seemed imminent, then the United States should "wrest" the prize from the grip of Spain.

Rumors of these recommendations soon leaked out, and the Whig press, especially the antislavery journals, excoriated the bandit-like Democratic administration of President Pierce. Actually, there was no "Ostend Manifesto," for a "manifesto" is a public pronouncement. This dispatch not only was secret but was never acted upon, for Spain ignored it. Nevertheless the stench of scandal remained.

Pierce did become involved in some rather dubious dealings in connection with the desperate struggle in "bleeding Kansas" between the free-soilers and the slaveryites. In order to placate the North, the President sent out as governor of the Kansas territory a Pennsylvanian by the name of Andrew Reeder. For speculative purposes, the new arrival improperly bought up land from the Indians, but these contracts were all disallowed by the Commissioner of Indian Affairs. Pierce is sometimes blamed for not having dismissed Reeder immediately on learning of these irregularities, but he temporized on the grounds that he did not want to antagonize the North further by removing a pro-Northern governor. Pierce finally and belatedly dismissed the speculator, largely on the grounds that the errant governor had not satisfactorily explained his shady land deals. Reeder charged that Pierce had tried to bribe him into resigning without a fuss, but this accusation was never proved.

Concurrently with the growth of the lusty young nation in the 1850s was the growth of bureaucracy, with its attendant scandals. Some of those mushrooming under Pierce continued under his successors. Worthy of mention was the postmaster of New York, Isaac Fowler, who was appointed by Pierce and kept on under President Buchanan. In 1860 Fowler fled the country, leaving his accounts in arrears by some $160,000. He had stolen government revenues and had ladled them out to Democratic candidates running for public office.

In 1859 came another exposé, this one of the practice of awarding navy yard contracts to companies that had been generous in their contributions to Democratic candidates for public office. Another scandalous case was that of Cornelius Wendell, a printer for the Washington government who shared some of his considerable profits with Democratic candidates and newspapers.

Franklin Pierce is not generally regarded as a strong President in the Andrew Jackson tradition. But he was a more honest man than the abolitionists would admit, despite the inevitable peculations of a few underlings. His worst crimes were that he seems to have believed in majority rule and that he felt an obligation to abide by his constitutional oath to enforce the laws. The real lawbrakers were the abolitionist minority who flouted the Fugitive Slave Act of 1850 and made a mockery of the compromise implicit in the Kansas-Nebraska Act of 1854. Antislavery historians have been less than impartial to Pierce.

A point to remember is that Pierce was a loyal Democrat, representing the national party of the North and South, as was his successor, James Buchanan. Lincoln, the Republican, was a minority President who represented the North. He evidently reached the White House in 1860 in part because his opponents, North and South, failed to unite with sufficient enthusiasm behind a single candidate. Pierce remained a Democrat, and in retirement opposed the Lincoln administration because it usurped power and destroyed personal and property rights. To the end Pierce was loyal to the concept of one flag and one nation.

CHAPTER 14

James Buchanan
1857–1861

I have had a hard time during my administration, but, upon a careful review of all my conduct, I should not change it in a single important measure if this were now in my power.

James Buchanan,
letter to *Philadelphia Times*,
September 21, 1861

James Buchanan of Pennsylvania, known to some as "Old Buck" Buchanan, was almost 60 years of age when the first Southern states seceded, forshadowing the Civil War. Some critics have blamed his supposed indecisiveness during the secession crisis on his presumed senility. He had never married but he was wedded to the Constitution, and his reverence for it was so deep that he could hardly have moved vigorously against the seceders, even if he had commanded adequate armed forces, which were conspiciously lacking. After the Civil War flared forth, Lincoln overrode the Constitution and became a national hero, with appropriate statues. Buchanan respected his constitutional oath, and has gone down in history without statues—way down.

One serious charge lodged against Buchanan, especially by the abolitionists of the North, was that he had proved to be an accessory to the owning and catching of slaves. It is true that he had a good many friends and supporters among slaveowning Southerners, but slavery was specifically sanctioned by the Constitution. Nor had Buchanan signed the Fugitive Slave Act of 1850, approved by President Fillmore. Yet he felt bound by his inaugural oath not only to support the Constitution but also to enforce the acts of Congress, regardless of whose toes were trampled on, Northern or Southern.

A damning charge of connivance brought against Buchanan related to the Lecompton constitution for the prospective state of Kansas. Late in 1857 the proslavery men in this territory contrived to draft a constitution at Lecompton in which they declared existing slave property to be inviolable within the prospective state. The drafters of the document then arranged for a popular referendum on "the constitution with slavery" and "the constitution with no slavery." If the free-soilers won, they would achieve only a dubious victory because, under existing arrangements, there still could be no interference with slave property already existing in Kansas. With the no-lose game thus partly rigged by the slaveryites, the free-soilers boycotted the polls, and by default the proposed "constitution with slavery" for Kansas was legally approved on December 21, 1857 by a vote of 6,226 to 569.

President Buchanan actively supported the double-dealing Lecompton constitution, and hence was savagely condemned, especially in the North, for openly conniving at fraud. He defended his position in his annual message to Congress on December 8, 1857, in a statement generally overlooked by Buchanan baiters and haters. Actually "bleeding Kansas" had suffered from irregularities and lawlessness on both sides, ranging from ballot-box stuffing and illegal voting to outright murder. Many Southerners felt a bitter sense of betrayal, for they had supported the principle of popular sovereignty or local option regarding slavery. The tacit understanding was that slave state Missouri on the east would turn neighboring Kansas into a slave state and that neighboring Iowa on the east would turn Nebraska into a free state. In Southern eyes the Northern anti-slaveryites were guilty of betrayal when they sought to "abolitionize" Kansas, contrary to the normal workings of popular sovereignty.

Buchanan declared in his annual message to Congress in

1857 that heretofore the normal procedure in admitting new states to the Union was for those settlers who owned slaves to retain them. Under the Lecompton constitution, established precedent was being followed, and besides that, the number of black slaves in Kansas was not significant. In truth slaveowners did not gladly take their valuable slave property into areas where the bullets were flying or were liable to fly.

President Buchanan concluded his justification of the Lecompton constitution by reference to the epochal Dred Scott decision, handed down some nine months earlier (March 6, 1857) by the South-oriented Supreme Court. In Buchanan's words, the judges had reaffirmed the principle that the owners of slaves who took them to free soil, even temporarily, could still retain title to them under "the common Constitution." The free-soilers of Kansas had been given an opportunity to vote; they had deliberately boycotted the polls; and they must abide by the result. Buchanan, the legalist and constitutionalist, thus contrived a strong argument for his position.

On March 23, 1858, the Senate followed Buchanan's recommendation and voted to admit Kansas as a slave state under its Lecompton constitution. Evidently the President had been able to persuade the Senators that such a course was reasonable and inevitable. But the House of Representatives refused to go along with him and voted to resubmit the land grant section of the Lecompton constitution to a genuinely popular vote. This was done and the free-soilers rallied to snow it under. The troubled territory remained outside the gates until January 29, 1861, after the secession of several Southern states had opened the door. Kansas was then admitted to the Union as a free state.

In the eyes of many Northerners, Buchanan was a traitor for "permitting" the first seven of the eleven Southern states to secede. He was restrained primarily by two considerations. First, he did not feel that he had the authority under his revered Constitution to make war on the sovereign states. Second, he did not have at his command an army capable of dragging the seceders bodily back into the Union. His policy of reconciliation and restraint was essentially the one followed by Lincoln, who had a civil war on his hands when the Confederates finally fired on Fort Sumter, April 12, 1861.

Buchanan can be acquitted of close collusion with slaveowners and of a traitorous mishandling of the secession crisis. But critics are on solid ground when they point out that clandestine graft was flowering on an unprecedented scale during Old Buck's unhappy four years. Most heavily involved were the federal post offices, the customhouses, the navy yards, and the public printing. Government publication was traditionally handled by private printers, conspicuously by those who also published newspapers. The typographical scandals finally became so notorious that in 1860, President Buchanan's next to last year, the federal government purchased a plant for its own printing.

In connection with the Democratic political campaigns of 1856 and 1858 various sleazy practices were employed by underlings. Buchanan clearly condoned some of these irregularities or engaged in them himself. An intimate personal friend of Buchanan was promised and received naval contracts in payment for campaign contributions. Isaac Fowler, the Democratic postmaster in New York City, also diverted large sums of government money for the support of Democratic candidates for public office. Printer Cornelius Wendell testified that he had funneled funds into Democratic coffers, actually more than $100,000 in a period of four years, dating from 1856 to 1860.

Much of the money diverted for these purposes was used to support campaign activities that were perfectly proper. But at least some of the political lubrication was used to buy votes, to naturalize numerous illegal aliens, or to transport these overnight voters in significant numbers to crucial states.

Buchanan clearly dirtied his hands in his determination to persuade Congress to approve the proslavery Lecompton constitution for Kansas. He dismissed friends of anti-Lecompton Democrats from federal jobs; he even went so far as to offer cold cash to key Congressmen. Senator Douglas bitterly opposed Buchanan on the issue of the Lecompton constitution, and the President secured revenge by appointing the Senator's enemy, Isaac Cook, to the Chicago post office. Cook had held the position before, but had left in disgrace as a defaulter. He managed to regain his job and began stealing again on a large scale, even robbing registered mail. Yet Buchanan, still feuding with Senator Douglas, kept the crook on despite outcries from outraged citizens.

A major scandal was the awarding of contracts to private printers for handling public printing, presumably by the lowest bidder. In practice these plums were given to friends of the President and of the majority party in Congress. The profits to the recipients were scandalously high, especially for newspapers that supported the party in power. In 1858 a congressional committee discovered that the official superintendent of public printing had privately extorted kickbacks or bribes from those printers to whom he awarded public business.

Much of the evidence concerning Buchanan's under-the-table dealings was exposed during the investigations by a House committee in 1860, headed by "honest John Covode." Covode's partisan Republican group was bent on uncovering and publicizing the alleged misdeeds of the Democrat Buchanan, and especially his efforts to influence Congress, whether by money, patronage, or other means. An outraged President sent two formal protests to the House of Representatives after it had ordered the damning report published. Brushing aside the ugly charges, Buchanan condemned the procedures of the House and the motives of his prosecutors. Like several of his successors, he righteously wrapped himself in the Constitution and insisted that he was not so much trying to save his own skin as to protect the presidency itself from legislative intrusion. Scholars have concluded that the sworn testimony before the Covode committee may generally be accepted as trustworthy. Perhaps the best that can be said regarding Buchanan is that national politics had gradually and naturally degenerated to this low level over a quarter of a century. Washington had become a peculator's paradise.

Strangest of all the scandals of his administration was Buchanan's involvement with his Secretary of War, the Virginian John B. Floyd, who later served as a general in the Confederate army. A Democratic committee investigating graft in the awarding of navy contracts cleared the Secretary of the Navy but was prepared to censure Democratic Secretary of War Floyd and the Democratic President Buchanan for excessive favoritism.

It would appear that Secretary Floyd was not so much an accomplished crook as he was a careless administrator who wanted to please his fellow Democrats. He sold government land to insiders for less than it was worth and bought other property from friends for much more than it was worth. He endorsed huge bills for army supplies before the money was actually appropriated by Congress, apparently unaware that this practice was illegal and that men had been jailed for less. At flood tide, about $5 million of these bogus bills, on which bank loans had been secured by the holders, were still outstanding.

When Buchanan learned of Secretary Floyd's tactics, he reprimanded his underling and ordered him to discontinue his illegal practices. But the defiant official refused to mend his ways, and Buchanan never did dismiss him. Perhaps he feared that a resigning Floyd would make confessions that would further discredit the already floundering administration. Floyd finally and belatedly resigned, using as excuse his disagreement with Buchanan's policy regarding the holding of Fort Sumter in Charleston harbor. He self-righteously refused to be associated any longer with a "dishonorable" regime that he had richly helped to dishonor.

Buchanan has been unfairly called a weak President because of his nonaction in the secession crisis. But he did have both the desire and the power to get Floyd out of his cabinet. Yet he failed to do so. Perhaps he reasoned that his regime was already in such bad trouble that the airing of this additional scandal would merely add dangerous fuel to the flames. Buchanan was desperately hoping to hand over the reins of a runaway republic to President Abraham Lincoln, and this he did.

As regards questionable conduct, Buchanan cannot be fairly blamed for permitting the seven Southern states to secede. He did not encourage them to do so, and he had no legal restraints under the Constitution, even assuming that he could deploy adequate military forces. But as regards serious graft, he stubbornly tolerated it or dirtied his own hands with some of it. Few of his successors whose administrations were besmirched by public scandals were so flagrantly involved in unlawful or otherwise irregular practices.

In fairness, we should note that Buchanan's sins or alleged sins generally involved politics, which even before his time had become a dirty business. He appears not to have enriched his own pocketbook from any of these irregularities. Unlike some predecessors and successors, he made it an inflexible rule while President to accept no gifts of real value, even from his most intimate friends. His niece, who was also mistress of the White House, took advantage of her position to use a public ship, named in her honor, for pleasure excursions. Close though Buchanan was to her, he advised her that such a practice would invite criticism, and he ordered the officials in charge to put an end to this privilege.

CHAPTER 15

Abraham Lincoln
1861–1865

Important principles may and must be flexible.

Abraham Lincoln, address,
April 11, 1865

"Honest Abe" Lincoln came to Washington as a newly elected President early in 1861. During the inauguration ceremony he laid a hand on the Bible and swore the prescribed oath to "preserve, protect, and defend the Constitution of the [then disunited] United States." Then, in a figurative sense, Lincoln used the same hand to tear holes in that Constitution. How does all this arbitrary action square with the honesty implicit in the sobriquet that the President had earned in Illinois: "Honest Abe Lincoln"?

The new chief executive had enough horse sense to perceive that if he folded his hands and watched the secession parade of the Southern states run its course, there would not be a Constitution of a United States to uphold. The elongated railsplitter was no hairsplitter, and the founding fathers probably expected the presidents to meet crises like the existing one by rising above constitutional restraints.

Congress was not in session when the Civil War burst forth, so Lincoln had to take all necessary action completely on his own. Brushing aside legal barriers, he boldly proclaimed a blockade of the key Southern ports, and his questionable order was later upheld by the Supreme Court. He also took the liberty of arbitrarily increasing the size of the United States Army, even though the Constitution lodges this power exclusively in Congress, which later obliged by upholding Lincoln's action. He ordered the Secretary of the Treasury to advance the sum of $2 million, wholly without Congressional appropriation, to three private agents for military purposes. This was a grave irregularity that flouted the Constitution.

Lincoln also suspended the precious privilege of the writ of habeas corpus so that pro-Southern Northerners, often called Copperheads, could be summarily arrested and lodged indefinitely in jail, as about 13,000 ultimately were at one time or another. In so acting, Lincoln defied a ruling of the Supreme Court that habeas corpus could be dispensed with only by the Congress. About two years later Congress upheld Lincoln's arbitrary action.

In other areas the Lincoln government was guilty of many arbitrary acts. Federal officials went so far as to order the suspension of certain pro-Southern newspapers and the arresting of their editors on the grounds of obstructing the war. The ancient Romans had a relevant saying, "In the clash of arms the laws are silent."

Among various high-handed acts, the Lincoln regime arranged for supervised voting in the slaveowning border states, whose sympathy for the Southern Confederacy was an object of suspicion. In at least one election the intimidated citizen was forced to hold a colored ballot revealing his party preference as he marched between two lines of armed troops. Courageous indeed was the voter who would display his sympathy for the South by holding a ballot not supportive of the Lincoln Republicans. This tactic was the kind later used by totalitarian regimes in Europe, where the voting results were often about 99 percent favorable to the dictators in power.

A notorious case involved a conspicuous Copperhead, Clement Valandigham. Too outspoken for his own good, he was tried by a military court for excessively free speech, although the civil courts in Ohio were then open, and legally he should have been tried in one of them. Lincoln decided that if the culprit liked the

Southerners so much, he should be banished behind their lines, and this is what "Tyrant" Lincoln proceeded to do.

War is the ultimate in waste, especially when a nation is unprepared and has to make ready in a hurry, regardless of the cost. During the Civil War, shoddy millionaires and other profiteers got rich in short order by providing poor-quality uniforms or shoes that fell apart in the first heavy rainstorm. In all the haste, the War Department and the Treasury Department made heavy overpayments to unscrupulous characters, and although such scandals always reflect unfavorably on the incumbent president, the slimy trail of corruption never led directly to Lincoln's door. Confusion and waste were more commonly involved than outright dishonesty.

Early in the Civil War the searchlight of scandal fell on General John C. Frémont, commanding the western department headquartered at St. Louis. President Lincoln finally dismissed him as an incompetent administrator who could not perceive what was going on around him but who was not demonstrably dishonest personally. His cronies managed to secure juicy army contracts without the competitive bidding required by law, and the railroad cars, mules, tents, and other required items they provided were of inferior quality. As one example, a friend of Frémont, an inexperienced contractor, received $191,000 to build some forts that should have cost one-third of that inflated sum.

The worst hotbed of waste and corruption was the War Department of Simon Cameron. So numerous were the complaints of extravagance and graft that a committee of the House of Representatives investigated Cameron's mismanagement and came up with an indictment consisting of 1,109 pages. The chief complaint of these investigators was that Cameron had ignored competitive bidding and had purchased only from favored middlemen, many of whom were patently dishonest. The result had been the acquisition at high prices of immense quantities of disintegrating blankets, spoiled pork, and diseased or dying horses, plus uniforms and knapsacks that fell apart in the rain. One purchasing agent in Boston, charging high commissions for his services, netted $20,000 in one week.

The stench of scandal in the War Department finally became so noxious that Lincoln decided to ship Secretary Cameron off to Russia as the American minister. Although the culprit had evidently not taken any of the graft in the form of kickbacks or other financial favors, he plainly had promoted shocking extravagance and waste. Politically Cameron had become too much of a liability, and he had to suffer the chill blasts of St. Petersburg. In a private letter Lincoln went so far as to praise Cameron for his "ability, patriotism, and fidelity to public trust." One may doubt that the President was completely candid.

Gideon Welles, Lincoln's Secretary of the Navy, became involved in practices that on the surface seemed like highly collusive nepotism. The navy urgently needed to improvise a blockading fleet, using largely privately owned vessels, and Welles's purchasing agent in New York turned out to be his brother-in-law. His commissions amounted to $95,000 in four and a half months of 1861.

Welles defended this cozy relationship with his brother-in-law when charges of collusion and corruption arose in Congress. The ships in question, he said, had to be purchased in a hurry; the brother-in-law had driven hard bargains; he had been charged only the going rates; he had saved the government money; he had procured excellent ships; and he had proved to be honest and reliable. Lincoln stood squarely behind Welles in this affair, and the Senate exonerated him by a vote of 31 to 5.

The Treasury Department, under Secretary Salmon P. Chase, became involved in a large number of irregularities, particularly in regard to stores of baled cotton made available to the invading Northern armies. Treasury agents were appointed to regulate the sale of this coveted fiber to the cotton-starved North. Like a swarm of flies attracted to honey, speculators with bribes appeared on the scene, and an unlovely situation developed, involving army officers and agents for the Treasury alike. Secretary Chase, himself admittedly an honest and honorable man, did his best to clean house, but the irregularities were so numerous and widespread that federal authorities were unable to stamp out all wrongdoing.

Whatever the shortcomings of his subordinates, Lincoln was unquestionably honest in dealing with personal money matters. In 1861 the Congress voted $20,000 for refurbishing the White House, and a spendthrift Mrs. Lincoln exceeded the appropriation by $6,700. The President thereupon declared that he would pay the overrun out of his own pocket rather than seek government funds to cover the deficit at a time when Yankee soldiers in the fields were short of blankets. Congress had the grace to include money to pay for this overrun in the budget for the next year.

Two of Lincoln's most memorable edicts were the preliminary Emancipation Proclamation of September 1862 and the final Emancipation Proclamation of January 1, 1863. In both pronouncements he was somewhat less than candid. Although generations of Americans have been brought up to believe that the Great Emancipator freed all the slaves by a stroke of his pen, these two manifestoes were not all that they seemed to be.

When the Civil War erupted in 1861, the abolitionists were quick to demand the liberation of all blacks held in bondage. But Lincoln was loath to move to a position of weakness, for to attempt to unchain the slaves by proclamation before the Confederacy was crushed would be to confess that the Union could not be restored by arms. An announced liberation of slaves in enemy territory would be but an empty gesture of defiance, designed to do with the pen what could not be done with the sword.

To quiet the clamor of the abolitionists at home and to win favor with the antislavery nations of Europe, Lincoln finally decided to issue a preliminary emancipation proclamation following the first significant victory over Confederate forces. General Lee invaded Maryland in September 1862 and was checked, though not decisively beaten, at the bloody battle of Antietam. But a draw with the redoubtable Lee was tantamount to a victory, and Lincoln issued his long-deferred preliminary Emancipation Proclamation on September 22, 1862. It proclaimed that in the final version, which was to become effective on January 1, 1863, he would declare free all slaves held in those parts of the Union still in rebellion against the United States.

Actually, the Emancipation Proclamation did not free a single slave overnight. It applied only to the blacks of those states or parts of states that were still in the hands of the rebels, yet there the Washington government was powerless to free anyone. About 800,000 slaves in the loyal border states were still shackled, notably in Missouri, Kentucky, and Maryland. An attempt to free them by proclamation, rather than by constitutional amendment, would probably drive their masters into the welcoming arms of the Confederates.

Where Lincoln could presumably free the slaves, he refused

to do so, partly because of constitutional restrictions upholding private property in slaves. Where he could not, he tried to do so, as a means of weakening the South's capacity to fight. The only liberation of slaves that resulted was of the do-it-yourself variety, which involved slaves that took to their heels in response to the grapevine rumors of the emancipation proclamations. Many of the fugitives simply flocked to the invading Yankee armies, where in some cases they badly cluttered up military operations.

Lincoln's paper blast was indeed of questionable legality. To deprive fellow citizens, loyal or not, of millions of dollars worth of valuable property, was stretching assumed war powers far indeed. Not until January 31, 1865, some two months before the shooting stopped, did Congress pass the Thirteenth Amendment. It was sent to the states and was finally proclaimed as approved by the requisite number in December 1865, including eight from the late Confederacy. They ratified under a form of duress, and as a consequence cast a temporary shadow on the validity of the epochal amendment.

Honest Abe Lincoln was no doubt one of the most honest of the presidents. His few departures from the straight and narrow path of rectitude came during a war in which the nation's very existence as a united nation was at stake. On those occasions he had to rise above both principle and the Constitution in pursuing what he regarded as the nation's interest. Some of his successors have done the same thing on occasion, but in none of these instances was the existence of the nation in anywhere near such desperate peril.

CHAPTER 16

Andrew Johnson
1865–1869

I am one of those who believe that a man may sin and do wrong, and after that may do right. If all of us who have sinned were put to death . . . there would not be many of us left.

Andrew Johnson, speech,
August 1866

"Old Andy" Johnson is generally regarded as a man of sterling honesty as far as his personal life was concerned. Yet he was impeached by the House of Representatives, for "high crimes and misdemeanors," by the lopsided vote of 126 to 47. He then escaped removal from his high office by the margin of a single vote in the Senate. The count fell one short of the necessary two-thirds because seven high-minded Republican senators placed consciences before careers and courted—and won—political oblivion. How can we reconcile Johnson's acknowledged personal honesty with the majority votes in both houses that condemned his so-called official dishonesty? The answer is to be found largely in politics and postwar passions.

Andrew Johnson was a Southerner who had been brought

up in North Carolina. Orphaned at an early age, he never attended school for a day, and in this respect was even more poorly educated than Abraham Lincoln. Apprenticed to a tailor, he fled to Tennessee where, while his former employer advertised for him as a runaway, he set himself up in his trade; hence the Tailor President or the Tennessee President. Entering the arena of politics in his adopted state as a Democrat, he gained notoriety as a rough-and-tumble stump speaker, and was elected successively to the Tennessee legislature, the United States House of Representatives, the governorship of Tennessee, and the Senate of the United States. As a poor white he harbored no love for the snobbish planter aristocracy of the South, although at one time he actually owned several slaves. When the Southern states left the Union in 1860–1861, he was the only Senator who did not secede with his state. He remained loyal to the Union and the Constitution to the very end; in fact, he requested that a copy of that hallowed document be used as a pillow for his head when he finally was laid away in a coffin.

In 1864, while the gory Civil War was grinding away with no end in sight, the Republican party was floundering. Although it renominated Lincoln at Baltimore, it cleverly assumed the temporary name Union Party in the hope of attracting more votes, especially from those Democrats who supported the North in the Civil War. To make the Union ticket even more attractive the Lincoln Republicans named for the vice presidency the Democrat Andrew Johnson, who had done commendable work with the rank of brigadier general as military governor of reconquered Tennessee. Little did these Republicans in Union clothing realize that they had chosen an unreformed Democrat with inborn sympathy for the South, the kind of sympathy that Lincoln had proclaimed in his second inaugural address, March 4, 1865. He then had urged his countrymen to bind up the nation's wounds, "with malice toward none, with charity for all."

Lincoln clung firmly to the view that the wayward states had never left the Union, partly because secession was not provided for by the Constitution. He would welcome the seceders back into the fold with a minimum of chastisement. President Johnson, a dyed-in-the-wool Southern Democrat, ultimately adopted essentially the same general policy. But he ran headlong into the radical Republicans. Then followed the overridden vetoes of "Sir Veto," and name-calling on both sides ("Judas Johnson"), while the unchained blacks and the defeated Confederates were caught in the middle of the new uncivil war.

What motivated the radical Republicans who wanted to reconstruct the South radically? Some of these politicians were old free-soilers who wanted to make sure that the emancipated blacks were not dragged back into a form of peonage that was not much better than the old slavery. Other Radicals feared that the Democratic voters of the readmitted states would join with the Democrats of the North to outnumber and then oust the nominally Republican regime in Washington. In this manner the defeated would undo the pro-Northern legislation that had been passed by the victors before and during the Civil War. One possible way to avert this calamity would be to disfranchise the white Democrats and enfranchise the blacks as Republicans.

At length the Republicans in Congress, weary of the protracted wrangling, vetoing, and name-calling, finally decided to rid the country of the bull-headed Johnson. The Constitution (Article II, Section 4) provides that "The President, Vice-President and all civil officers of the United States shall be removed from office on impeachment for, and on conviction of, treason, bribery, or other high crimes and misdemeanors." Under the Constitution the House votes the impeachment charges by a simple majority; the Senate can then convict the president on these charges, but only with "the concurrence of two-thirds of the members present."

It should be noted that the Constitution does not define "high crimes and misdemeanors." In later days one prominent member of the House of Representatives, Gerald R. Ford, truthfully observed that a "high crime and misdemeanor" is whatever the House says it is. This not only happens to be true but also explains why the doors of the House of Representatives can be thrown wide open to partisan prosecution and persecution.

As for Johnson, on December 7, 1867 the House voted, 108 to 57, against impeachment because of the absence of a specific act of high misdemeanor. Less than three months later this same body reversed itself and resolved by a vote of 126 to 47 that Johnson be impeached for "high crimes and misdemeanors in office." A battle over the Tenure of Office Act had reached a climax in the interim.

In March 1867 the fateful Tenure of Office Act had passed Congress, as usual over the futile veto of President Johnson. The new legislation required, contrary to precedent, that the president must secure the approval of the Senate before he could remove appointees that had been approved earlier by that august body. The radical Republicans hoped to freeze into the cabinet the incumbent Secretary of War, Edwin M. Stanton, who was not only a holdover from the Lincoln administration, but was secretly serving as both a spy and an informer for the radicals in Congress. Another obvious purpose of the Tenure of Office Act was to goad President Johnson into flouting the new law, and thus trump up a plausible pretext for his removal.

An annoyed Johnson, regarding the Tenure of Office Act as unconstitutional, was eager to bring a test case before the Supreme Court. He therefore dismissed the two-faced Stanton early in 1868. The President did not believe that the law applied to President Lincoln's holdovers, even though the radicals claimed otherwise. The Supreme Court, 58 years later, in the case of *Myers* v. *United States* (1926), ruled in Johnson's favor by declaring that Congress may not limit the president's removal power. No president should have the legislative branch force on him an unwanted holdover, loyal or disloyal.

Aroused radicals in the House of Representatives struck back swiftly in February 1868, when, by a vote of 126 to 47, they agreed to impeach Johnson. Most of the specific accusations stemmed from the President's flouting of a Tenure of Office Act that he correctly believed to be unconstitutional. Two added charges accused Johnson of verbal assaults on Congress, including "disgrace, ridicule, hatred, contempt, and reproach."

Sitting as jury, the Senate came within one vote of mustering the necessary two-thirds for unseating Johnson in May 1868. Although more than half of the Senate regarded the ousting of Johnson as necessary for their political schemes, seven high-minded Republicans courageously forsook their radical comrades and held out for acquittal. In defending what he thought the Constitution stood for, the President was clearly guilty of bad speeches, bad judgment, and bad temper, but hardly of "high crimes and misdemeanors."

Some critics of Johnson still claim that he sinned by not "executing the laws of Congress," as stipulated in the Constitution he had formally sworn to uphold on inauguration day. But the oath that the president always takes binds him to "faithfully execute the office of President of the United States." Nothing is said spe-

cifically elsewhere about his enforcing laws that he deems unconstitutional, only that "he shall take care that the laws be faithfully
executed." But Johnson, as a strict constructionist, evidently did
not feel that his presidential oath bound him to execute "faithfully" unlawful statutes. There were and are so many federal laws
on the books, including those that involve drugs, illegal aliens,
and a host of other problems, that a broad interpretation of
"faithfully" would find many presidents with serious shortcomings.

In truth, some federal laws are literally unenforceable. President Jefferson tried desperately to enforce the Embargo Act of
1807 but finally had to throw up his hands in despair, and the
hated measure was repealed in 1809. In 1831 the ordinarily hot-
tempered President Jackson viewed with equanimity the deadlock
that developed when the state of Georgia thrice defied the Supreme Court in regard to its claim of jurisdiction over the Cherokee Indians.

The anti-alcohol Eighteenth Amendment was written into
the Constitution in 1919. The Volstead Act, designed to implement the amendment, passed Congress that same year. The successive administrations of Wilson, Harding, Coolidge, Hoover,
and Roosevelt tried to uphold the statute but found it unenforceable, as is often true when a majority of the people, or even a
large minority, oppose a federal enactment. Many of the laws
dealing with the unrepentant South were impossible to enforce
effectively, and an awareness of this weakness may have some
bearing on Johnson's negative course, particularly regarding legislation that he personally deemed unconstitutional.

Like Lincoln, who first saw daylight in the border state of
Kentucky, Johnson was a Southerner who was not notoriously
vindictive. He was also a Democrat tacked onto the makeshift
Republican ticket to snare Democratic votes for Lincoln. The radicals were unhappy when their strategy backfired, and they finally
set out to dethrone and disgrace a man they had hoped would be
a puppet.

In connection with laws for reconstructing the South drasti-
cally, Johnson repeatedly tempered the wind for the shorn
(white) lambs, especially in connection with the law establishing
the Freedman's Bureau for helping former slaves. But most of
these so-called lapses from duty were relatively minor. When we
remember how desperately eager the radicals were to get rid of

Johnson, and when we note how little dirt they managed to dig up, we are forced to conclude that Johnson had developed high standards of personal honesty.

There were, of course, minor instances of graft in some of the federal departments, but these had been occurring since early days, and often on a more scandalous scale. So eager were the radical Republicans to oust Johnson that they certainly would have paraded these minor derelictions if such had held promise of bringing down the President. Instead, they focused on the Tenure of Office Act which, to Johnson's posthumous credit, turned out to be unconstitutional.

CHAPTER 17

Ulysses Simpson Grant
1869–1877

It was my fortune, or misfortune, to be called to the office of Chief Executive without any previous political training.

> U. S. Grant,
> message to Congress,
> December 5, 1876

As a war-hero President, Grant proved to be the only graduate of West Point to reach the White House except for Dwight D. Eisenhower in 1953. The tragic Civil War had torn the nation apart for four years, during which an enormous amount of profiteering and outright graft had flourished. Civil conflict tends to bring out both the best and worst in people. The period immediately after the war continued to provide a happy hunting ground for the greedy and unscrupulous. A saying was that the man in the moon had to hold his nose when passing over America.

Upon this treacherous terrain stepped a military man almost totally without experience in public life. This handicap, combined with other drawbacks, fostered the continuance of scandals in the major departments of the national government on a scale hitherto without precedent in American public life. Only the most spectacular irregularities will command our attention.

As an unimpressive farm boy from Ohio, Grant entered West
Point and graduated in 1843 near the middle of his class but with
a reputation as a superb horseman. After fighting with distinction
in the Mexican War, he found himself stationed as a captain at a
gloomy, rain-drenched fort near Humboldt Bay, in northern California. Separated from his family, lonely, bored, and unhappy,
he began to drink so heavily that in 1854 he was forced to resign
from the army to avoid a court martial for drunkenness.

Having failed to achieve financial success in farming and real
estate, Grant was working in his father's leather store in Galena,
Illinois, for $50 a month—hardly the standard American success
story—when the Civil War broke out. Heeding the call of the
country, he offered his military expertise and was first commissioned a colonel and then a brigadier general of the volunteers.
From then on his rise was spectacular, and the war ended with his
victory over General Lee at Appomattox.

The gratitude and generosity of Northerners knew almost
no bounds. Citizens of Philadelphia, Washington, and Galena
presented Grant with a house in each place. Grateful New Yorkers tendered him a check for $105,000. The once-poor Grant
accepted all of these benefactions with open arms, as though citizens of the republic owed such lavish gifts to him for his having
brought them victory. He appears not to have realized that people
who give favors are inclined to expect favors in return, especially
if the recipient happens to become president of the United
States.

Politically, General Grant was a greenhorn, and naive enough
to think that he could govern the once sundered sections of the
North and South with as much ease as he had commanded armies. So popular was he and so weary was the nation of the prolonged quarrel between President Johnson and Congress, that
Grant probably could have had the nomination for president at
the hands of either Republicans or Democrats. To his enthusiastic
backers it seemed logical that success in the Civil War would guarantee success in civil office. Yet Grant had not actively identified
himself with either political party; his one vote in a presidential
election had been cast for the Democrat Buchanan in 1856.

The hero of Appomattox had never succeeded financially in
private life, and he enjoyed the company of wealthy men who

had. Some of them were unsavory characters who took full advantage of Grant, especially if they had been involved in showering him with gifts. The ugly face of scandal revealed itself in the major departments of the national government under Grant to a more disturbing degree than under any preceding administration. Included were the Navy Department, the Post Office, and the ever-corrupt custom houses. In some cases Grant had nothing to do with these irregularities, notably the notorious Tweed ring in New York City, but in other instances he showed a reluctance to clean house that was not seemly in the President of the United States. Whether he was obtuse, blindly loyal to friends and supporters, unwilling to rock the boat, confused, misled, or simply naive cannot be determined with certainty in all cases. Yet at heart he seems to have been an honest man; probably his chief weakness was a reluctance to crack down on crooks, especially his own associates.

From the outset President Grant revealed that his mind had been firmly cast in a military mold. As a former general, he expected prompt, heel-clicking obedience to orders. Four of his secretaries were generals, and at one stage even the White House butler was a former mess sergeant. Like a good general with top-secret plans, Grant chose his Cabinet with great confidentiality, and the results surprised and even shocked the nation. His choices did not reflect the usual political and geographical niceties. To outsiders his selections appeared to have been motivated in part by a desire to reward those gift-givers who had sponsored a house for Grant, or a check for Grant, or some other substantial favor. Today such benefactions would be called "payola."

Previous presidents had been cautious or completely negative about putting relatives on the public payroll, a practice that had come to be called nepotism, including "nephewism." Grant had married Julia Dent in 1848, and he finally proved to be a godsend to the in-laws of the Dent family, many of whom ultimately found themselves on the government payroll.

At the outset Grant was mildly favorable to civil service reform. But a designing group of politicians soon changed his views, after plying him with choice wines, expensive cigars, and fast horses. These hangers-on not only frequented the White House but also persuaded Grant that the path to virtue lay in a partisan Republican course. The President's initial disposition to reconstruct with leniency the South that he had defeated was similarly sidetracked. He who had been magnanimous in war thus became vindictive in peace, in spite of his famous saying when accepting the Republican nomination, "Let us have peace."

The infamous Black Friday scandal of September 1869 besmirched Grant's first year as President. Two crafty financial manipulators, millionaires Jim Fisk and Jay Gould, schemed to corner the gold on the New York market, force up the price, and scoop up millions of dollars. Yet this plot could succeed only if the Washington Treasury would hold back its funds when the squeeze was on. The conspirators approached Grant directly, telling him that a high price for gold would help international trade, and also through his brother-in-law, who received $25,000 for his role. On Black Friday (September 24, 1869) Fisk and Gould, evidently believing that Grant would cooperate, bid the price of gold to new highs, while scores of ordinary businessmen went to the wall. The pressure ultimately became so intense that the Treasury, despite what may have been Grant's earlier assurances to the contrary, was compelled to release its gold, and the bubble burst. A Congressional investigation concluded that Grant had been stupid and indiscreet, but not crooked. Himself relatively honest, he served as a front for dishonesty.

Also in 1869 Grant became deeply involved in a fruitless attempt to acquire the Caribbean republic of Santo Domingo, with attendant scandal. The president of this bankrupt republic was undertaking to salvage what he could for himself by annexing Santo Domingo to the United States, which would assume the public debt and then take care of the scheming ruler financially. Self-seeking American speculators also had their fingers in the potential pie.

The whole proposal was tainted with scandal, but the morally insensitive Grant was unduly impressed with the strategic advantages of the island. As a Civil War general, he remembered that the Union had been handicapped in blockading the South by not owning a base in the Caribbean. Grant finally arranged to have a treaty of annexation drawn up and submitted to the Senate for approval. He fought with all the weapons at his command for his pet scheme, but the anti-expansionist Senators, smelling the rank odor of scandal, flatly rejected the pact. An unseemly public row developed over the issue between President Grant and Senator Charles Sumner, chairman of the Senate Committee on Foreign Relations. Sumner won when the treaty was rejected, but Grant gained a victory of sorts when he spitefully arranged to have the Senator removed from his chairmanship.

The Crédit Mobilier was an inside company that milked extortionate profits of some $20 million from building the government-backed Union Pacific Railroad, completed in 1869. Congressmen were bribed to look the other way, and James A. Garfield, the future President, was indelibly tainted. Grant was not involved in this pre-1870 scandal, but its revelation was further symptomatic of the polluting of American public life.

The "Salary Grab Act" also reflected these morally malodorous times. The President's salary of $25,000 was obviously inadequate for all his expenses, and Grant's friends in Congress undertook to raise it to $50,000. At the same time the Congressmen increased the pay of certain other public officials and boosted their own salaries from $5,000 to $7,500. In the final amending of this bill, the Senate and House decided to add for themselves a take-home bonus of $5,000. This figure would represent a retroactive increase for the two-year term that they had already served. Hence the term "salary grab."

Grant gladly signed the amended act on the last day of his first term, March 3, 1873. He expressed no regret or protest whatever. The Constitution states that the president's compensation "shall neither be increased nor diminished during the period for which he shall have been elected." Grant had one day remaining on his first elective term, but the four-year period for which he had been reelected began the next day. If Grant had read the relevant part of the Constitution carefully he could hardly have avoided some doubts as to the propriety of doubling his own stipend at this particular time. A chastened Congress, responding to a popular outcry, repealed all salary increases in January 1874 except those affecting the president and the justices of the Supreme Court.

As Grant's "eight long years of scandal" drew to a close the stench of corruption continued to hang over Washington, including the local government itself and its "Boss" Shepherd. To detail all the crookedness in the various departments would result in wearisome and repetitive detail. Yet two episodes that particularly disturbed the country involved the Treasury Department and the War Department.

In 1875 the public was shocked to learn that a gigantic Whiskey Ring had been robbing the Treasury of millions of dollars of internal revenue. President Grant sounded a welcome note when he insisted, "Let no guilty man escape." But when he discovered that his own trusted private secretary, General Orville E. Babcock, was among the defendants, his old sense of loyalty to friends and subordinates took command.

The trial of Babcock went forward before a jury in St. Louis. Witnesses were suborned to give false testimony. Grant appeared before the chief justice in Washington to record a sworn statement favorable to the accused, and it evidently carried much weight with the judge and jury. Babcock was acquitted despite strong evidence of his complicity.

A host of observers expected that Babcock, once a gallant officer under Grant in the Civil War, would be dismissed as Grant's private secretary, but he was kept on. Republican supporters of the President greeted Babcock as though he were some kind of hero. Wealthy admirers made up a purse of some $30,000 to defray legal expenses and other costs incurred by Babcock in his struggle to stay out of prison.

Another damaging scandal involved Secretary of War William W. Belknap. In 1876 word leaked out that this official, married successively to two extravagant wives, had been engaged in graft. He had netted some $24,000 by selling the privilege of disbursing supplies, often shoddy material, to the Indians. In short, he had been robbing both the government and the luckless natives. The evidence of Belknap's guilt was so overwhelming that the House of Representatives, by a *unanimous* count, voted to impeach him. The Senate failed to muster enough votes to convict him of the charges, primarily because there were doubts as to senatorial jurisdiction. President Grant had come to Belknap's rescue by accepting his resignation. The question consequently arose in the Senate as to that body's authority to find a Secretary of War guilty of "high crimes and misdemeanors" when he was no longer Secretary of War.

Grant complicated the problem when he not only accepted Belknap's resignation but did so "with great regret." Did this mean that the President regretted the Secretary's dishonest conduct or regretted the necessity of having to dispense with a loyal Secretary in order to take the accused off the impeachment hook? When we consider Grant's moral callousness, his insensitivity to graft, his stubborn sympathy for loyal subordinates and benefactors, it is difficult to escape the conclusion that the President was trying his best to help Belknap escape the consequences of his criminality.

As an addendum to the Belknap scandal, a New York newspaper reported that Orvil Grant, the President's brother, had presented some interesting testimony to a Washington committee investigating expenditures in the War Department. The witness admitted that he had obtained from President Grant four lucrative Indian posts, and that he had shared the profits with his partners. The favored brother kept the posts, and no action was taken against him. Possibly nothing more serious than nepotism was involved.

Grant evidently had his priorities confused. To a degree Grant was loyal to friends, grateful to benefactors, and inexperienced in the ways of politicians. He does not seem to have changed much during eight years of costly on-the-job training. In his final annual message to Congress (December 5, 1876) he inserted a farewell apology of the "you're another" variety. Grant declared, "Mistakes have been made, as all can see and I admit, but it seems to me oftener in the selections made of the assistants appointed to aid in carrying out the various duties of administering the government. . . . History has shown that no administration from the time of Washington to the present has been free from these mistakes. But I leave comparisons to history, claiming only that I have acted in every instance from a conscientious desire to do what was right, constitutional, within the law, and for the very best interests of the whole people. Failures have been errors in judgment, not of intent."

Grant's attempt to blame his troubles on subordinates is not completely convincing. A man has no business running for President who can make as many bad appointments as he did—and who then sticks with them when they are caught with a hand in the cookie jar. If Grant had been as good a judge of human character as he was of horseflesh, there would have been less need to apologize.

History itself makes no comparisons, for it is singularly mute; historians and non-historians pronounce judgments. Whatever Grant's motives, the various departments of the national government evidently were more riddled by scandal than ever before or since in the nation's history. It is hard to believe that Grant's saving of Babcock's skin in the Whiskey Ring scandal was in "the very best interests of the whole people." But the President's inter-vention was indisputably in the interests of Babcock.

Blind to his ineptitudes, Grant showed a disquieting willing-ness to challenge the no-third-term tradition and try for a third term. The designing politicians around him wanted the "Old Man" to run again so they could benefit further from this era when corruption was rampant. But the House of Representatives administered a stinging rebuke when it passed an anti-third-term resolution by the overwhelming bipartisan vote of 233 to 18. Con-gress thus warned the country (and Grant) of the dictatorial implications of breaking a tradition established by George Wash-ington.

After leaving the White House, Grant embarked on a pro-longed world tour, during which he was hailed as a conquering hero. His backers, licking their chops for "four more years of good stealing," wanted to run him again in 1880, arguing that a third non-consecutive term was entirely proper. Obtusely enough, the scandal-bedaubed General was quite willing to be used. At the Republican convention in Chicago he actually led on the first 35 ballots, and the deadlock was finally broken when the delegates stampeded to a dark horse, James A. Garfield. To the very end Grant evidently believed that his "eight long years of scandal" had been a considerable success, and that by serving a non-consecutive third term, he would not be seriously in conflict with the hallowed third-term tradition.

CHAPTER **18**

Rutherford Birchard Hayes 1877–1881

. . . In politics, in morals, in public and private life, the right is always expedient.

Rutherford B. Hayes, speech
September 4, 1867

A virtue such as personal honesty cannot be easily or accurately measured, yet by any such test Hayes deserves a secure place near the top of the presidential roster. His record is all the more remarkable when we note that he came to the White House at a time when confidence in the Washington government had sunk to a low point in the aftermath of the post-Civil War scandals, especially those that had surfaced during the "eight long years" of Grantism.

Sterling honesty was built into Hayes's makeup, and it shone through in his public pronouncements. He was the first elected President to proclaim in his letter accepting the nomination of his party that under no circumstances would he be a candidate for a second term. To put it bluntly, Presidents all too often act in the interests of their re-election rather than in the interests of their country, and those who do so are not completely honest. As Hayes proclaimed in his inaugural address, "He serves his party best who serves the country best."

From the standpoint of political strategy a public official imposes a serious handicap on himself by spurning all possibility of re-election at or near the outset of his term. Subordinate politicians are put on notice that they no longer need to feel under obligation to the president, and that they are free to go their own way. In short, Hayes was a lame duck President even before he took office.

Like Grant, Hayes had served honorably in the Civil War, rising to the rank of major general and suffering a severe wound in an arm. But, unlike President Grant, Hayes was a political veteran, having served a term in the national House of Representatives and having been elected governor of Ohio three times.

Hayes was by no means a dark horse when the Republican national convention met in 1876 in Cincinnati. He was nominated on the seventh ballot after the weary warhorses of the party, men like James G. Blaine and Roscoe Conkling, had shot their bolt. Hayes's triumph was especially pleasing to the reformers in the party and to the Civil War veterans, while not particularly offensive to the Old Guard Republican politicians. This hardshell group was not then fully aware of the sterling honesty of their nominee.

The irony is that Hayes, a paragon of integrity, was seated as President following probably the most corrupt and certainly the most controversial presidential election in American history, the battle of the ballots in 1876. An arresting fact to emerge from the nationwide balloting was that the Democratic candidate, Samuel J. Tilden, polled 247,448 more popular votes than Hayes out of more than eight million cast. On its face, Tilden had clearly won not only the popularity contest but also the election. He needed only one more electoral vote out of the 20 in dispute in four states.

The 19 electoral votes in three Southern states were most seriously in dispute: Louisiana, South Carolina, and Florida, and on them hinged the election. Republicans and Democrats alike dispatched partisan wirepullers to these areas, and consequently each of the three states submitted two sets of returns, one Democratic for Tilden and the other Republican for Hayes. Unless the Republican returns, including all 20 votes, were accepted as valid, Hayes would surely lose. In the disputed Southern states there had been gross irregularities on both sides, including bribery, forgery, ballot-box stuffing, intimidation, shootings, and outright murder. Undoubtedly a large number of freed slaves, eager to vote for the redeeming Republican party of Abraham Lincoln, were "bulldozed" or frightened (Ku-Kluxed) away from the polls. "His honesty," Rutherford B. Hayes, personally came to believe that in a fair election he would have won.

The Democrats were so sure they had been robbed of the presidency that there was ugly talk of seizing arms and fighting a new Civil War. But more sober counsels finally prevailed, and a supposedly impartial Electoral Commission was set up consisting of eight Republicans and seven Democrats from Congress and the Supreme Court. Not surprisingly, they voted a strictly partisan eight-to-seven to validate the Republican returns from the three Southern states in dispute. The Tilden supporters could not get even the necessary one vote among the 20 in dispute.

The outraged Democrats, feeling betrayed, prepared to negate these unwelcome results by a filibuster, but behind the scenes the Republicans offered attractive inducements if the Democrats would only choke down the election of Hayes. Among various concessions, the negotiators committed a victorious Hayes to withdrawing the intimidating federal troops from the two Southern states where they still remained: Louisiana and South Carolina. As a consequence, the Republicans would abandon the Negro voters and the solid South would solidify as Democratic. To many battle-scarred Southerners, home rule was somewhat more desirable than rule in Washington. The South was also promised a place at the presidential patronage trough, which was partially made available. There was also to be financial support for a Southern transcontinental railroad—support that was never forthcoming.

A rough appraisal of the disputed election of 1876 would be that the Democrats stole the presidency from Hayes, and that the Republicans stole it back in "the great steal of 1876." All things considered, it would have been more honorable to have lost than to have won this election. Yet Hayes evidently convinced himself that the sins of the Democrats eclipsed those of the Republicans, and that the Devil had to be fought with fire. Certainly he would be breaking faith with his own Republican party to concede the election to the Democratic "party of the rebellion," after a war in which he had fought with great gallantry.

The irony is that the transparently honest Hayes was forced to suffer in silence from the slings and arrows of the losing Democrats. He was dubbed His Fraudulency, The Fraud President, Old Eight to Seven, Boss Thief, Usurper, and Rutherfraud (Rutherford) B. Hayes.

With the advent in Washington of President Hayes and his wife, a purer atmosphere swept through the White House than had existed in the alcoholic days of Grant. Family prayers were offered daily, and because Hayes and his wife, Lucy, were temperance advocates, they ran a wineless White House. The "cold water" administration of "Lemonade Lucy" was the butt of much ridicule.

Hayes boldly withdrew the federal troops from their menacing Southern stations, pursuant to the pre-presidential bargain. Also honoring such commitments, he placed in his Cabinet as Postmaster General, a former Confederate general. Outraged Republican spoilsmen complained that Hayes was the kind of man who, if Pope, would have felt obliged to appoint a few Protestant cardinals.

Yet Hayes had bad news for the spoilsmen. At the outset he vowed, unlike Grant, to appoint no one to federal office who was related to him by blood or marriage. He fell considerably from grace when political pressures forced him to hand out a few political plums to Southern carpetbaggers from the North, conspicuously those who had helped to procure his election by irregular means. Hayes was upbraided by the reformers for office-mongering and by the spoils seekers for not having ladled out more political gravy. The President further offended the spoilsmen in June 1877 by issuing a sweeping executive order against political activity by officeholders and against the practice of assessing them for political contributions. This edict was widely disregarded.

For decades the New York Custom House had been a veritable hotbed of graft and other forms of iniquity. It was also a vital part of Republican Senator Roscoe Conkling's political machine. In July 1878 Hayes summarily removed the Collector, the future President Chester A. Arthur, plus a subordinate, for objectionable political activity. Senator Conkling put up a bitter fight against Senate confirmation of the two new appointees, but in the end President Hayes triumphed. The old line Republican politicians condemned the President as "Granny Hayes" and as a

"Goody Two Shoes" reformer, especially after he had written an open letter to the new Collector of the Port of New York in February 1879 ordering him to conduct his office in accord with the reformist rules of the Civil Service Commission.

Another source of peculation was the federal Post Office Department, but surprisingly President Hayes did little about it. The sorry tale involved the "Star Route frauds," which had developed in the Far West, where the carrying of mail by the railroads and steamships was supplemented by the horseback riders, wagon trains, and stagecoaches. Contracts were drawn up for these more primitive operations, which were designated in listings by asterisks or stars—hence the term "Star Route."

Unscrupulous Star Route operators would petition Washington for increased subventions to cover the cost of supposedly improved service, and these sums would be granted by the Post Office and Treasury Departments, with the consequent enrichment of the insiders involved. Neither Congress nor President Hayes was as concerned about probing these under-the-table dealings as they should have been. The best that can be said of Hayes is that he probably regarded the problem as one of extravagance rather than of outright corruption. Whatever the verdict, millions of dollars were illegally diverted to the pockets of swindlers.

President Hayes believed firmly in gold-standard money, also known as "hard money," "sound money," or "honest money." In 1878 the silverites pushed through Congress a bill to improve the status of silver in relation to gold. Hayes, the champion of honest money, emphatically vetoed this measure but the controversial Bland-Allison Act was repassed over his veto. Yet this victory for silver proved to be rather hollow and something of a disappointment to the silverites.

Hayes sincerely believed that honesty was the best policy in foreign as well as in financial affairs. In the 1870s violence developed in California against the inpouring of Chinese laborers, whose chief sin was a willingness to work hard for lower wages than the whites. Congress bowed to all this uproar by passing a bill that severely limited the entrance of Chinese "coolies." But Hayes believed that this slamming of the door on Oriental fingers violated an existing treaty with China, so he vetoed the bill. Angered Californians burned "Missey Hayes" in effigy, but the only reasonable solution was to negotiate a new treaty with China. This was done in 1880, following which appropriate measures were taken in later years to stem the flood of Orientals.

In another area of foreign affairs, Hayes did his duty ruthlessly. A French company under Ferdinand de Lesseps, the conqueror of the isthmus of Suez, was proposing to construct the long-needed transoceanic canal through Panama. Hayes opposed this foreign project as one liable to generate serious friction with France, which might violate the Monroe Doctrine.

A clever de Lesseps sought to form a propagandistic "advisory committee" in the United States to quiet current suspicions. He approached the Secretary of the Navy, Richard W. Thompson, whom President Hayes warned not to have anything to do with this barefaced scheme. But the official permitted himself to be seduced, because the duties of this additional job were light and the salary of $25,000 was munificent for those days. The resulting conflict of interest was so obvious that President Hayes accepted Secretary Thompson's resignation before it was even tendered. The sacked official was reputed to have questionable ethical standards, and to the members of Hayes's official family not even the breath of scandal was to be tolerated.

CHAPTER 19

James A. Garfield
1881

I would rather be beaten in Right than succeed in Wrong.

James A. Garfield, Maxims

As the presidential election of 1880 neared, the Democrats were on fire to undo the "Great Fraud" of 1876 and boost Samuel J. Tilden into the Presidential chair that they regarded as rightfully his. But Tilden was four years older and sicker, and with no stomach to go through the ordeal of another tempestuous run for the White House.

The retired President Grant, laden with honors from his journey around the world, was quite willing to run for a non-consecutive third term. Frustrated Republican partisans, fed up with Hayes's honesty and purity, rallied behind Grant in a formidable phalanx. They believed, or many of them did, that there were four more years of rich plunder in Washington.

The Republican stalwarts, attending the national nominating convention in Chicago, not only marshalled a solid bloc of 306 votes for Grant but he held the lead over James G. Blaine for an extraordinary 35 ballots. On the thirty-sixth ballot the delegates ended the deadlock by stampeding to James A. Garfield of Ohio, who had advertised himself favorably to the convention by eloquently managing the candidacy of John Sherman, also of Ohio. There were those who felt that Garfield had been guilty of betrayal by running off with the nomination himself, but such accusations seem to have been greatly exaggerated.

Partly to appease Senator Conkling and his pro-Grant stalwarts, the convention that nominated Garfield for President chose Chester A. Arthur as its candidate for Vice President. Conkling and his crowd were neither appeased nor pleased. As for Arthur, he had recently been dismissed from his lucrative post as Collector of Customs for the important Port of New York by President Hayes. The charge was not graft but objectionable political activity. Arthur will be heard from again as a President-by-bullet.

In the heated election campaign of November 1880, the Republican General Garfield defeated the Democratic General Hancock by the tiny margin of only 9,464 popular votes out of more than 9,000,000 cast. Much more reassuring was the electoral count, 214 to 155.

The campaign of 1880 displayed tactics that neither the Democratic nor the Republican candidate, if honest, could have easily condoned. The Democrats came up with a forged letter addressed to one H. L. Morey, in which candidate Garfield supposedly advocated the importation of cheap Oriental labor for employment in factories. The Republicans promptly denounced this "roorback" as a fraud, but the Democratic National Committee gave it wide publicity. Presumably as a result, the anti-Chinese Californians awarded the Democratic candidate five of the six electoral votes of their state.

For their part, the Republicans raised a slush fund and then spent money freely in purchasing votes. Levies were extracted from manufacturers, while assessments on federal officeholders were commonplace, especially in the closely contested state of Indiana. Candidate Garfield was aware of some of these extortions, but in his defense one should note that in 1880 such contributions for "job insurance" were not yet outlawed by federal statute.

At a famous victory banquet in New York City early in 1881, Vice President-elect Chester A. Arthur delivered a speech in honor of the secretary of the Republican campaign committee, whose special concern was Indiana. Monetary "soap" had bought votes and lubricated the political machinery in that state. Arthur baldly proclaimed: "Indiana was really, I suppose, a Democratic state. It had been put down on the books always as a state that might be carried by close and perfect organization and a great deal of . . . (laughter). I see the reporters are present, therefore I will simply say that everybody showed a great deal of interest in the occasion and distributed tracts and political documents all through the state."

Two old charges of scandal were dredged up by the Democrats to discredit Garfield in the presidential campaign of 1880. During the Grant administration, when the Credit Mobilier railroad construction scandal was fully exposed, evidence presented to the Poland Committee of the House of Representatives showed that Garfield had been one of several Congressmen who had accepted stock and a check for $329 in dividends. The scheme was to bribe the members of Congress with the stocks and permit them to pay, if at all, from the dividends. Garfield, among others, cashed his check. Before the Poland Committee he appears to have testified falsely. In the presidential campaign of 1880 cynical Democrats chalked the telltale figure of $329 on countless stones and fences.

Connected with the $329 scandal was the valid charge that, as a member of Congress, Garfield had accepted a retaining fee of $5,000 for legal services rendered to a company desirous of furnishing the city of Washington with wooden-block pavements. His response to this accusation was that he had no connection whatever with the government agency awarding the contract, and that his services were basically no different from those rendered by other members of Congress who practiced law in the federal courts. In any event, both of these scandals were laid before Garfield's constituents when he successfully ran for reelection to Congress in 1874.

As the last President to be born in a log cabin, Garfield was a poor Ohioan who acquired an excellent education. He ultimately became president of Hiram College ("The Teacher President") and then a distinguished member of the House of Representatives. He also had served on the Electoral Commission that had thrown the disputed election of 1876 to President Hayes, despite gross irregularities on both sides.

As a devout Christian and an eloquent preacher of the Church of Christ ("The Preacher President"), Garfield was expected to maintain high standards of morality in the White House. He did so, quite in contrast to the unsavory misdeeds under Grant and in conformity with the high levels of integrity established by President Hayes. On the inauguration platform Garfield turned and kissed his mother, who was the first woman to witness the installation of her son as President.

The Star Route frauds in the postal service were a cinder in the public eye during Garfield's tragically shortened administration, which lasted only 199 days, instead of the expected four years. It is unfair to blame these scandals on Garfield, as is sometimes done, for they had been proliferating during the era after the Civil War. One estimate was that over a five-year period preceding the Garfield term about $4 million had been mulcted from the postal service.

As earlier noted, the practice had developed of permitting contractors in Washington to bid for many of the 9,000 or so "Star Routes" or those designated on lists by an asterisk or star. These involved the transportation of mail, especially in the West, by stagecoach, private carriages, or horseback riders, rather than by steamboats and railroads. The successful bidders in Washington would then sublet the actual work to local carriers, who were paid what their services were presumably worth. The lucky bidders would then appeal to the Washington government for a juicy but unwarranted increase in the payments to themselves for alleged cost overruns.

The magnitude of the scandal struck the Garfield administration with full force when the second assistant postmaster general, Thomas J. Brady, asked for a deficiency appropriation of about $1,700,000. Most of this sum would presumably line the pockets of the local bidders in Washington, not the actual carriers in the field. Following an earnest investigation, Brady was dismissed in April 1881, and a list of 93 suspected "Star Routes" was turned over to the press.

Some of the money thus siphoned off from the Treasury by the Star Route contracts had found its way into the Republican slush funds used to elect Garfield in 1880, so the party wheelhorses cautioned the President to go easy on any investigation of the Star Route contracts. Such a warning Garfield flatly rejected when he issued these instructions: "Cut the ulcer out, no matter whom it hurts. I have sworn to uphold the Constitution and the laws. I shall do my full duty."

On June 29, 1881, Garfield complained to the postmaster

general that the government agents probing these cases were moving too slowly. He stated that "they should be more earnest in their work, and that they should have the accused parties indicted and tried." Three days later Garfield was shot. Charges that he was trying hard to quash the Star Route investigations are not supported by evidence.

A reverberating political row involving President Garfield and Senator Conkling of New York probably motivated the assassination of the President by Charles Guiteau. We remember that Senator Conkling of New York, a last-ditch supporter of Grant in 1880, belonged to the spoilsman or Stalwart faction of the Republican Party. James G. Blaine was regarded as a member of the Half-breed element in the Republican camp—that is, half Stalwart and half reformist. The elected President Garfield not only sympathized with Blaine but appointed him Secretary of State, a post then regarded as the premier position in the cabinet. Evidently these two Half-breeds were conspiring to pass out the juiciest patronage plums of office to fellow partisans, all to the discomfiture of the leading Stalwart, Senator Roscoe Conkling.

A political explosion occurred when President Garfield, evidently working hand in glove with Secretary Blaine, appointed an archrival of Conkling to the high-paying and politically potent post of Collector of the Port of New York. An aroused Senator Conkling fought this objectionable appointment in the Senate with all of the weapons at his command. When he discovered he could not prevail, he decided to resign, return to Albany, New York, and there be triumphantly reelected by the state legislature in a vote of confidence. He persuaded the junior Senator from New York, Thomas C. Platt, to resign also, and thereafter this not-too-clever politician was dubbed "Me Too" Platt.

The "Battle of Albany" thus ran its heated course. New fury was added when Vice President Arthur, formerly a henchman of the "Stalwart" Conkling, journeyed to Albany and there worked hard for the vindication and re-election of both Conkling and Platt. As vice president, Arthur presented the unlovely spectacle of stabbing his new chief, President Garfield, in the back while supporting his old political cronies from New York. The resignation scheme finally backfired badly when both Conkling and Platt failed of reelection and were retired from public life, Platt temporarily. Two new Senators were chosen by the legislature in their places.

The whole sorry affair was more than an intraparty squabble between two factions of the Republican party; it was full-fledged political warfare. These passions evidently inflamed the mentally deranged Charles J. Guiteau, a disappointed officeseeker. He managed to shoot and mortally wound President Garfield while in a Washington railroad station, and then was reported to have cried before being seized, "I am a Stalwart. Arthur is now President of the United States." The implication was that Conklingites would now get good jobs from the ex-Stalwart Arthur. The culprit went so far at his trial as to ask for contributions to his defense fund from those who supposedly had benefited politically from his insane deed. He was found guilty of murder and hanged.

It is not greatly to Garfield's credit that he died as the result of a bitter intraparty struggle over the spoils of victory. But in Conkling he was battling a spoilsman who was seeking to regain control over the crooked and politically potent New York Custom House, with its 1300 or so employees. He won this struggle but lost his life. Although politically motivated, Garfield took his stand on the side of good government, notably in his determined efforts to cleanse the Post Office Department of the long-notorious Star Route frauds. His tragically truncated administration showed promise of lining up foursquare on the side of honest government.

CHAPTER 20

Chester Alan Arthur
1881–1885

Men [like Garfield] may die, but the fabrics of our free institutions remain unshaken.

Chester A. Arthur,
inaugural address, 1881

"His Accidency," President Chester A. Arthur, was a wealthy New York lawyer-politician whose abundant wardrobe and extravagant life-style caused him to be dubbed "Elegant Arthur," "Prince Arthur," and "The Dude President." Notorious as "Friend of the Stalwarts," he had earlier held only one civilian office of importance, that of Collector of the Port of New York. This key post had been notorious as a hotbed of political spoilsmanship and graft, with the "Stalwart" Senator Roscoe Conkling acting as the political power behind the throne. Arthur served capably and honestly in this position from 1871 to 1878 under appointment by the naive President Grant. Elegant Arthur lost this prize political plum when the reformist President Hayes summarily removed him, not for graft but for objectionable political activity in connection with the Conkling machine.

We recall that in 1880 Vice President Arthur was placed on the Republican ticket in an effort to mollify Roscoe Conkling, the Senator who had lost out in his desperate attempt to win for former President Grant, the friend of spoilsmen, a third presidential nomination. We also remember that Vice President Arthur had been in Albany, supporting his old friend Conkling in the partisan fight with President Garfield at the very time the President was felled by the fatal bullet. Many stunned Americans reacted with, "My God! Chet Arthur, President of the United States." But the shock of new responsibilities evidently caused the "Gentleman Boss" to rise to new heights. This Friend of the Stalwarts, turning his back on his slippery old associates in the Stalwart camp, gave the country a more honest and constructive administration that it deserved for having elected him to the vice presidency.

An unwelcome legacy slopping over onto the new accidental administration was the prosecution of those swindlers deeply enmeshed in the notorious Star Route scandals of the Post Office Department. Greatly to the new President's credit, he appointed an able and well informed prosecutor as Attorney General. He also reported to Congress in his first annual message (December 6, 1881) that the railroads had helped to decrease the length of the horse-supported star routes, which now had been reduced by 3,949 miles in length and $364,144 in cost. The nature of the problem is glaringly revealed by the experience of one contractor, a rider who carried over the mountains the entire bag of mail in his boot. His services alone cost the government $50,000 a year.

As for prosecution of frauds already unearthed in the days of Garfield, President Arthur reported in his first annual message that he had alerted the officials concerned to "the duty of prosecuting with the utmost vigor of the law all persons who may be chargeable with frauds upon the postal service." The subsequent prosecution did not proceed with noteworthy haste, but in February 1882 eight defendants were finally brought to trial. Included were the two main culprits, Thomas J. Brady, Assistant Postmaster-General, and ex-Senator Stephen W. Dorsey of Arkansas, who had thrust his fingers deeply into the Washington Treasury.

The prosecution did not go forward smoothly, partly because the defense had available enough tainted money to employ the most skillful and obstructive lawyers. Various kinds of irregulari-

ties surfaced, including attempts to intimidate or even bribe witnesses. The result was a hung jury, which voted 10 to 2 to convict
Postmaster Brady and 9 to 3 to convict Senator Dorsey.

The abundant evidence of criminality warranted a new trial,
which began late in 1882. As President Arthur reported to Congress in his second annual message of December 4, 1882, "If any
guilty persons shall finally escape punishment for their offenses,
it will not be for lack of diligent and earnest efforts on the part of
the prosecution." A new trial was staged, also with gross irregularities. Nine months after it opened the jury returned a verdict
of "not guilty as indicted." The beneficiaries of the Star Route
frauds had ample funds with which to bribe jurors, but suspicions
that they did so were not proved conclusively.

A third major trial seemed senseless, but a few persons were
indicted for bribery, and a number of government employees
were dismissed from their jobs for offenses connected with the
trials. Others, curiously, were retained, even promoted. Critics
have claimed that the prosecution was poorly conducted, for the
charge brought against the defendants was conspiracy, which is
usually difficult to prove.

Whatever the shortcomings of the prosecutors, President Arthur evidently threw no monkey wrenches into the machinery of
justice. Attorney General Brewster later testified that Arthur had
instructed him to do his work "earnestly and thoroughly," and
had said, "I desire that these people shall be prosecuted with the
utmost vigor of the law. I will give you all the help I can. You can
come to see me whenever you wish to, and I will do all I can to
aid you." Brewster continued, "he did so all the way through,
without a moment's hesitation—always stood by me and strengthened me and gave me confidence."

As collector of the Port of New York for nearly seven years,
Arthur had been intimately associated with the political machine
of Roscoe Conkling. When Arthur, the Gentleman Boss, was elevated to the presidency by the bullet that killed Garfield, the
reformers feared that the new President would revert to his earlier habits of spoilsmanship.

The practice of levying political assessments on officeholders
was already well established. The normal procedure was to have
the party in power "invite" government employees to contribute
"gifts" annually to the party coffers, usually two percent of the
giver's salary. Such exactions were supposedly voluntary, but to
many donors these contributions were in the nature of job insur-

ance, and hence not freely given. No employee could be sure that non-payment would not be held against him, with a consequent loss of his promotion or even his job.

The reformist law of 1876 prohibited these political assessments, but such deeply rooted practices continued to flourish widely under President Arthur. In 1882 the Republican Congressional Committee sent out its usual letter of solicitation to all employees of the federal government, including lowly scrubwomen, assuring them that such "gifts" would elicit no official objections. But the implication was that a contribution would insure retention of one's job.

As events turned out, the non-assessment law of 1876 was widely flouted or watered down. The Attorney General ruled that the elected members of Congress were technically not "officers," and hence the statute was not applicable to them. President Arthur further weakened the law of 1876 by declaring that officeholders might give or not, without fear of losing their jobs. If one may judge from the "gifts" that continued to pour in to the Republican campaign coffers, the officeholders were taking no chances.

Zealous reformers criticized President Arthur severely for shying away from his declared support of civil service reform. General N. M. Curtis was convicted of violating the law of 1876 by serving simultaneously as a Treasury agent and as a member of the New York Republican state committee. Yet President Arthur refused to pardon him, although appealed to by fellow Republicans. They claimed that General Curtis had sinned only by doing what many others had done more or less routinely with impunity.

President Arthur fell further from grace when William W. Dudley, commissioner of the Pensions Office, arranged for a leave of absence so that he could campaign in the national election of 1884. He took with him about 100 special examiners from his office, many of them with formal leaves of absence. He concentrated on the key states of Indiana and Ohio, the home of many Civil War veterans, a good many of whom were beneficiaries of government pensions—or hoped to be. Word rapidly circulated that a vote for the Republican ticket would expedite favorable action on pension claims. This huckstering of government favors was nothing less than scandalous, as highly vocal reformers, especially Democrats, were not slow to point out.

President Arthur, to his discredit, was obviously aware of this scandalous situation but did nothing about it. He could not have had a personal stake in the outcome of the election of 1884, for James G. Blaine, not Arthur, was the official presidential nominee of the Republicans. Why Arthur did not act is something of a mystery; perhaps he wanted to avoid stirring up further dissension within Republican ranks.

Yet President Arthur deserves much credit for his strong support of the Pendleton Act of 1883, the so-called Magna Carta of civil service reform. Garfield's murder and subsequent political scandals had generated a tidal wave of pressure for wholesome change.

The Pendleton Act, as signed by Arthur, instituted a number of desirable changes for the better. It prohibited, at least on paper, assessments from officeholders, whether Senators or scrubwomen. The new statute established a merit system that involved appointments based on competence rather than "pull." The law created a Civil Service Commission, which was to administer open competitive examinations to applicants for positions in the "classified service." But openings not designated as classified remained the pawns of politicians.

From the beginning the success of the new anti-spoilsman Pendleton Act depended heavily on the backing of the notorious ex-spoilsman, President Arthur, the onetime Gentleman Boss. Fortunately for good government, he cooperated handsomely in promoting what cynics called "snivel service reform." By 1884, his last full year, he had set aside or classified 14,000 federal jobs, or about 10 percent of the total. Subsequent Presidents, especially in the next century, gradually increased the number to about 90 percent. Ironically, the fully flowered new system spawned problems of its own, including smugness, laziness, insolence, and the extreme difficulty of separating an uncivil or otherwise undesirable employee from his civil service job.

In the field of foreign affairs, President Arthur demonstrated courage in standing up for decency in the teeth of riotous opposition, especially from California. The Treaty of 1880 with China had given the United States the right to "regulate, limit or suspend" but not "absolutely prohibit" the immigration of Chinese laborers. But Congress in 1882 passed a bill suspending immigration from China for 20 years. President Arthur, regarding this prolonged blockage as close to complete exclusion, vetoed the bill.

Arthur's reasoning was set forth with complete clarity and forthrightness in his veto message of April 4, 1882: "A nation is justified in repudiating its treaty obligations only when they are in conflict with great paramount interests. Even then all possible reasonable means for modifying or changing those obligations by mutual agreement should be exhausted before resorting to the supreme right of refusal to comply with them."

Arthur's courageous veto triggered an uproar in the West, where in San Francisco flags were hung at half-mast and merchants draped their stores in black. Congress, forced to reconsider its action, passed the act of 1882, which suspended Chinese immigration for a much more reasonable 10 years, as compared with 20. President Arthur signed the new bill, and the West rejoiced with restrained enthusiasm over this temporary relief.

The President's stern veto of a wasteful Rivers and Harbors bill in August 1882 met with no success whatever. Recognized by cynics as the usual log-rolling or "pork barrel" measure, it appropriated some $18 million for the alleged improvements of waterways in Congressional districts where the voters would be pleased with the jobs created. But all too often such expenditures were both unneeded and extravagant. Arthur's valiant attempt to counter the "demoralizing effect" of such vote-snaring waste proved ineffective. Vote-greedy congressmen, eager to scratch each other's backs, promptly passed the pork barrel bill over the President's veto.

If, as the proverb tells us, one good turn deserves another, one good term deserves another. President Arthur, the onetime political spoilsman and Friend of the Stalwarts, gave the country an administration of such conspicuous fairness and honesty that he richly deserved renomination and re-election in his own right. But he had gravely offended the Conklingite politicians of the Stalwart stripe and the Blaineite politicians of the Half-breed stripe. He was finally passed over by the Republicans in their Chicago nominating convention of 1884. The high honor fell to James G. Blaine, whose personal honesty was widely distrusted. The next year Arthur died of a cerebral hemorrhage, leaving a legacy of presidential uprightness that tended to cancel out his earlier career as a friend of spoilsmen.

CHAPTER 21

Grover Cleveland
1885–1889

Your every voter, as surely as your chief magistrate, exercises a public trust.

Grover Cleveland, inaugural
address, March 4, 1885

"Old Grover" Cleveland ranks high among the Presidents as a man of homespun honesty and sterling integrity. Physically, he presented a portly figure, and one unfriendly critic quipped that he had so much backbone that his stomach stuck out in front.

Stephen Grover Cleveland was born in New Jersey in 1837 but his roots were finally transplanted deep into the soil of the electorally potent state of New York. Schooled in the law, he became an attorney in Buffalo and a lifelong foe of the corrupt Democratic machine in New York City known as Tammany Hall.

As fate ordained, Cleveland's father was a pious but penurious Presbyterian preacher. In the home, young Grover learned the virtues of honesty and devotion to duty. In his attorney's office, he became a stickler for the strict letter of the law.

When the Civil War erupted in 1861, Cleveland was nearly 24 years of age and presumably able-bodied cannon fodder. Two

124

of his brothers served, so Grover was needed at home to support his widowed mother. As was commonly and openly done, he hired a substitute to go in his place, in this case a Polish immigrant for $150. The absence of a war record hurt Cleveland politically in later years, especially when he had to deal with pension bills for the aging Boys in Blue who had faced the bullets and bayonets of the Confederates.

Cleveland's devotion to orthodox Presbyterian principles was more evident in his public life than in his early private life. The blunt truth is that in his twenties and early thirties bachelor Grover hung around during much of his spare time in saloons, where he evidently developed a protruding beer belly. More than that, he consorted with the widowed Maria Halpin, to whom a son was born. Ever the man of principle, Cleveland quietly acknowledged his responsibility for the paternity of this unwanted bundle from heaven, and made financial provision for its support.

Cleveland's meteoric rise in politics was distinguished by a painful dedication to duty. Elected sheriff of Erie County (New York) in 1871, he made commendable headway in cleansing the county of dishonest contractors. Two common criminals were scheduled to be hanged, and Sheriff Cleveland performed this disagreeable duty with his own hands, although he probably could have foisted the execution off onto subordinates. For his addiction to duty he came to be known by his enemies as "The Buffalo Hangman." As often happened, he saw his duty and overdid it.

Acclaimed as a man of unimpeachable honesty, "The Beast of Buffalo" was elected mayor of his home city on a platform of political reform. Taking his new office seriously, Cleveland proceeded to push for a housecleaning, much too energetically, in fact, for the slippery politicians of the old school. He not only tried to make good things happen but also used his busy pen to make bad things not happen. He thus came honestly by the title of "Veto Mayor."

Elected "Reform Governor" of New York State in 1883, Cleveland gained office as the "Unowned Candidate" who had won the enmity of the Democratic politicians in New York City's Tammany Hall. He further antagonized the party wheelhorses and other seasoned professionals by refusing to play the questionable game of parceling out the election spoils and other benefactions. Not surprisingly, Cleveland's vigorous use of the veto club earned him the unsolicited title of "Veto Governor."

A popular bill passed by the state legislature in Albany lowered the fare on the elevated railroads of New York City from 10 cents to 5 cents—prospectively a great boon to the poor working class. But such a measure was a clear-cut violation of the existing state contract with the transit companies. As between humanitarianism and legalism, a governor with Cleveland's cast of mind was bound to do the legally correct thing—and he imposed a highly unpopular veto.

The Democrats had not elected a President for 24 long years, and by 1884 the country was ripe for a seasoned Chief Executive who favored reform. The orator who placed Cleveland's name before the Democratic nominating convention in Chicago praised Old Grover's courageous record as a "reform governor," and lauded him "for the enemies he has made." Strong men tend to make strong enemies, and Cleveland had made many of the right kind, especially among nest-feathering politicians of his own party.

Against Cleveland, still a bachelor, the Republicans pitted a prominent family man, James G. Blaine of Maine, who was tainted with some damning political dishonesties or rumors of dishonesty. The Democrats carried on in high glee until the devastating news leaked out of Cleveland's bastard offspring.

The now-blackened "Grover the Good," to the consternation of his backers, flatly refused to "lie like a gentleman." "Tell the truth," he instructed his crestfallen followers. He also allegedly suppressed evidence brought to him that cast doubt on Blaine's faithfulness to the marriage vows. Cleveland was evidently willing to permit the other side of have a monopoly of all the dirt in this campaign.

Taken aback temporarily, the Democrats claimed that their nominee enjoyed an impeccable record in public life, to which he was seeking election. Blaine, on the contrary, displayed a disgraceful public life, from which he should be retired to adorn the private state of matrimony. The Democrats claimed that the issue was forgivable private immorality versus unforgivable public dishonesty, and here Cleveland had an advantage. He was elected President in 1884 by an extremely narrow margin, as crowds in the streets shouted "Ma, ma, where's my pa? Gone to the White House, ha, ha, ha!"

President Cleveland's first task was the staggering one of trying to satisfy the horde of officeseekers that poured into Washington elbowing for jobs. The crush was intensified by the prolonged political drought: the last Democrat to enter the White House had been Buchanan in 1857, 28 years earlier. In the interim the Southern states had seceded, had been made temporary outcasts, and then had worked up a ravenous appetite for offices while being excluded from the political plums. The Northern Democrats, for their part, were hardly less demanding.

A fair-minded Cleveland outraged Northern veterans of the Civil War, especially Republicans, by appointing two ex-Confederates to his Cabinet, one of them a former general. At long last the once rebellious South was to receive something approaching fair recognition. Cleveland also believed in the merit system. To him "a public office was a public trust," but the pressures became so intense that he turned over to the first assistant postmaster general the formidable task of uprooting some 40,000 entrenched Republican postmasters. Even so, Cleveland's grudging concessions won few friends. Dislodged Republicans cried that Old Grover went too far; office-hungry Democrats condemned him for not going far enough. Advocates of genuine civil service reform were aghast.

Cleveland's perplexities were deepened by the confusion over pensions for Civil War veterans. He was trapped in an awkward position, for he not only was a Democrat but he had hired a substitute, as was then thought proper, to fight the war in his place. Existing pension legislation made it possible for ex-soldiers with service-connected disabilities to secure compensation from the time of their discharge to the filing of the necessary disability claims.

At a maximum the pensioning process could involve payments reaching back for about 18 years. If the Pension Bureau rejected the claim of the ex-soldier, he could readily persuade his Congressman to introduce a special bill covering his case. The legislative handout would be passed by Congressmen who in due season would expect similar favors for their constituents from cooperative colleagues. The door was thus thrown open to a vast amount of fraud and other skullduggery, especially when pension-chasing attorneys entered the scramble.

Cleveland believed that the pension roll should be an honor roll and not a swindle sheet concocted by deserters, malingerers, and other dollar-grabbers. Ever a slave to conscience, he read these special bills painstakingly and sternly vetoed several hundred of them. In doing so he laboriously penned individual veto messages, in which he repeatedly exposed the greed and misrepresentation of the applicant, including one who had suffered a "terrific encounter with the measles." More than that, in 1887 Cleveland successfully vetoed the Dependent Pension Bill, which awarded an overgenerous pension to any Union veteran who had served 90 days and was now unable to earn a living. The "Veto President's" laborious penny-pinching at the expense of Union veterans, worthy or unworthy, stirred up a storm of vituperation, especially among Republicans in the North.

The defeated states of the Confederacy, as losers, had to deal with their own pension problems. As a conciliatory gesture, Cleveland ordered the return of certain captured Confederate flags, with consequent outraged cries of "treason" in the North. The President revoked the order, not in response to the uproar, but when he found that only Congress could legally authorize a return of the banners. Eighteen years later this transfer of battle flags to the South was quietly achieved under the Republican administration of Theodore Roosevelt.

Grover Cleveland, though a devotee of honest government, would not meddle with business or take an active role in social reform. We recall that as reform governor of New York he had vetoed a bill designed to reduce car fares to five cents. In 1887, he vetoed humane legislation by Congress designed to provide seeds for the drought-stricken farmers of Texas. "Though the people support the government," he bluntly insisted, "the government should not support the people." This hands-off approach made especially heartless reading in the days of Franklin Roosevelt's lavish New Deal.

Yet Cleveland displayed humaneness and honest stubbornness in forthrightly tackling the tariff issue. One problem was that the Treasury had accumulated an embarrassing surplus of about $145 million, chiefly from import duties. American manufacturers were thus able to charge higher prices for their goods behind the protective wall of the tariff. In addition, the unneeded surplus in the Treasury was a standing invitation to cooperative Congressmen to log-roll through Congress pork barrel legislation for extravagant and unnecessary projects in their respective districts.

In 1887 Cleveland, his jaw set, decided to awaken the country to the tariff problem by devoting his entire annual message to Congress to the necessity of revising existing duties downward but not abolishing them. Democratic politicians, who had expected to ride into office on his coattails, were aghast. The President could be confident of re-election in 1888 if he did not rock the boat with such a call for drastic change. But a bull-headed Cleveland replied, "What is the use of being elected or re-elected unless you stand for something?" He stubbornly submitted his bombshell tariff message to Congress; the Republicans unfairly cried "free trade"; and Cleveland was defeated for re-election by a narrow margin. Actually he polled about 100,000 more popular votes than his rival, Benjamin Harrison, although losing in the Electoral College, 233 to 168.

No one can say with certainty that Cleveland's stubbornness on tariff reduction—not abolition—cost him re-election. But it certainly did him little good. What may have hurt him more was an indiscreet letter penned by Sir Lionel Sackville-West, the British Minister in Washington. A clever California Republican had written to the envoy asking how one should vote in the current contest for the presidency between the Democratic Cleveland and the Republican Harrison. The uncautious Sackville-West responded in effect that a vote for Cleveland was a vote for England.

The gleeful Republicans arranged for the publication of this indiscreet letter in the newspaper press. The resulting uproar, especially among normally Democratic Irishmen, shook the nation, as the Irish vote seemed to be slipping away from Cleveland, especially in New York State. The politicians urged Cleveland to bundle the "damned Englishman" off home before election day, without waiting for the formality of his recall. Cleveland resultantly did so, thus providing one of the few conspicuously weak acts of his entire political career. At least he showed he was human.

Often overlooked in appraising Cleveland's concern for the underdog and his antipathy to graft was his role in rescuing public lands from predators who had come by them irregularly or dishonestly. Among the offenders were "cattle barons" and the railroad "octopus." In his fourth annual message to Congress, December 3, 1888, Cleveland noted with much satisfaction that over 80 million acres had been saved from "illegal usurpation, improvident grants, and fraudulent entries and claims." These lands had been made available to ordinary citizens to be home-steaded by "honest industry." Unforgiving foe of fraud, Grover Cleveland remained ruggedly honest and independent to the end.

CHAPTER 22

Benjamin Harrison
1889–1893

A high sense of duty and an ambition to improve the service should characterize all public offices.

Benjamin Harrison, inaugural
address, March 4, 1889

The Republican Benjamin Harrison, who defeated Grover Cleveland in 1888, was the grandson of Old Tippecanoe Harrison. The older statesman had served as President for only 31 days in 1841 before dying of pneumonia. The younger Harrison—"Young Tippecanoe"—was a stumpy, colorless figure, often cartooned as rattling around in his grandfather's oversized military hat. A splendid orator on the political platform, the grandson was so reserved in meeting people in his office as to be dubbed the "White House Iceberg." As a Presbyterian elder, he was unquestionably a man of integrity, although he could not have been proud of certain questionable dealings that went on under his nose during his administration.

The Republican platform on which "Little Ben" ran called for "the integrity and purity of elections," yet the contest in which he triumphed was blackened by scandalous irregularities. The frightening prospect of a lowered tariff spurred Republican campaigners into frenzied action. They succeeded in raising a war chest of about $3 million, largely by "frying the fat" out of panicky industrialists. The resulting funds were used to seduce corruptible "voting cattle," popularly called "repeaters" or "floaters." In Indiana, a key state, the price of a purchased vote shot up to $20. The key figure in this scandal proved to be W. W. Dudley, the treasurer of the Republican National Committee. He was accused of having written a letter to the county leaders of Indiana instructing them to line up the purchasable voters for the Republican Harrison. "Divide the [footloose] floaters into blocks of five," the instructions ran, "and put a trusted man with necessary funds in charge of these five and make him responsible that none get away and that all vote our ticket."

Loyal Republicans stubbornly insisted that the incriminating letter was a forgery. Candidate Harrison, claiming that he had not seen the original statement in question, flatly refused to pass judgment on its authenticity. The Republican leaders felt let down, while the Democrats assailed Harrison's failure to clean house. Partly because the election day was imminent, Harrison kept the allegedly wrongdoing Dudley on as treasurer of the Republican National Committee.

As a man of integrity, Harrison could hardly have been so naive as not to realize that his election had been bought. But like President-elect Hayes in 1876 he realized that probably more than enough Republican black voters had been disfranchised in the Democratic South to offset Republican irregularities. When the crunch comes, even respectable politicians will sometimes turn a deaf ear to the voice of conscience.

As for the spoils of office, the incoming Republicans under Harrison found themselves in an awkward position because they had been the party of the outs for four barren years. During this unhappy interim the Democrats had scooped up the prize political plums, and the unhappy Republicans had come out flatly in their platform of 1888 for "the reform of the civil service."

But the shoe was now on the other foot, and a hungry horde of Republican officeseekers poured into Washington and other areas where the patronage counter was open for business. The incoming President Harrison, to his credit, observed the strict letter of the Pendleton Civil Service Act, but he decapitated politically many disappointed and resentful Democrats. Also to his credit, he appointed to the Civil Service Commission a hyperactive New Yorker, the redoubtable young Theodore Roosevelt. The future Rough Rider had received this honorable office as a reward for having campaigned with unrestrained energy and oratory in the recent heated campaign for Harrison. Oddly enough, his new job was to prevent such crass spoilsmanship.

Yet Harrison is to be commended for having upheld both the letter and spirit of the Pendleton Civil Service Act. He actually raised the number of classified positions from 27,000 to 38,000. Those officeholders so categorized were subject to open competitive examinations. Yet, on the whole, Harrison managed to please neither partisan Republicans nor extreme civil service reformers. He who steers a fair middle course often suffers brickbats from both sides.

The burden of a surplus, which had greatly vexed President Cleveland, was rather quickly disposed of by extravagant Congressional appropriations under Harrison. "Czar" Thomas B. Reed, Speaker of the House, railroaded through the House of Representatives expensive Republican legislation that gave the name of "Billion-Dollar Congress" to the fifty-first Congress—the first one in peacetime to appropriate approximately this then-prodigious sum.

"Brave Ben" Harrison, himself a Civil War brigadier general, had a soft spot in his heart for his aging comrades-in-arms. He believed with the Republican platform that no man who had worn the blue Union uniform worthily should "become the inmate of an almshouse, or dependent upon private charity," especially in view of the presence of an overflowing Treasury.

President Harrison unwittingly generated a costly scandal when he appointed ex-Corporal James R. Tanner as Commissioner of Pensions. The new director, who had lost both legs in the Civil War at the battle of Bull Run, promised to drive a six-mule team through the Treasury and to wring from the hearts of many the prayer, "God help the surplus!" He even remitted overdue pensions to surprised veterans who had not even applied for them, and also extended his generosity to civilian employees of his office. Yet he appears not to have appropriated surplus money for himself.

In the face of these lavish and sometimes illegal handouts, Harrison forced Corporal Tanner to resign in less than a year.

The embarrassed President proved reluctant to take action in the teeth of the potent veteran vote, but finally he did act. A surplus in the Treasury has not been a real problem since Tanner's debauch. The Republican Congress cooperated generously when it passed the openhanded Pension Act of 1890, signed by Harrison. When the President left office in 1893 the annual pension bill had skyrocketed from $81 million to $135 million—large sums for those days.

In dismissing Corporal Tanner, Harrison had assured him, "Your honesty has not at any time been called into question." Tanner's real sin appears to have been excessive generosity to others with public funds. His replacement was G. B. Raum, whom critics accused of accepting substantial loans from lawyers to expedite their pension cases. Committees of the House of Representatives twice investigated these ugly charges but split along Republican and Democratic lines. For their part, the Democrats concluded that Raum had "prostituted his office for the purposes of private gain." Harrison, a staunch Republican, held firmly to the party line, despite considerable evidence of wrongdoing under his nose. Democratic critics felt that although the President might not himself be dishonest, he was covering for a dishonest man. The party in power is less inclined than "the outs" to feel that everything must be above suspicion.

President Harrison proved to be a peaceful expansionist who backed Secretary of State Blaine in promoting limited reciprocal trade arrangements with the nations of Latin America. But his unsuccessful attempt to achieve the annexation of the Hawaiian islands was much more vulnerable to criticism.

In 1893 Hawaii was ruled by a native monarchy headed by the Queen Liliuokalani of the legendary Hawaiian dynasty. White men, chiefly Americans, had come to control the major agricultural industry of the islands—the growing of sugarcane. These planters came to grief in 1890 when the Congress of the United States erected the high McKinley tariff barriers against their product. Annexation under the American flag seemed to be the only way to get out from under this burden.

Unrest among the white minority in Hawaii deepened as Queen Liliuokalani began to display increasingly anti-foreign tendencies. Especially disturbing to the planters was her insistence that the native majority, not the white minority, should control these idyllic islands. In short, Hawaii for the Hawaiians, or genuine democracy.

A small band of disgruntled whites finally organized a revolt against the Queen in Honolulu in January 1893. The uprising probably succeeded primarily because the American minister John L. Stevens, though totally without authorization from Washington, had authorized the landing of about 150 American marines from a warship in Honolulu harbor, together with some artillery. Though presumably present to protect American lives and property, these troops were actually stationed where they could menace the native forces. Thus confronted with the unauthorized power of the United States, the Queen in effect threw herself on its mercy, while a handful of white rebels took control of the Honolulu government.

A triumphant white commission—four Americans and one Englishman—rushed a treaty of annexation to Washington shortly before the end of the incumbent administration. President Harrison promptly submitted the pact to the Senate with high hopes of adding these island jewels to the national crown. Overlooking the marines and the American minister Stevens, his special message gave assurance that "the overthrow of the monarchy was not in any way promoted by the government."

But delays prevented speedy action, and the newly re-elected President Cleveland withdrew the rush-order treaty on the grounds that it had not been justly negotiated, as indeed it had not been. An unauthorized American Minister had used the threat of unneutral military intervention to dethrone a legal ruler on behalf of a self-serving white minority, mostly American. Grover Cleveland could see all this clearly but Harrison, blinded by the prospects of tropical expansion, either could not or would not. His precipitate pushing of the treaty indicates that on occasion his ethical standards would permit him to be a willing partner in international skullduggery—all in the national interest.

In another quarter, a slight scandal sprang from Harrison's policy regarding gifts from private sources. The Constitution states clearly that no public official holding a national office shall accept any kind of present from any "king, prince, or foreign state" without the consent of Congress. The intent is clear. But nothing bars a public official from accepting any gift of real worth from private individuals, foreign or domestic.

With a few exceptions most Presidents, for the sake of appearances, have declined to receive gifts of substantial value. To do otherwise would raise questions of undue influence or suspected influence. President Harrison departed from this general rule early in June 1890, when his wealthy Postmaster General, John Wanamaker, joined by some Philadelphia friends, presented Mrs. Harrison with an attractive new cottage at the popular resort of Cape May, New Jersey.

When this gift—or was it a bribe of sorts?—first came to public notice President Harrison made no comment. Somewhat later he protested that all along he had intended to buy the cottage in question, once Mrs. Harrison had given it the stamp of her approval. Shortly thereafter she visited the cottage and found the gift to her liking. The President then sent Postmaster General Wanamaker a check for $10,000. There is no way of knowing whether or not Harrison was unduly influenced by this gift, but the acceptance of it must have made it more difficult for him to decline when his benefactors came around expecting or requesting special presidential favors. In 1890, $10,000 was no trifling sum.

CHAPTER 23

Grover Cleveland
1893–1897

I do not believe that nations any more than individuals can safely violate the rules of honesty and fair dealing.

Grover Cleveland, 1886

Defeated for re-election in the Electoral College in 1888, but not by the popular vote, Grover Cleveland took up residence in New York City, not Buffalo. He evidently became even more conservative as he rubbed elbows with wealthy clients, although he seemed undisposed to extract exorbitant fees.

Cleveland's two-fisted crusade for a lowered tariff in 1887–1888 had won many converts, especially after the enactment of the towering Republican McKinley tariff of 1890. The former President, after being overwhelmingly nominated by the Democrats in St. Louis on the first ballot, rather handily ousted the high-tariff Benjamin Harrison in the national election of 1892.

Three days after taking office for the second time, Cleveland summarily withdrew from the Senate the recent rush-order treaty for the annexation of Hawaii. He strongly suspected—as his later investigation proved—that the native queen had been dishonor-ably overthrown in favor of a white oligarchy, which enjoyed the unauthorized connivance of the American minister in Honolulu. But since the Queen would not promise to pardon the conspirators when restored to her throne, Cleveland had no choice but to leave the white regime in control of the Hawaiian government. American public opinion, especially in the Democratic and anti-black South, simply would not stand idly by and watch the native queen wreak vengeance on white men. In 1898, under a less scrupulous president and in a changed international atmosphere, the Hawaiian islands were admitted to the American fold as a territory. But Cleveland's role in this insular episode testified eloquently to his determination to steer the nation on an honorable and anti-imperialistic course.

Cleveland's second four years were bedeviled by the Panic of 1893. It helped bring to a head the clash between the high-tariff and low-tariff zealots, as well as the one between the silverites and the "gold bugs." Cleveland continued to be dedicated to a low tariff and sound money. The "honest" gold standard, in the eyes of conservatives like Cleveland, would safeguard the dollar against an inflationary deluge of cheap silver dollars.

Alarmingly, the constant drainage of gold from the Treasury threatened the soundness of the dollar. A major source of this leakage was the Sherman Silver Purchase Act, passed by Congress in 1890 under President Harrison. Ever the sound-money man, Cleveland summoned Congress into special session to end the buying of silver and to bolster the gold standard. Pursuing what he regarded as the only honest course, he managed in 1893 to engineer a repeal of the Sherman Silver Purchase Act of 1890, but in so doing he split his Democratic party wide open.

Cleveland was both less successful and less true to his rigid principles in the struggle to lower the extortionate Republican tariff of 1890, which bore the name of William McKinley, soon to be President. A reasonable bill to lower existing duties was introduced in Congress, whereupon the smooth-talking lobbyists got busy, especially those for the sugar trust, and in the end 630 amendments were added. The resulting Wilson-Gorman Bill lowered the existing rates of the McKinley tariff from an average of 48 percent to 41 percent, but this was not the kind of reduction envisaged in Cleveland's Democratic platform. That pronouncement had denounced the McKinley act "as the culminating atrocity of class legislation" and had promised its repeal "as one of the beneficent results that will follow the action of the people in intrusting power to the Democratic party."

President Cleveland was disheartened by this anemic tariff reform bill, which to him seemed like a gross betrayal of Democratic pledges in the official platform. He angrily denounced the new legislation as "party perfidy and party dishonor," to the unrestrained glee of partisan Republicans. But he realized that to use his well-inked veto pen would leave untouched the even more restrictive McKinley tariff. He finally chose the lesser of two evils when he took a weaker course not at all characteristic of him: he simply allowed the Wilson-Gorman bill to become a law without his signature.

A scandal rapidly developed involving the American Sugar Company, a monopoly that managed to have included in the new tariff bill self-serving benefits worth a sweet $20 million a year. The allegation was that the corporation had contributed some $100,000 to Secretary of the Treasury Carlisle to seal the bargain. A Senate investigating committee completely exonerated Carlisle but implicated several Senators in sugar-stock speculation.

The withering panic of 1893 had brought in its wake a severe strain on the Treasury, which continued to hemorrhage gold at an alarming rate. Early in 1894 only a disheartening $41 million remained, and the Washington government was confronted with the suicidal prospect of going off the gold standard. Cleveland finally concluded that the only feasible stopgap was to sell federal bonds for gold and deposit the proceeds in the Treasury. He arranged to have two bond issues floated in 1894, for a total of more than $100 million, but all of this backing melted away as worried citizens lined up to present paper money for redemption in gold.

Early in 1895, in a last desperate throw of the dice, Cleveland made contact with financier J. P. ("Jupiter") Morgan and a Wall Street syndicate. The bankers finally agreed to lend the Treasury $65 million in gold, but charged a costly commission of about $7 million, as they were in a position to do. With the aid of these funds and one more loan, Cleveland surmounted the financial crisis.

In the eyes of the poor, especially the silverites, Wall Street loomed as an unprincipled and oppressive monopoly, with J. P. Morgan the chief financial ogre. Rumors multiplied that the President and his advisers had unlawfully sold out the national government to brigands. Cleveland, falsely accused of being "Morgan's errand boy," responded defiantly by declaring, "Without shame and without repentance I confess my share of the guilt." Extensive Congressional investigations turned up no real evidence of wrongdoing of any kind. "Grover the Good" was acting only in what he conceived to be the best financial interests of the nation, and the results seemed to prove him right.

In the area of foreign affairs Cleveland had early shown a disposition to side with the wronged underdog, notably in the case of Queen Liliuokalani in Honolulu. But this affair was a minor squabble when compared with Cleveland's willingness to go to the brink of war with Great Britain over an ancient boundary dispute between faraway Venezuela and British Guiana. Yet the President declined to intervene at all in the nearby revolt in Cuba against the autocratic rule of Spain. Indeed, Cleveland went to considerable lengths to enforce the leaky neutrality laws that were only partially checking the flow of men and munitions from the United States to the Cuban insurgents.

A dispute over the boundary line between Venezuela and Great Britain had been simmering off and on for more than a half-century before Cleveland got a finger in the pie. As events proved, the claim of the Venezuelans was extravagant, and the British had consequently declined to submit the dispute to arbitration. Arbitrators all too often tend to split the difference.

Cleveland cherished no great love for Britain, and he was a foremost champion of righteous dealings for the underdog, whether in Hawaii or Venezuela. He evidently was unduly influenced by the Venezuelan propagandists, and instructed his Secretary of State to send a lengthy and peremptory diplomatic note to London virtually demanding that the current dispute be submitted to impartial arbitration. Cleveland, who was prone to put his foot down rather than slide it down, himself dubbed this famous note a "20-inch gun" blast.

Oddly enough, Cleveland tried to justify his intervention on behalf of the underdog by invoking the Monroe Doctrine of 1823. He reasoned that Britain, by claiming disputed territory, was extending her extensive territorial domain in the Americas, contrary to the warning of President Monroe. Yet this kind of problem was certainly not what Monroe had in mind.

London took four leisurely months to respond to the intemperate blast from Washington. Cleveland's hot temper had already reached the boiling point when the bored British in a toplofty note responded that the Monroe Doctrine was not relevant and that arbitration was out of the question. In short, the President had stuck his nose into somebody else's quarrel, and he was told in careful diplomatic language to pull it out.

President Cleveland was infuriated by the condescending British reply. He sent a bristling message to Congress urging funds for a commission of experts who would determine where the boundary line should rightfully run. His implication was that if the British would not accept this fair boundary, then the United States would fight for it.

Such was Cleveland's misguided effort to be honest and stand up for a distant underdog. There was ugly talk of war on both sides of the Atlantic, a clash in which the British would have 32 battleships to only 5 for the United States. The ominous international situation, involving also the bellicose German Kaiser, helped to induce the British to back down. At long last London agreed to arbitrate the boundary dispute with Venezuela, and ironically the arbiters awarded to the British the bulk of what they had claimed from the beginning. The historian can only conclude that the upright but ill-informed Cleveland went overboard in his championing of righteousness.

As for the civil service, Cleveland believed with his Democratic platform that a "Public office is a public trust." He undertook to carry out the existing legislation that related to civil service reform. In May 1896 he published civil service rules designed to improve the system, thus blanketing 85,000 additional employees under the Civil Service Commission.

High-level officials, including cabinet members and diplomats, were still beneficiaries of the spoils system. After all, the President does not welcome or even need intimate advisers from the opposition party. But one curious case arose that probably proved more embarrassing to the supposed beneficiary than to Cleveland.

Traditionally some of the major embassies, notably those in London and Paris, have been so expensive to maintain that only wealthy persons can afford to hold these posts. In 1892 James Van Alen, a rich Rhode Islander, had contributed about $50,000 to the Democratic campaign coffers. Despite appearances and warnings, Cleveland appointed him Minister to Italy in the time-honored fashion, except that Van Alen was better qualified for the post than many of his predecessors and successors. The liberal press raised a storm about a "purchased office," but Cleveland, fully conscious of his own rectitude, believed that critics and potential critics should not challenge the purity of his motives. The Senate, with a number of Republicans also voting for Van Alen, finally confirmed the appointment. Having received this vindication, the controversial recipient, embarrassed by all the uproar, resigned his post.

In private, Cleveland bitterly attacked Van Alen's critics, and wrote to a friend, "No one will accuse me of such a trade"—that is, a diplomatic post for a campaign contribution. The fact is that many partisan critics believed the worst, despite the President's self-righteous assessment of his own motives. But that was the way that the game of politics was often played—and to some extent still is.

Cleveland, the sound-money champion, was virtually a man without a party when his second term ended on March 4, 1897. The inflationary free-silverites had seized control of the Democratic Party, and had nominated the silver-tongued William Jennings Bryan at Chicago in July 1896. The delegates, shouting insults at the absent Cleveland, put on the unprecedented and suicidal act of condemning his administration by a vote of 564 to 357. Bryan subsequently lost to the sound money "gold bug," Republican William McKinley, in the frenzied free-silver campaign of 1896. Conservative Democrats helped out the Republicans by splitting their party and nominating their own antisilver candidates.

Cleveland retired to Princeton, New Jersey, where he kept a modest hand in local and national affairs. On his deathbed in 1908, he is reported to have said, "I have tried so hard to do right."

CHAPTER 24

William McKinley
1897–1901

*Nothing in the . . . world is worth so much, will last so long, and serve its possessor
so well as good character.*

William McKinley, speech,
December 18, 1898

William McKinley has traditionally been portrayed as a weak, ear-to-the-ground politician, who served as a tool of Republican big business as exemplified by "Dollar Mark" Hanna. In more recent decades scholars have concluded that although McKinley was a kindly and compassionate man, he did have a mind of his own and a sincere dedication to conservative principles. His personal honesty was commendable, and although he was guilty of occasional mistakes, they were made by a man of integrity on the basis of such information as was available to him at the time.

As a former member of Congress and a governor of Ohio, McKinley ran for the presidency in 1896 on the Republican ticket as the gold standard candidate. Pitted against him was the leading champion of free silver, William Jennings Bryan, "The Boy Orator of the Platte," who had swept the Chicago nominating convention off its feet by assailing the gold standard as a "crown of thorns" pressed down on the brow of a crucified mankind.

In the frenzied battle between the gold and silver standards that ensued, McKinley won handily. His mentor, Mark Hanna, "shook down" the worried businessmen and financiers for a then enormous campaign fund. The great bulk of this sum was not used to buy votes outright, as had sometimes been done, but through pro-gold leaflets and other propaganda designed to frighten people into voting against Bryan and his free-silver heresy. This strategy was then regarded, and still is, as the way the game of politics is legitimately played.

McKinley was fully aware that he owed Mark Hanna a lasting debt for having boosted him into the presidential chair. As a reward, Hanna coveted a seat in the Senate of the United States, but there was no vacancy. Yet the aging Senator John Sherman was induced to leave his place in the Senate to take over the prestigious post of Secretary of State. The vacancy thus created was filled when the governor of Ohio obliged McKinley by appointing Hanna to the Senate.

This episode could be written off as just another political deal, not as a scandal, if it had worked out well for Secretary Sherman and the United States. The ex-Senator, now "kicked upstairs," was well into his seventies, and his loss of memory was so pronounced as to cause serious embarrassment in delicate negotiations then involving several foreign countries. More or less put on the shelf, he resigned in 1898 as a protest against the expansionist war with Spain.

McKinley's handling of the crisis in Cuba has raised several nagging questions about his capacity for honorable dealing. When he entered the White House in 1897, a renewed insurrection in "The Pearl of the Antilles" against Spanish rule was claiming the headlines. American trade and investments were being adversely affected, as were a few naturalized American citizens of Cuban background. The yellow press clamored for intervention to abate a nuisance, but a determined McKinley set his face like flint against involvement.

In February 1898 Americans were aroused to a fighting pitch when the United States warship *Maine,* on a peacetime visit, blew up in Havana harbor, with the loss of 260 officers and men. An official investigation by the U.S. Navy reported that the vessel had been destroyed by an external submarine mine. On the other hand, the official Spanish investigation found for an internal accidental explosion. A new American inquiry in 1976, headed by Admiral H. G. Rickover, concluded 78 years too late that the Spaniards were indisputably right.

When evidence of presumed Spanish treachery was officially released by the Navy in 1898, the American public threw restraint to the winds. The demand for armed intervention against Spain's Cuba rose to hurricane force. McKinley resisted such pressures as best he could; in fact, he was driven to sleeping pills to quiet his nerves. Critics hanged him in effigy and proclaimed that he did not have "the backbone of a chocolate eclair." They did not seem to realize that backbone was needed to stay out of this war rather than plunge into it.

McKinley, to his credit, first tried the quiet channels of diplomacy, and there he had some illusory success. Madrid agreed to end the reconcentration camps for Cuban civilians and to offer an armistice to the rebels in arms. But just as it takes two to tango, it takes two in this kind of situation to make an armistice. We now have persuasive evidence that the insurgents would have kept on fighting until they had won their complete independence.

It is not true that McKinley, having won a great diplomatic victory over Spain, cynically tossed the whole burning issue into the lap of a war-mad Congress. The President had reluctantly come to the conclusion that because the war would grind on anyhow, the wisest course would be to abate the nuisance of the Cuban pesthouse. The American people were clamoring for armed intervention, and in a democracy the people are entitled to what they overwhelmingly want, even if it may not be good for them. Nor could McKinley have been so stupid as not to perceive that war would help his chances of reelection in 1900, when presumably McKinley's gold standard would again be pitted against Bryan's silver standard. As far as the President was concerned, a victory for a free Cuba was preferable to a triumph for free silver.

The Spanish-American war, although begun with high ideals, turned out to be a major scandal in the Philippines and as such reflected unfavorably on President McKinley. The irony is that in all the major battles with Spain the Americans emerged victorious. The Spaniards, as became painfully evident, were even less well prepared for war than their Yankee foe, partly because they were forced to fight in Cuba or Cuban waters or in the Philippines and Philippine waters, thousands of miles from their home base.

At the outbreak of war, Commodore George Dewey, then

stationed in Chinese waters with six American warships, received orders from Washington to descend on Manila in the Philippines. There he destroyed a fleet so wretchedly prepared that one vessel was a moored hulk without functioning engines. The Spaniards lost nearly 400 men killed and wounded; Dewey did not sacrifice a man. He waited in Manila Bay from May 1 to August 13, 1898, for troops to arrive from America, whereupon the Americans, supported by Filipino insurgents, wrested the city of Manila from the Spaniards.

By 1898 Spain had stationed about 100,000 soldiers in Cuba, most of them scheduled to fight the slippery insurgents. After much disorganization and confusion, the Americans landed about 17,000 troops in the vicinity of Santiago, although Theodore Roosevelt's Rough Riders were forced to leave behind in the United States most of their horses in the haste to get into action. A main objective of the invaders was to capture Santiago and force out the harbor the fleet of overmatched and ill-prepared Spanish warships. With the city thus jeopardized, the Spanish ships made a suicidal run out of the harbor, only to have the four armored cruisers completely destroyed by the American fleet of seven major vessels. The Spaniards lost 474 killed or wounded, and 1,750 taken prisoner; the Americans lost one killed and one wounded.

On the face of it, such smashing victories were a tribute to the superior organization, preparedness, and skill of the Americans. Actually, the Spaniards were disorganized and outgunned in both of the headline battles. The ugly truth is that the Americans were so wretchedly prepared to fight in the tropics that Europeans were wont to say that God looked after "drunkards, fools, and the United States of America." Among various blunders, training camps were set up in the Southern states in typhoid-infected areas, where many strong recruits suffered inglorious death. In Cuba the soldiers were even fed canned meat that was spoiled—the so-called embalmed beef. The fighting men finally found themselves in tropical Cuba with flannel shirts that had been intended for use in the snows of Montana.

After the Spaniards surrendered in Cuba, the American army of occupation there began to melt away from the inroads of malaria, typhoid, yellow fever, and dysentery. Under pressure from the commanding officers, about 25,000 men, 80 percent of them ill, were transferred to chilly Long Island, New York, where their light summer clothing finally reached them. In the entire war nearly 400 American soldiers lost their lives in battle, but over 5,000 succumbed to bacteria and non-combat causes.

These scandalous statistics cried out that all was not well, whether as the result of gross mismanagement, grafting suppliers, sheer ignorance, or criminal negligence. A "goat" had to be found, even though the American people themselves were to be blamed for demanding war at a time when their country was singularly unprepared for waging war, especially in the tropics. The "goat" turned out to be Secretary of War Russell A. Alger, who might have gone down in history as a competent Secretary of War if there had been no war.

Alger had been a poor choice for this responsible position. As a former governor of Michigan and past commander of the Civil War veterans' organization called Grand Army of the Republic, he was essentially a political appointee. Yet despite mounting criticism, President McKinley retained and publicly supported him, while himself helping to direct overall strategy. Perhaps McKinley felt that throwing Alger to the wolves would be a confession that he himself had mismanaged the war—and he had his eye on re-election for a second term in 1900.

A formal investigative commission was appointed to probe into Alger's War Department. In Feburary 1899 this body issued its nine-volume report, which was expected to arrive at some conclusions as to possible corruption and criminal negligence. It came up with scanty solid evidence but with much in the way of conflicting testimony. Perhaps the major finding was that the army was not guilty of deliberate negligence or major corruption.

Alger was cleared of official wrongdoing, although he had selected a fellow Michiganer, General William Shafter, to command the invasion of Cuba, rather than General Nelson A. Miles. Actually, Shafter was obscenely obese and so seriously incapacitated during much of the Santiago campaign that he had to be carried around on an unhinged door. After Secretary Alger had ceased to be the storm center of controversy, McKinley gently eased him out of the Cabinet.

As a nation, the United States already had many of the attributes of a world power before Commodore Dewey's guns boomed at Manila Bay on May Day 1898. But there can be no doubt that the United States emerged from the Spanish-American War as an imperialist world power, with new and immense overseas liabilities. In taking on some of these tropical burdens, McKinley on occasion did some violence to his personal beliefs and ethical standards, at least as they had existed before he entered the White House. He was both an ear-to-the-ground politician and a true believer in democracy. Accordingly, when the crunch came, he tended to go along with the expansionist majority, even though what they clamored for might not have been good for them. In fact, McKinley was frequently confronted with confusing alternatives, none of them desirable. His formidable task was to peer into the unseeable future and choose the course that appeared to be the least bad.

First came the idyllic Hawaiian islands. McKinley did not suffer from Cleveland's qualms about the injustice done to the Queen Liliuokalani and her native Hawaiians. He was actually pressing for a new treaty of annexation in the Senate, but was getting nowhere. Then came Dewey's exhilarating victory and the need or the presumed need for the Hawaiian islands as a convenient supply station for Dewey's reinforcements. Distrustful of Senate delays, the annexationists rammed through a hurry-up joint resolution in both houses of Congress by a simple majority vote, and McKinley gladly signed the measure. So much for justice to Queen Liliuokalani. Circumstances do indeed alter cases —and ethical standards.

The Americans had not conquered the Philippine islands, although they did command the waters of Manila Bay. The peace protocol ending the shooting was not signed in Washington until August 12, 1898. Ignorant of the signing, the next day the American armed forces attacked and captured Manila from the Spanish troops. So it was that the Americans, in the peace treaty signed at Paris some four months later, agreed to pay impoverished Spain the sum of $20 million for this insular liability. It was one of the best bargains that a defeated nation has ever made with the conquering foe, and it bespoke a certain sense of honor in the McKinley administration.

McKinley wrestled long and prayerfully over whether or not to take the Philippines. The easiest and most irresponsible course would be to turn them over to the natives, who had been resisting Spain's rule, as the Cubans had, for many years. But the islands might well lapse into anarchy, and one or more of the great powers might rush into the scramble for spoils and trigger a world war into which the United States would be sucked. Overseas markets and products were of growing concern to American businessmen in this era of expansionism, and the more the mineral, agricultural, and other resources of the Philippines became known, the less capable the natives seemed of self-government.

The commercial exploitation of the Philippine islands may well have been the deciding factor. It certainly was present in the mind of Mark Hanna, President McKinley's powerful sponsor. Regarding annexation, Hanna cried out, "If this be commercialism," then "for God's sake let us have commercialism." McKinley's final decision to take the Philippines and perhaps give them independence later, has been slyly summarized by one historian as "God directs us—perhaps it will pay."

For various reasons, some of them strategic, the United States also relieved Spain of both Guam and Puerto Rico, which proved to be an expensive, burdensome, and ungrateful liability. Cuba had a different but subordinate status, for at the time of declaring war in April 1898 the Congress had passed the Teller Amendment. It ringingly proclaimed that when the United States had overthrown Spanish misrule, the Cubans would receive their freedom. Yet in June 1901 Congress approved the Platt Amendment under which the United States made Cuba a virtual protectorate for about 33 years. During this probationary period the United States repeatedly intervened in Cuban affairs, and until the coming of Fidel Castro in 1959, local patriots insisted that the island was enslaved by the golden chain of Wall Street.

McKinley's decision to retain the Philippines saddled the United States with a frightfully expensive burden that proved difficult to defend. As we see the picture now, the President, whether motivated or not by commercial instincts, would have served the best interests of the United States and possibly those of the Philippines by leaving the inhabitants to their own devices.

Commodore Dewey had brought back from exile on the Asiatic mainland, when he sailed for his memorable attack on the Spanish fleet, a Filipino patriot named Emilio Aguinaldo. Led to believe that his people would be freed when the Spanish colonizers were ousted, he and his native forces cooperated fully with their American saviors in the final attack on Manila. Dewey denied that he had made any commitment to Filipino freedom, but Aguinaldo almost certainly would not have assisted as he did in the absence of such assurances, whether concrete or tacit.

Blunders were made on both sides, but probably the worst

was the failure of the United States to assure the Filipinos that they would ultimately be freed, somewhat as the Cubans had been. But the Senate, fatally bitten by the imperialistic bug, narrowly refused to make such a commitment. Friction between the "betrayed" natives and the occupying American "liberators" continued, and it finally erupted in open insurrection in February 1899.

The Filipino insurrection, like the jungle-cursed Vietnam War of the 1960s and 1970s, soon became both an international scandal and a black eye for the Americans, including the administration of the kindly William McKinley. The "splendid little" Spanish-American War lasted only four months; the miserable and prolonged Filipino insurrection lasted some inglorious 38 months before degenerating into jungle warfare, with the Americans the pursuers. The invasion of Cuba had involved only some 16,000 American troops. Yet a total of about 120,000 U.S. soldiers were brought into the fighting in the Philippines. American casualties, including battle losses and the dead from disease, exceeded the toll taken by the Spanish-American war by about 1,500 men. Little glory could be extracted from battling half-naked savages whose greatest sin was their struggling to be free, as the Americans themselves had done in the Revolutionary War.

As in Vietnam, the level of the fighting degenerated to the level of the primitive people being fought. Lurid tales reached the press about captured Americans being smeared with honey and left half buried in the jungle to be eaten alive by ants. Such barbarities were also practiced by rival tribes against their own people. On the island of Samar an entire company of 48 American regulars was attacked but not taken prisoner; they were slaughtered to the last man, like Custer's command at the Little Big Horn River in 1876.

Fighting fire with fire, the American invaders retaliated with various tortures, including the "water cure." It consisted of pouring water into the victim until the pain became so great that he invariably talked, especially if military secrets were wanted. Following the massacre of the 48 American regulars, General Jacob ("Hell-Roaring Jake") Smith issued iron-toothed orders (never fully carried out) to kill every male over 10 years of age on the island. The Americans also set up reconcentration camps for civilians who might aid the insurgents, somewhat as the maligned Spaniards had done under "Butcher" Weyler in Cuba. News of these activities was carried in the press of the world, and did much to tarnish the good name of the United States, formerly regarded as the haven of the underprivileged and oppressed of all races and climes.

McKinley was a kindly and compassionate man who no doubt was cut to the quick by all these scandals. There can be little doubt that he would have acted differently toward the Philippine islands if he could have foreseen the future. But foresight, rather than hindsight, is what statesmen are supposed to employ as they weigh alternative courses of action, and when they guess wrong their reputations suffer accordingly. One is tempted to conclude that statesmen are successful politicians who were lucky enough to guess right.

CHAPTER 25

Theodore Roosevelt 1901–1909

A man should in his public as well as private life strive to conform his conduct to the principles laid down in those two ancient guides to conduct, the Decalogue [Ten Commandments] and the Golden Rule.

Theodore Roosevelt, New York, 1898

In examining the public addresses of President Theodore Roosevelt, who was elevated to the White House in 1901 by the bullet that killed McKinley, the reader cannot avoid concluding that this dynamic "Rough Rider" far eclipsed all predecessors or successors in his vehement concern for honesty and honor. He repeatedly preached on such themes as the need for honesty in government, honesty in public life, and honesty in politics. One contemporary congratulated him on his original discovery of the Ten Commandments, while another described him as an interesting combination of Saint Paul and Saint Vitus.

The blunt truth is that behind the scenes Roosevelt resorted on occasion to devious dealings that in retrospect seem out of step with his noisy commitment to such principles as his much-trumpeted Square Deal. Particularly in the arena of foreign affairs,

Roosevelt did not emerge completely untainted. A pugnacious man who loved war and who gloried in armed combat, he adopted the proverb, "Speak softly and carry a big stick, [and] you will go far." Using the threat of often superior naval and military power, he employed the big stick to bully weaker nations into accepting, albeit reluctantly, "my policies."

Late in 1902 a crisis developed involving principally Britain and Germany on one side and dictator-ridden Venezuela on the other. The European powers, unable to collect the overdue debts owed to them, established a tight blockade. German warships sank two Venezuelan gunboats, and later bombarded a town. The Venezuelan dictator then hastened to accept the arbitration that he had earlier spurned, and the State Department in Washington transmitted his acceptance to the European powers involved. There was no hint of a real crisis as far as the United States was concerned.

Fourteen years later, that is in 1916, when ex-President Roosevelt was deeply aroused by German aggression in World War I, he made public a sensational tale. His story was that in 1902 he had summoned the German ambassador in Washington, presented an ultimatum to him, threatened to send Admiral Dewey's powerful fleet to Venezuelan waters, and forced Germany to arbitrate.

No contemporary record of such big-stick pressure has yet been found, whether in the German or American archives, and many historians have written Roosevelt off as both a meddlesome braggart and a barefaced liar. Yet it is possible that Roosevelt did approach the German ambassador in Washington informally, and that the envoy did not see fit to relay the warning to a Berlin that was already preparing to consent to arbitration. We should also note that Roosevelt's private papers reveal that several years before he left the White House he was excited about some kind of tale relating to the secret pressure that he had put on the German Kaiser in 1902. The main outline of the story was evident in his mind before Germany invaded Belgium and France in 1914.

There can be no doubt that President Roosevelt repeatedly championed a "square deal" for everybody, from the poorest laborer to the richest capitalist. But he gave the British and Canadians an unfair deal in connection with the combustible boundary dispute between the Canadians and the Americans in the panhandle of Alaska.

In 1903 Roosevelt consented to an agreement under which "six impartial jurists of repute" would settle the dispute. Three of them would be Americans, two of them Canadians, and one of them British. This was not true arbitration, only an imitation of it, for if the three Americans voted the way that Roosevelt made sure they would, the United States would come out with no less than a tie.

Not all of the six "jurists" were men of "repute," and certainly all or most of them were not "impartial." Roosevelt privately assured himself of the full cooperation of the Americans before he appointed them to the tribunal. On the British side were two Canadians and one prominent British jurist, Lord Alverstone. The two Canadians would undoubtedly support the maximum claim of Canada, with the result that the avoidance of a deadlock rested squarely on the British Lord.

An aroused Roosevelt indiscreetly made it known through indirect channels that if the tribunal failed to decide properly— that is for the extreme American claim—he would occupy the disputed area with troops and run the boundary line the way he thought it ought to go. Resort to armed intervention could only mean war between Britain and America, with this terrible responsibility for the shooting bedeviling Lord Alverstone. As events turned out, the noble Briton voted for the main American contention, leaving the final count at four to two. Whether or not Alverstone yielded to pressure from Roosevelt is still a disputed point, but he certainly created the suspicion of having done so. Roosevelt was elated, the Canadians were outraged, and the British were relieved to have a solution without shooting.

The rigged settlement of the Alaska boundary dispute did not represent Roosevelt's finest hour. Apostle of the Square Deal, fair play, and good sportsmanship, he sullied the good name of the United States. But he did get results that in the long run were beneficial to the nation. Yet Roosevelt's acquisition of the Panama Canal the next year raised even more serious questions of wrongdoing—on an even larger scale.

For more than fifty years the possibility of constructing a trans-isthmian canal in Central America had been a subject of discussion and debate. The dream moved closer to reality in 1901 when the British, abandoning their restrictive Clayton-Bulwer Treaty of 1850, gave the Americans a free hand to build and control an isthmian canal.

The next question was where to construct the vital waterway. In the 1880s a French company had tried its hand in Panama, but had made only a partial excavation before succumbing to disease, construction problems, poor financing, and other obstacles. The New Panama Canal Company had taken over the remains of the bankrupt old one, and was asking $109 million for its holdings, including the partial excavation and the rusted machinery. When Congress began to show disquieting signs of favoring the Nicaragua route, the New Panama Canal Company, represented by the unscrupulous young French engineer, Philippe Bunau-Varilla, dramatically dropped its price from $109 million to the fire sale figure of $40 million.

This startling financial concession, combined with evidence of volcanic activity in Nicaragua, helped turn the decision toward Panama. In June 1902, Congress authorized the President to secure a right of way from Colombia across Panama. If he could not do so "within a reasonable time and upon reasonable terms" he was to turn to Nicaragua. This qualification does much to explain Roosevelt's sudden eagerness to make the dirt fly. As the incumbent vice-president and as a candidate for election as President in his own right in 1904, he was quick to perceive that visible progress with the proposed canal would be a giant feather in his cap. He simply could not tolerate undue delay. "Damn the law," he reportedly exclaimed. "I want the canal built."

Great pressure was now put on the Colombian Chargé in Washington to approve a treaty granting the United States the necessary canal rights in Panama. He signed reluctantly and with serious misgivings on January 22, 1903, but three days later came a telegram from Bogotá instructing him to take no action but to await new instructions.

This critical pact with Colombia, approved by the Senate of the United States, chimed in nicely with Roosevelt's plans. It granted a canal zone six miles wide for only $10 million, plus an annuity of $250,000. Yet the Colombian Senate in Bogotá unanimously rejected the pact, regarding the money as quite inadequate for the surrender of the nation's most valuable natural resource. Yet the Bogotá regime indicated some willingness to settle for an additional $15 million.

The Washington government was willing to pay—and finally did pay—the French creditors $40 million for their abandoned holdings in Panama. These rights were due to expire in 1904, somewhat more than a year later, at which time the Colombians could take over and claim the $40 million for themselves. Delay was obviously to their financial advantage, but not to that of Roosevelt, who was frantically eager to begin the digging and further endear himself to the electorate in the upcoming presidential election of 1904. He ignored the well-known fact that the Senate of the United States had repeatedly delayed or rejected treaties, and he excoriated, chiefly in private, the "inefficient bandits" and "highwaymen" serving as the "black-mailers of Bogotá."

Fortunately for President Roosevelt's objectives, the subordinate political entity known as Panama was ripe for revolt. Over the years, the Panamanians had launched numerous unsuccessful uprisings against the regime in Bogotá, and the rejection of the treaty with the United States raised fears in Panama that the dream of canal-spawned prosperity was not to be realized. The chief agent of the New Panama Canal Company, the wily French chief engineer, Philippe Bunau-Varilla, had a large hand in engineering the revolt.

The success or failure of the revolution depended on the clandestine cooperation of President Roosevelt. The yellowing treaty of 1846, negotiated with Washington when Colombia was known as New Grenada, entitled the United States to intervene in Panama to protect "free transit" across the isthmus by land. On seven different occasions prior to 1903 the United States had landed troops to protect free transit during disturbances, and in every instance, except one, such forces had been employed with the prior approval or consent of the Colombian government. Only once had American armed men interfered with the movement of suppressive Colombian troops, and for this intrusion the Washington government had later expressed regret. Obviously the treaty of 1846 had envisaged American intervention only to prevent foreigners or revolutionists from gaining control, and until 1903 the pact had been so interpreted by both sides.

With the ill-concealed encouragement of Roosevelt, the handful of Panamanian revolutionists went ahead with their plans for a coup. American naval forces, acting under orders from Washington, openly prevented Colombian troops from landing and thus crushing the revolt. The United States thus protected traditional free transit by improperly denying it to the Colombian authorities.

This sequence of events throws a lurid light on the United

States and Roosevelt. On November 2, 1903, the American naval force arrived in Panamanian waters. Thus encouraged, the Panamanians rose in revolt the next day, November 3. On November 4 the newborn republic proclaimed itself a sovereign nation. About an hour after being informed of this welcome event, Roosevelt authorized formal recognition, and it was granted on November 6, 1903. Such unseemly haste gave further support to the widespread belief that Roosevelt had connived at and encouraged the Panamanian uprising.

The slippery Bunau-Varilla, though a French citizen, managed to have himself made the first minister from Panama to Washington. On November 18, 1903, twelve days after the formal recognition, he concluded a treaty or convention with the United States for the canal zone which, like the earlier one, provided for $10 million down and $250,000 a year. But the canal zone was widened from six miles to ten. The $40 million that Bunau-Varilla demanded was paid to the French government, with $25 million earmarked for the original company of De Lesseps and $15 million for the New Panama Canal Company. Widespread allegations that Roosevelt or persons connected with him shared in this huge payment remained unproved, and in the case of Roosevelt seem highly improbable.

Roosevelt would never concede that he had wronged Colombia by his tortured interpretation of the ancient treaty of 1846 or that by his "indecent haste" he had brought "scandal, disgrace, and dishonor" to himself and his country. The fiery President claimed that he had a so-called mandate from civilization to get the canal started. To his dying day he resisted any suggestion of an apology to Colombia, but in 1921, after his death and thanks largely to the discovery of oil there, the United States finally voted Colombia "canalimony" in the sum of $25 million. But that amount is an apology in any language. The irony is that the payments of $15 million in 1903 might well have resulted in the approval of the original treaty by Bogotá, with the elimination of all the uproar caused by big-stick tactics. Roosevelt may or may not have said in his Berkeley speech of 1911, "I took the Canal Zone . . ." But that is essentially what he did.

Angered by the accusations of graft and other wrongdoing, Roosevelt sent a special message to Congress on January 8, 1906, in which he flatly denied all allegations of corruption in connection with the projected canal. On December 15, 1908, he submitted another special message, accompanied by what he insisted was documentary proof of his innocence. He later pressed proceedings for criminal libel against his chief accusers, the *New York World* and the *Indianapolis News,* thereby raising the issue of freedom of the press. In both cases the federal courts rejected Roosevelt's claims by concluding that the evidence had proved neither malice nor libel. Widespread suspicions of scandal continued to fester, but not enough evidence could be mustered to prove them. To this day we do not know precisely the fate of all the $40 million paid to the French for their bankrupt rights.

Thanks in part to his spectacular intervention in Panama, Roosevelt was easily renominated for President in his own right. But he was disturbed by the comparative lethargy of the Chicago nominating convention, and decided to bring it to life by a cheap electioneering trick unworthy of a democratic leader who preened himself on his high ethical standards.

In May 1904 Greek-born Ion Perdicaris, allegedly a naturalized American citizen, had been seized in Morocco by a native chieftain named Raisuli. American warships were speedily rushed to Tangier, and provision was made for the release of the captive. Yet Roosevelt arranged to have his Secretary of State fire off a cablegram to the American consul in Tangier demanding "Perdicaris alive or Raisuli dead." When read to the Chicago convention, it electrified the delegates, just as Roosevelt had planned.

This heroic message was not necessary for Roosevelt's renomination or for Perdicaris's release, which already had been secured. Born a Greek subject, there was doubt as to whether or not the victim was yet a naturalized American citizen. When the evidence was brought to Roosevelt, he waved it aside. A confession that he had jumped the gun would be further evidence of his notorious impetuosity.

In November 1904 Roosevelt was overwhelmingly elected President, vanquishing a colorless Democratic rival. Exhilarated by the joy of victory, the Rough Rider issued a ringing statement to the effect that his three and a half years as accidental president constituted "my first term," and that "under no circumstances will I be a candidate for or accept another nomination." Four years later, a shyster-like Roosevelt declared that this unequivocal statement really applied only to consecutive terms. He enthusiastically accepted the nomination of the Progressive party in 1912, split his own Republican Party, and ensured the election of the Democratic Woodrow Wilson, whom he hated. Four years later this Rough Rider of high principle again accepted the nomination of the Progressives, then left them hopelessly in the lurch when he forsook them to rejoin the Republicans.

A President who could dishonor his pledge not to run for a third term would surely have few qualms about reinterpreting the immortal Monroe Doctrine to his own liking. This Roosevelt did in 1904 and formalized his action by an agreement with Santo Domingo in 1905.

Revolution-rent Santo Domingo proved to be the focus of the new Roosevelt doctrine in the Caribbean, where defaulted debts owed to European creditors posed explosive problems. The President feared that the Germans or other Europeans might come as bill collectors. If they arrived in force, they might stay, thus presenting a frontal challenge to the Monroe Doctrine that could involve the United States in war.

So it was that Roosevelt adopted the intrusive policy of "preventive intervention," popularly called the Roosevelt corollary of the Monroe Doctrine. Under it the United States would do the intervening, take over the graft-ridden custom houses in the Caribbean, pay off the foreign debts, and keep the worried European creditors on the other side of the Atlantic. Roosevelt believed that the United States itself had a moral obligation to become an international bill collector, since he would not permit Europeans themselves to act in that capacity.

Employing such self-serving logic, Roosevelt began operations in the Caribbean with his big stick in 1905, and finally formalized his intervention by a treaty with Santo Domingo in 1907. The local grafters in the custom houses found such meddling highly distasteful. There were other big stick interventions in the Caribbean as well, and the great powers of Europe did refrain from armed intervention. Roosevelt's misapplication of the Monroe Doctrine did not proclaim, as Monroe had said in effect, "You keep out," but rather, "We'll go in so that you will stay out."

Roosevelt's perversion of the Monroe Doctrine actually worked, despite the pained outcries of embezzlers in the banana republics. But the big-stick approach contributed immensely to the bad relations that continued until the Good Neighbor Policy of President Franklin Roosevelt. What one Roosevelt took away a later Roosevelt restored after he reached the White House in 1933.

During his White House years Roosevelt gained exaggerated fame as a "trustbuster." He did succeed in curbing or breaking up a few of the most offensive trusts, but his critics claimed that he used a padded stick and that his real achievements were much overpraised. But it is undeniable that he launched, with a fair degree of success, a number of prosecutions during his incumbency.

In his campaign for reelection in 1904, Roosevelt managed to amass a huge campaign fund, much of it from the most powerful trusts. Rumors began to circulate that representatives of the larger corporations or trusts had contributed "protection money" after receiving assurances that their generosity would be properly rewarded. Roosevelt noisily branded such reports false and labeled their authors liars. The testimony of witnesses is so conflicting that the charges of extortion, promises of favored treatment, and other improper conduct have not been convincingly proved against Roosevelt.

Where there is smoke there must be some fire, and it is difficult to imagine hard-bitten executives of big business pouring out hundreds of thousands of dollars to elect a hostile Roosevelt unless they had received assurances, or thought they had, of tender treatment. After the election, industrialist Henry C. Frick was quoted as having lamented, "We bought the son of a bitch and then he did not stay bought."

One aftermath of this unsavory scandal is crystal clear. As a result of Roosevelt's repeated urgings, Congress finally took belated action. In January 1907 it enacted legislation that prohibited monetary contributions by national banks and corporations in elections involving federal officials. But corporate officers acting as individuals were placed under no such restriction.

In 1907 a painful "rich man's panic" hit the United States, centering chiefly in Wall Street. Hoping to ride out the crisis, Roosevelt permitted the potent United States Steel Corporation to acquire the wobbly Tennessee Coal and Iron Company, with the clear understanding that the federal government would not invoke the antitrust legislation. The President's primary motive appears to have been a desire to forestall the misery to the public that would result from a prolonged panic. His enemies, of whom he now had many, accused him of violating the antitrust laws by an under-the-table deal with a giant corporation. The accusation was at length appealed to the Supreme Court, which ruled on

March 1, 1920—more than a year after the Rough Rider's death —that Roosevelt had been guilty of no wrongdoing.

Roosevelt's twilight months in office were marred by an unseemly altercation between him and the members of Congress. They angrily charged that the President was using the Secret Service as an "army of federal spies," instead of for such legitimate duties as protection of the Chief Executive and the arrest of counterfeiters. In 1909 a resentful Congress passed legislation limiting the Secret Service exclusively to investigations involving the Treasury Department. Roosevelt circumvented this slap by creating within the Department of Justice a new detective agency that eventually evolved into the Federal Bureau of Investigation, better known as the FBI.

The Rough Rider's enemies in Congress charged that Roosevelt, the busybody, was flouting the separation of powers written into the Constitution. But Congress has routinely embraced a few crooks, who, when exposed, are generally handled with kid gloves by their colleagues and reelected by their constituents. The voters evidently approve of crooks if they can do enough for their district. Even so, there was a strong suspicion that Roosevelt went out of his way to incriminate Congressmen who were conspicuously unfriendly to "my policies."

A listing of Roosevelt's faults without a glance at the credit side of the ledger is unfair to an immensely popular leader. Most of what he did was, at least in his own judgment, in the national interest, including his election in his own right in 1904. He did take giant steps in the conservation of land and other national resources; he did tackle the trust evil with a commendable degree of success; he did stand for fair play and a square deal for the Japanese immigrants in their difficulties with Japan; he did win the Nobel Peace Prize in 1906 for having mediated an end to the sanguinary Russo-Japanese War; and his administration did arrange to return to China an undeserved part, some $18 million, of the Boxer indemnity fund. Roosevelt was an impatient, impetuous, direct actionist, at heart a lover of war, but far more restrained in word and deed than his enemies feared he would be when the assassin's bullet felled President McKinley.

CHAPTER 26

William Howard Taft 1909–1913

The principles of the fathers are maintained by those who maintain them with reason, and according to the fitness of the thing, and not by those who are constantly shaking them before the mass of voters when they have no application.

William H. Taft, address,
May 8, 1909

President Taft was a transparently honest man, and what appear to have been his few slips from grace were either relatively minor or in some other way excusable. Trained as a lawyer and experienced as a judge, he possessed a judicial temperament, and his greatest aspiration was to become a member of the Supreme Court—a dream that was finally realized. His wife and other members of his family were evidently more ambitious for him to become President than he was himself.

One of Taft's biggest problems was that Roosevelt's brandishing of the big stick against strikers, trusts, and nations was a hard act to follow. Unlike the Rough Rider, "good old Bill Taft" did not have a "bully time" herding emperors and kings, and after all the Rooseveltian fireworks the country felt let down under the new President. Unlike Roosevelt, Taft believed in a government of laws, not men. He knew that the law was often dismayingly slow, but he would have cringed if he had heard Roosevelt cry out, "Damn the law! I want the canal built!" Taft did not possess his predecessor's skill in magnifying his achievements and minifying his errors. He simply could not stoop to cheap electioneering tricks, such as Roosevelt's "Perdicaris alive or Raisuli dead."

One of Taft's greatest handicaps lay in his ability to swim with the rising tide of progressivism. He was no doubt mildly progressive, but the liberal elements were now moving so fast to the left that he seemed to be floundering. Something seemed bound to explode, and the outburst came in 1912 when ex-President Roosevelt took over leadership of the renegade "Bull Moose" Progressive party.

The protective tariff had long been a football of politics, and the last general tariff law had been the Dingley Act of 1897. It established the highest rates thus far in American experience. The heated antitrust movement that followed made clear that many of the giant trusts were no longer infant industries that needed protection. Rather, the consuming public needed protection against the trusts.

"Teddy" Roosevelt, the born fighter, had been much too clever a politician to get embroiled in a free-for-all over the protective tariff. But the Republican platform on which Taft ran in 1908 came out "unequivocally" for a tariff revision but equivocally declined to state whether the revision should be higher or lower. Honest old "Bill Taft," the political novice, forthrightly announced that this evasive pledge was in support of a downward revision. More than that, he further tempted fate by summoning Congress into a special session in the first month of his administration. After extensive debate, the House passed the Payne Bill (later the Payne-Aldrich Bill) which provided for modest reductions in the existing protective tariff.

The Senate, known as "the millionaires club," then got into the act. Dominated by politicians friendly to the trusts, the responsive Senators engineered 847 changes in the Payne Bill, most of which were upward. Although the downward revisions were numerically significant, many of them related to items that were insignificant, including canary birdseed. But the foes of the trusts did manage to force into the Payne-Aldrich Bill the modest beginnings of a tax on corporation profits.

What was "Honest Bill" Taft to do, after having promised a genuine tariff revision? A rugged Grover Cleveland probably would have vetoed the Payne-Aldrich monstrosity, thus disrupting the party. But Taft set greater store by loyalty to those people who had elevated him to his exalted office. After all, the controversial bill contained some significant reductions, more in fact than the party platform had really promised. Besides, the new measure contained a few redeeming features, including the trifling one percent tax on corporation profits and the provision for a fact-finding Tariff Commission.

A blundering Taft, afflicted in some degree by foot-in-mouth disease, unwisely went out onto the stump to defend the new legislation. He conceded that the Payne-Aldrich patchwork was not perfect but at Winona, Minnesota, he defended the new law as "the best [tariff] bill that the Republican party ever passed." This statement was near the truth, for the Republicans had passed some controversial tariff legislation in the past. But the headlines had Taft acclaiming the Payne-Aldrich Act as "the best tariff in history," which was not true, and he was never able to squelch this perversion. One proverb tells us that honesty is the best policy but another maintains that at times silence is golden.

Following elsewhere in Theodore Roosevelt's giant footsteps, Taft achieved commendable progress in the conservation of public lands, mineral resources, and water-power sites. But these praiseworthy achievements were largely blotted out in the public mind by a scandalous bureaucratic row in which President Taft became involved.

The storm center of the uproar was Secretary of the Interior Ballinger, a lawyer with expertise in land law. President Roosevelt, often contemptuous of legalities, had overstretched existing statutes in his zeal for conservation. Ballinger, a stickler for a rigid interpretation of the law, felt obligated to reverse some of Roosevelt's hasty and questionable actions. In so doing the legalistic Secretary threw open to private exploitation certain water-power sites in Wyoming and Montana that Roosevelt had reserved. Valuable coal lands in Alaska were also made available to big business, in conformity with the law as Ballinger interpreted it.

The rescuing of public lands from the clutches of corporate exploiters had been one of the most popular features of Roosevelt's recent administration. Quick to take up arms against Secretary Ballinger was the flaming conservationist, Gifford Pinchot,

Chief of the Division of Forestry of the Department of Agriculture, and also a former member of Roosevelt's "Tennis Cabinet."

As a former Secretary of War under Roosevelt, Taft was a stickler for administrative efficiency, and he would not tolerate fighting within his official family. Feeling compelled to uphold Ballinger, the President dismissed Pinchot for insubordination. A Congressional investigation subsequently cleared Ballinger, amid loud cries of "whitewash" from the conservationist admirers of Theodore Roosevelt. A minority report from the same committee, dictated partly by Republican insurgents, fired an angry blast at Secretary Ballinger.

Taft, not one to dismiss a subordinate unfairly under fire, loyally retained Ballinger for about a year and a half. The embattled Secretary finally resigned in March 1911, after his usefulness was compromised, and he returned to practice law in Seattle. Evidence turned up later indicates that Ballinger had a stronger legal position regarding conservation than many of his critics would concede. Yet the whole disagreeable episode served to widen the growing rift between Taft and Roosevelt.

After examining the Ballinger controversy more closely, a critic may fairly conclude that Taft was more a loyal chief than a clever politician. A man of lesser fiber might well have thrown his subordinate to the conservationist wolves. He did fudge a bit when he ordered a key memorandum to be predated in such a way as to indicate that he had found the time to read and digest all of it. But this sin was a minor one.

Taft embraced President Roosevelt's interventionist corollary to the Monroe Doctrine, and in the new administration American troops were landed in Honduras and notably Nicaragua. Some 2,500 Marines went ashore there in August 1912, following the establishment of control of the customs by the United States during the previous year.

Roosevelt's foreign policy had featured a combination of the Big Stick and the interventionist Roosevelt corollary to the Monroe Doctrine. On the other hand, Taft was a practitioner of "dollar diplomacy," a concept that had two phases. One was for the national government to promote American commercial and monetary interests abroad by encouraging peaceful foreign investment, and then to protect such ventures with American armed forces, if necessary and possible. The other phase was to defend American strategic areas abroad by encouraging American bankers to pump their dollars into places, such as those near Panama, in which the United States had a heavy stake. In short, as Taft told Congress in 1912, this was a policy of "substituting dollars for bullets"—or the big dollar for the big stick.

Liberal voices in the United States protested vehemently against the entanglements of Dollar Diplomacy, but there was nothing clearly dishonest about it. To promote prosperity abroad, especially in strategic areas, was something that all the other imperialistic powers were doing, as evidenced by "pound sterling diplomacy," "franc diplomacy," "mark diplomacy," and other such policies. In response, American anti-imperialists argued that something was wrong when Wall Street bankers invested in places like Nicaragua, where the high interest rate reflected danger. Then the U.S. Marines, supported by all the taxpayers, were sent in to remove the risks.

In 1912 Congress passed an act providing for the operation of the Panama Canal, which was due to be opened for business in 1914. The most controversial feature of the new measure was an exemption from paying tolls that was granted to American coastwise shipping, including that from San Francisco to New York. This stipulation seemed to be in direct violation of the Hay-Pauncefote Treaty with Great Britain in 1901. The pact in question stated in plain English that "all nations" observing the rules would be required to pay the same rates. Taft and fellow legalists construed this clause to read, as did American public opinion, that "all nations other than the United States" would have to pay. But this was not what the treaty stated.

The American view, shared by Taft, held that the United States, at an enormous cost in money and considerable loss of life, had itself constructed the canal. The nation was therefore entitled to special benefits for its coastwise shipping, in which foreigners could not legally participate anyhow. What Taft and other Americans would not concede was that the total costs of operating the canal would result in higher tolls for foreign shipping if American coastwise shippers were the beneficiaries of a free ride.

"Big Bill" Taft was an honest man and certainly not a stupid one, for in 1921 he was made Chief Justice of the United States. The relevant clause in the Anglo-American treaty of 1901—relating to "all nations," not all other nations—was not even ambiguous. Yet, Taft's reading made it ambiguous. Possibly the explanation is that in August 1912, when he signed the canal legislation, he was in the thick of a desperate three-cornered race for reelection. Tolls exemption for American shipping was highly popular, especially with the anti-British vote of the Irish-Americans. President Wilson, Taft's successor, finally engineered a repeal of the Panama Canal tolls exemption, but he waited until one year after his inauguration before making his plea to Congress. By then the political atmosphere was more favorable to repeal.

The closing months of Taft's administration were marred by a bitter public quarrel between ex-President Roosevelt and his creation, President Taft. No doubt Taft had turned out to be less progressive than the Rough Rider had expected, and Roosevelt was soured by highly colored reports to the effect that Taft had sold out to the trusts and other big-money interests. In February 1912 Roosevelt formally tossed overboard his pledge of no third term and threw his hat into the ring in the expectation of wresting the Republican nomination from President Taft.

Roosevelt did well in the Republican presidential primaries, but in the Chicago convention of 1912 the Taft forces controlled the driver's seat of the political steamroller—ironically the steamroller that Roosevelt had used four years earlier to ram through the nomination for Taft, then the fair-haired boy. A critic can hardly blame Taft for permitting his lieutenants to play politics at this convention in the conventional way.

An angered and disappointed Roosevelt, long a sportsman but now a poor sport, accepted with enthusiasm his nomination for a third term at the hands of the seceding Progressives of the regular Republican party. The ensuing political struggle degenerated into an unseemly brawl. Taft bluntly branded his former friend a "dangerous egoist" and a "demagogue." Roosevelt assailed Taft as a "fathead" with the brain of a "guinea pig." Taft was nearer right than Roosevelt, but in neither case were the two combatants dishonestly concealing their real feelings.

As Roosevelt must have known, his candidacy would split the Republican vote, and thus probably ensure the election of the Democratic candidate, Woodrow Wilson. This is precisely what happened, and consequently cast an undeserved shadow on the basic honesty and effectiveness of the Taft administration.

CHAPTER 27

Woodrow Wilson
1913–1921

America will come into the full light of day when all shall know that she puts human rights above all other rights and that her flag is the flag not only of America but of humanity.

> Woodrow Wilson,
> address in Philadelphia,
> July 4, 1914

Any appraisal of Woodrow Wilson's integrity must take into account the high standards he set for himself and how well he adhered to them. First of all he was a religionist, the son of a Presbyterian minister, and himself a lay preacher of great power and persuasiveness. In the bosom of Wilson's family, with wife and daughters present, Bible reading and prayer were routine.

Born in Virginia five years before the Civil War erupted, young Tommy Wilson was reared in war-ravaged Georgia, South Carolina, and North Carolina. He evidently absorbed the sensitive concern for honor so prevalent in the South, the last stronghold in the United States of the man-to-man duel. As a hater of war and all it entailed, he could be categorized as a pacifist, but not a doctrinaire one. All this may explain why his initial reaction to the sinking of the British *Lusitania,* with 128 Americans lost, was that the United States was "too proud to fight." Yet fate finally forced him into the bloodiest general conflict thus far in the nation's history, whereupon he became an inspiring war leader but a less than ideal peacemaker.

After failing at law, the youthful Wilson entered the academic world, wrote several impressive books as a political scientist, taught large college classes with rare eloquence, and ultimately became the distinguished president of Princeton University. Zealous for reforming both the academic and social structure of the university, he enjoyed initial success, but finally ran into a man as stubborn as he was, Dean Andrew West. The two men became involved in a bitter quarrel over the precise placement of the building designed to house the new graduate college.

During the heated controversy over the graduate college, Wilson seems to have lied. When testifying regarding a booklet earlier published by Dean West, Wilson stated that he had never read it, although he had himself written a laudatory preface for it. Even if he had perused only a small part of the manuscript, he had been guilty of deception. On the eve of his first inauguration as President of the United States, Wilson told Colonel House privately that a man in his exalted position would be justified in lying only if the honor of a woman or an issue of public policy was involved.

Princeton finally became so uncomfortable for Wilson that he began to cast his gaze outward for greener pastures. Luckily for him, the Democratic bosses of New Jersey were looking for a winning candidate with a liberal outlook. The party leaders evidently thought they had an understanding with Wilson that he would not wreck their well-oiled party machine with ultraliberal policies. Wilson either understood otherwise or, bit in teeth, just proceeded to do as he pleased. With great zeal he drove through the first session of the state legislature a reformist program designed to combat the monopolistic and predatory practices of the powerful trusts and other moneyed interests. Seeking greater honesty in business, politics, and government, he also secured a primary election law, a strengthened public utilities act, a corrupt practices act, and an employer's liability act.

The state of New Jersey, once known as "The Mother of Trusts" (including Standard Oil), was thus transformed into a showpiece in the nationwide agitation for reform, with Governor Woodrow Wilson a knight in shining armor brandishing the sword of righteousness. His enemies charged that he was a college professor "gone Bolshevik," so strong were his strictures against the capitalists and manufacturers of the United States. On the other hand, Wilson described himself as "a Progressive with the brakes on."

The political atmosphere in 1912 demanded a presidential candidate dedicated to reforming the hidebound capitalistic system, and the Democrats turned to Woodrow Wilson as their presidential nominee in 1912. Luck was with him, for the Republicans broke into two snarling factions, with Taft leading the Republicans and Roosevelt spearheading the secessionist Progressives, as his Bull Moose party was called. Thanks to this split, Woodrow Wilson won handily, although netting only 41 percent of the popular vote.

Early in his administration, President Wilson seized the reins of leadership when he appeared before Congress in person (the first since John Adams to do so) to plead for what he regarded as desperately needed reforms. The fruits of his eloquent leadership of Congress were a significant lowering of the tariff in 1913 that had been fattening American capitalists, the enactment of urgently needed banking reform (the Federal Reserve Act of December 1913), and the passing of laws in 1914 designed to protect the ordinary citizen. These last-named measures took the form of the Federal Trade Commission and the Clayton Antitrust Act.

An idealistic Wilson was bitterly opposed to Taft's "dollar diplomacy," which seemed to him to use the contributions of ordinary taxpayers to swell the coffers of opulent Wall Street bankers. In the interests of simple honesty and non-involvement abroad, Wilson struck a heavy blow at his predecessor's policy in China during the early days of his administration. A group of Wall Street bankers had been preparing to invest in a six-power loan of $125 million, but Wilson bluntly informed them that they could expect no support whatever from the Washington government. Wilson feared that this financial scheme to benefit the bankers would compromise the sovereignty of China and possibly entangle the United States.

Inconsistency is normally not a major sin, yet it is not often regarded as a virtue. The outgoing Taft administration, in pursuance of its foreign policy, had negotiated a treaty with Nicaragua which secured naval-base rights and an option in perpetuity on a second trans-isthmian canal route. For such privileges the United States would pay $3 million, thus enabling the Nicaraguan government to reimburse American bankers.

Wilson detested Taft's "dollar diplomacy" but he recognized the value of an alternate canal route. Accordingly, he threw his weight behind the proposed treaty, which the Senate approved in 1916, including Republican members. In this way they applauded Wilson's belated and partial conversion to Taft's dollar imperialism.

Other disturbing events in the Caribbean forced the pacifistic Wilson to embrace not only Taft's distasteful "dollar diplomacy" but also Roosevelt's corollary to or perversion of the Monroe Doctrine. American armed forces would again be used to restore order and thus prevent Germany or some other unfriendly European power from intruding and causing trouble.

First Haiti became an ugly trouble spot. In 1915 a murderous dictator was literally torn to pieces by a frenzied mob. To protect American lives and also the property of Wall Street investors, Wilson dispatched troops to restore order and to force Haiti to become a protectorate of the United States. In the course of "pacifying" this country an estimated 2,000 Haitians were killed. Armed occupation by the United States continued for 19 years, until 1934, while some fiscal control continued until 1947.

Haiti's eastern neighbor, the Dominican Republic, shared a somewhat similar but less bloody fate. In 1914 the "insurrectionary habit" brought a U.S. warship, and in 1916 the Marines, who found it necessary to shoot a few of the inhabitants. These troops were withdrawn in 1924, after an eight-year stay, but the customs receivership lasted until 1941. Such were the fruits of protecting the Panama Canal, excluding foreign intervention, and safeguarding American investments.

Oddly enough, Wilson also emerged as something of a minor league imperialist. After the World War broke out in 1914, the danger loomed that Germany would invade Denmark and then scoop up the Danish West Indies. These once defenseless islands could be used as a naval base, thus jeopardizing the approaches to the Panama Canal. In 1916 the United States under Wilson purchased the whole lot of otherwise inconsequential islets for a whopping $25 million.

In two other areas of conflicting national interests, Wilson acted more like the honest idealist that he professed to be. One was California, where in 1913 the white people of the Golden State were antagonizing Japan by taking steps to prohibit Japanese immigrants from owning land. Gigantic protest meetings in Japan indicated that a war could conceivably break out over this provocative issue. Hoping to avert such a calamity, Wilson dispatched Secretary of State Bryan to California in an effort to persuade the citizens of this famed state to listen to reason.

The legislature in Sacramento, brushing aside the great orator's eloquent pleas, proceeded to bar Japanese from owning land. But the legislation was so ingeniously worded as not to mention Japan, convey a direct affront, or violate the strict letter of existing treaty obligations. Wilson's conciliatory attitude and attempted fairness helped to mollify the Japanese, whose prospective attack on the Philippines was postponed for 28 years.

The engineering marvel known as the Panama Canal, scheduled to be opened for traffic in August 1914, gave President Wilson an opportunity to appear at his high-principled best. We recall that President Taft, the legalist, had questionably read the relevant treaty with Great Britain to mean that American coastwise commerce could be exempted from paying tolls. As a result, there would have to be higher tolls for all other traffic, including that of a protesting Great Britain. This problem lay uneasily on the White House doorstep when the new President assumed power.

Wilson found himself in a most embarrassing bind politically. Congress had already passed and Taft had signed a bill exempting American coastwise traffic from paying tolls. Wilson had been elected on a platform that enthusiastically supported exclusionary legislation, and this Panama plank was highly popular among anti-British Irish-Americans, a mainstay of Wilson's Democratic party.

After churning the problem over in his mind, the President, to his credit, adopted a policy of "politics be damned," and courageously opted for the honorable course. As he personally proclaimed to a divided Congress, the United States was "too big, too powerful, too self-respecting a nation to interpret with too strained or refined a reading the words of our own promises just because we have power enough to give us leave to read them as we please."

Repeal of the canal tolls exemption, after a bitter fight, received the stamp of Congressional approval in June 1914, just a few weeks before the opening of the Panama Canal and the outbreak of World War I in Europe. This strain on British-American relations was thus removed, thereby making easier America's involvement in the great conflict on the side of Great Britain. To Wilson's everlasting credit, he had the courage to place national honor above political expediency.

If Wilson's armed interventions in Haiti and the Dominican Republic were relatively minor extensions of Taft's maligned dollar diplomacy, the new President's formidable military intrusions into Mexico were different. Oddly enough, they came about largely as the result of Wilson's idealistic concern for the Mexican masses and the success of their democratic revolution. American bankers and other investors, having ventured their capital in Mexican oil and other resources, clamored for wholesale intervention in that revolution-torn country. Prominent among the agitators was the newspaper tycoon, William R. Hearst, who had acquired land holdings in Mexico approximately the size of the state of Rhode Island.

As for Mexico, the background may be briefly sketched. Since 1877, when Porfirio Diaz began his three-decade dictatorship ("Diazpotism"), relations with the United States had been generally calm. By 1913 there were more than 50,000 American citizens living in Mexico, and their investments totaled about one billion dollars. But in 1911 the desperately poor Mexican masses arose and drove dictator Diaz into exile. The plot thickened when the liberal leader, Francisco Madero, was murdered in cold blood, evidently in response to orders from the ambitious Victoriano Huerta.

An idealistic Wilson righteously refused to recognize the bloody-handed regime of Huerta, even though the usurper had managed to establish himself precariously in power. Prior to this time the policy of the United States had been to extend the right hand of recognition to any regime that was obviously in control, regardless of how it had managed to get there. Yet Wilson stated in an interview, "My ideal is an orderly and righteous government in Mexico; but my passion is for the submerged eighty-five percent of the people of that republic who are now struggling toward liberty." Rejecting "government by murder," ex-Professor Wilson told a visiting Briton, "I am going to teach the South American republics to elect good men."

If Wilson had really wished to avoid trouble, he would have closed his eyes to conditions south of the border. A critical Republican journalist cried out, "What legal or moral right has a President of the United States to say who shall or shall not be President of Mexico?" But Wilson, troubled by his Christian conscience, could not get the downtrodden Mexican masses out of his mind. He also suspected that foreign oil interests, British and American, were backing the "unspeakable Heurta."

Stubbornly denying recognition to the new regime in Mexico, Wilson pursued what he called a policy of "watchful waiting," which his opponents, mostly Republicans, branded "deadly drifting." From 1913 to 1915, 70 Americans were slain in Mexico, as patriotic Americans clamored for armed intervention. Fight-thirsty Theodore Roosevelt, on fire for action, snarled at Wilson, "He kissed the blood-stained hand that slapped his face."

The pacifistic President Wilson, that hater of war, was ultimately trapped in a no-win dilemma in Tampico, Mexico, in April 1914. A small boat of the United States Navy, with colors plainly in view, was engaged in securing supplies for the offshore patrol. Two members of the crew were arrested by Mexican authorities for having violated martial law, but were speedily released with apologies for the misunderstanding. But Admiral Mayo, commanding the American fleet in these waters, evidently wanted to make Mexico crawl. On his own responsibility, he demanded a more formal disavowal and apology, punishment of the offending officer, and a 21-gun salute of the American flag by Huerta.

These humiliating terms magnified the Mexican offense out of all proportion, and Huerta understandably balked at saluting the flag of a nation that refused to recognize him. Strange to relate, the pacifistic Secretary Bryan and the no less pacifistic Wilson backed Admiral Mayo on the grounds that the dignity and honor of the United States demanded the further abasement of the Huerta regime. Wilson had shown his political courage in the Panama Canal tolls dispute, and there is reason to believe that if he had accepted Mexico's earlier apologies as adequate, the storm would have blown over without undue harm. Probably Wilson's loathing of "the unspeakable" Huerta colored his judgment.

Accordingly, Wilson went before Congress on April 20, 1914, to ask for authority to intervene in Mexico by force of arms, and that body responded affirmatively after two days of debate. American marines and sailors stormed ashore, after a heavy bombardment of key centers of the city. Of the attackers, 19 men were killed and 71 wounded; of the defenders about 126 were killed and 195 wounded, of all ages and both sexes. The hated conquerors held the city for about six months.

Wilson was profoundly moved by the 19 American dead. Speaking at their funeral rites. he declared that he had been striving to "serve the Mexicans" by freeing them from the iron grip of Huerta, and that it was "a proud thing to die" in a "war of service." The 300 or so Mexican casualties were less appreciative of this "war of service"; their foremost thought had been to repel the hated Yankee invader from their soil.

Wilson now found himself writhing on the horns of a dilemma. He could not face the humiliation of withdrawal without some abasement of Huerta; yet he could not, as a lover of peace, risk a full-fledged war that would be costly, bloody, and uncertain in its outcome. Fortunately for him, the three leading powers of South America stepped forward with an offer of mediation, which Wilson gratefully accepted. The conferees met at the Niagara Falls on the Canadian side, but the plan agreed upon proved ineffectual because Carranza, the foremost rival of Huerta, spurned it. Yet Wilson won his main objective when the "unspeakable Huerta," yielding to mounting pressure, fled to Europe.

Worse was yet to come. The newly installed Carranza was unable to control the bloody excesses of a colorful rival, Pancho Villa. This "bandit" not only massacred 18 American citizens in cold blood at Santa Ysabel, Mexico, but also invaded New Mexico early in March 1916, sacking the town of Columbus and leaving behind 17 slain Americans. President Wilson, the peace-lover, painfully concluded that he had no alternative but to send General Pershing, with about 10,000 authorized troops, spearheaded by cavalry, in pursuit of the invader. The remarkable chase after Villa by the "perishing" expedition proved fruitless, except perhaps to demonstrate America's will to avenge and its unreadiness for military operations. As Carranzista troops began to shoot it out with the hated invader, and as war with Germany became increasingly imminent, Wilson withdrew the American invaders. The upshot was that, willy-nilly, he permitted the Mexicans to have their own revolution in their own sanguinary way. He evidently had learned that nothing much was to be gained by "shooting men into self-government."

In August 1914, about a year and a half after Wilson's inauguration, Europe burst into the flames of World War I, as the German invasion of Belgium and France captured the headlines. The waging of the war and the making of the peace cast a lengthening shadow over the two administrations of Woodrow Wilson.

At the outset Wilson, the pacifist, issued the usual proclamations of neutrality. He went even further when he called upon his fellow citizens, most of them descendants of Europe immigrants, to be "impartial in thought as well as in action." This course obviously could not be followed. Unneutral actions could be restrained with comparative ease, but hardly unneutral thoughts. Wilson himself was unneutrally pro-British, as might be inferred from his ancestral background, his summer travels in England, and his admiration for British government, statesmen, and political philosophers. By one way of reckoning Wilson's unneutral policies led directly to his successful appeal to Congress in 1917 for a declaration of war on Germany.

The course that the war finally took caused Wilson's professions of neutrality to seem two-faced. Germany was well stocked with munitions when she invaded Belgium in 1914, but the British and French Allies needed and procured enormous shipments of needed arms from the United States. By one way of reckoning, there was nothing unneutral about these huge sales, because American manufacturers would have been delighted to work both sides of the street and sell weapons to the Germans as well. But such traffic could not force its way through the British blockade of Germany. Even so, the German view was that there was something immoral about the making of thousands of German widows and orphans with explosives manufactured in America.

This "one-sided" traffic in munitions had another and more entangling side. As the frightfully wasteful war ground on, the financially pinched British and French governments sought immense loans from Wall Street to finance their overseas purchases. It was one thing morally to sell munitions to kill Germans; it was something else again to advance the money with which to make the sales.

Secretary of State Bryan, more of a peace-lover and war-hater than Wilson, voiced strong opposition. Money was not then regarded as contraband of war, but Bryan sagely observed that "money is the worst of all contrabands because it commands everything else." Yet Wilson overruled Bryan when he quietly informed the interested bankers that Washington would permit private credits and loans.

Circumstances suggest that the President allowed politics and economics to overrule his more humane instincts. At the outbreak of war in Europe, the United States had been wallowing in a severe economic recession. But the immense sales of arms to the Allies had brought feverish prosperity, which presumably would melt away if the munitions traffic ground to a halt for want of funds. Not only would the country probably be plunged back into a depression, but Wilson's chances of re-election in 1916 would doubtless suffer. A good politician can easily reason that what is good for the country is also good for him as a candidate, and Wilson's thinking may have run along these lines.

Much later, in the 1930s, Congress took a backward look at Wilson's policies and then passed a series of neutrality acts. Among the stipulations that reflected on American conduct prior to entering World War I were those that prohibited loans or credits to the belligerents, embargoed direct or indirect shipments of munitions, and forbade Americans to travel on the passenger or merchant ships of belligerents, especially liners like the ill-starred *Lusitania*.

Early in the blazing conflict of 1914–1918, Great Britain established a unique long-range blockade against Germany, including a mining of the North Sea. Largely because of lurking German submarines, the British regarded the conventional close-in blockade of enemy ports as too dangerous. All neutral ships approaching harbors with direct or indirect access to German territory were forced to stop at British ports and be searched for contraband cargo. If transporting innocent freight, these vessels would be shepherded safely through the minefields by British pilots. Ships approaching Great Britain from the Atlantic would be intercepted on the high seas and sent to British ports, where a careful and leisurely search of their cargo would follow. If the neutral steamer was carrying no contraband, it would be sent on its way rejoicing. If not, the vessel or its cargo or both might be confiscated, in some cases with compensation to the owners.

This practice clashed so sharply with international law as to be an outrageous violation of freedom of the seas, by which President Wilson set great store. Yet the British rewrote international law to fit what they called the "unusual" or "peculiar" conditions of a war that had unveiled the lethal German submarines. These fragile marauders had found it hazardous to emerge and give a warning signal.

The Washington government protested hotly to London against the seizures of a number of American ships, and in some cases secured a release or partial monetary redress for the owners. But the amazing fact is the State Department never did protest formally against the unorthodox British blockade. Belatedly, and only after the break in relations with Germany over the submarine on February 3, 1917, did Secretary of State Lansing advise London that the Washington government must "reserve generally all of its rights in the premises." Compare this gentle slap on the wrist with the repeated demands of the United States that Berlin abandon its "unlawful" submarine blockade. As Secretary of State Bryan later wrote, the delicate scales of neutrality were thrown out of balance by the notes which were not written rather than by those that were written.

Why Wilson, with his dedication to both neutrality and freedom of the seas, did not protest promptly and emphatically against the illegal British blockade remains something of a mystery. Perhaps the answer may be found in his pro-British bias, for his action did not square with his deep-felt humanitarianism. The British actually established an inhumane hunger blockade of Germany, and kept it clamped on for more than seven months after the Armistice of 1918.

Probably the deciding factor with Wilson was that the retaliatory German submarine blockade, begun in February 1915, deliberately sent men, women, and children to watery graves. On the other hand, the British blockaders merely confiscated property, which in a number of cases was paid for in whole or in part by the London government. Wilson seems not to have fully realized that tens of thousands of blockaded Germans were to die slow deaths from hunger, malnutrition, and disease—many more than perished as a result of German torpedoings without warning.

Responding to the illegal mining of the North Sea and the consequent British naval blockade, the Germans retaliated in February 1915 with an illegal submarine blockade around the British Isles. Berlin announced in effect that its deadly U-boats would destroy all enemy merchant ships found within the designated zone. The Germans also declared that they would try not to sink neutral vessels, including those of the United States, but conceded that mistakes probably would occur.

At this point the President made perhaps the most tragic mistake of his career. He who had not protested at all at the time the illegal British blockade was proclaimed, promptly announced after a wait of only six days that Germany would be held to "strict accountability" for any attacks on American vessels or citizens. Wilson's holding of Germany to accountability sucked a badly prepared United States into World War I in 1917. By contrast, Sweden, Norway, Denmark, and the Netherlands—all under the shadow of German military might—managed to keep out of the nearby bloodbath, although they suffered severe losses in ships and seamen to the German marauders. These weak neutrals studiously avoided holding the German government responsible because there was little they could do short of inviting a hopeless, all-out war.

After several rather minor incidents involving Americans, the *Lusitania,* a palatial British passenger liner, was torpedoed and sunk without warning on May 7, 1915, near the British Isles. The loss totaled 1,198 persons, many of them women, children, and babes in arms. All told, 128 Americans lost their lives. Secretary of State Bryan had repeatedly urged the President to keep American travelers off munitions-carrying passenger ships, but Wilson stood inflexibly for the right of American citizens, even at the risk of death, to travel on belligerent merchant ships and thus serve as a shield for shipments of explosives.

We now know that the *Lusitania* was in effect a swift blockade-runner transporting a considerable cargo of munitions and counting on her superior speed for her safety. The captain was carrying official orders to ram on sight any enemy submarine, and a stickler for international law could argue that these instructions transformed his liner into an offensively armed warship. What Wilson had flatly refused to accept, Congress actually did decree when its neutrality legislation of the 1930s strictly forbade American passengers to travel on belligerent passenger ships.

Wilson was profoundly shocked by the *Lusitania* tragedy. But he was enough of a realist not to invoke promptly his threat of strict accountability and lead a woefully unprepared nation into a fearsome war. Three days later the *Lusitania* disaster, he addressed a large audience in Philadelphia. Stressing America's great moral mission, he declared, "There is such a thing as a man being too proud to fight. There is such a thing as a nation being so right that it does not need to convince others by force that it is right."

Here was Wilson, the man of Southern honor, refusing to dirty his hands on an outlaw Germany. War would not prove who was right, only who was stronger or luckier. But red-blooded Americans, including ex-President Theodore Roosevelt, unloosed an uproar against Wilson's "too proud to fight" pacifism. The President, whether motivated or not by his hoped-for reelection the next year, fired off a series of "strict accountability" notes to Berlin, the second of which was so resolute as to cause the resignation of Secretary Bryan, a truer pacifist. The dispute was still not completely resolved when the United States declared war on Germany in 1917, although Berlin had finally agreed to pay a suitable indemnity for the lost American lives.

Surprisingly, Wilson talked tough to imperial Germany at a time when American military preparedness had fallen so far behind that he had no Rooseveltian big stick—and the Germans knew it. He also managed to scuttle two Congressional resolutions that would have kept American citizens from sailing into the danger zones on armed merchant vessels of the belligerents. He explained to Congress that if such a ban were imposed, "the whole fine fabric of international law might crumble under our hands piece by piece." This was obviously an exaggeration, for the illegal blockades of both camps of belligerents had already caused international law to crumble.

In August 1916 the Germans sank another British passenger liner, the unwarned *Arabic,* with the loss of two Americans. Responding to pressures from Wilson, Germany reluctantly agreed to destroy no more unarmed and unresisting passenger ships without warning. Berlin honored this pledge for about six months, when a German U-boat, evidently by mistake, torpedoed a French cross-channel passenger ship, the *Sussex,* in March 1916.

Wilson reacted angrily. He informed Germany in ringing phrases that she would have to renounce the inhumane practice of sinking merchantmen without warning or the United States would be forced to break diplomatic relations, a step in these feverish days that would be an almost certain prelude to war. The Germans replied that they would accept these terms, but on one condition. The United States would have to persuade the Allies to respect the letter of international law in conducting their blockade. Wilson rather disingenuously accepted the pledge without accepting the condition. His action in effect handed Germany a blank check. Whenever Berlin chose to reopen attacks on un-warned merchant ships, the United States would have no honor-able choice but to plunge into the war against Germany.

In June 1916 Wilson, the so-called pacifist, achieved renomi-nation by a wildly cheering convention in St. Louis. The winning slogan became, "He Kept Us Out of War." This battle cry had the merit of being true, if one overlooked the undeclared incursions into Haiti, Santo Domingo, and Mexico, while focusing on Ger-many. But Wilson disliked this slogan because it carried an im-plied promise that he would continue to keep the nation out of war with a Germany that had the initiative in its own hands. But if he had publicly renounced the slogan, as no politician in his right mind would have done, he almost certainly would have lost the election, which he actually won by the narrowest of margins. In a sense, he received a popular mandate to continue to keep out of war, and an observer would not have expected a man of his high moral standards to provoke Germany into attacking Ameri-can shipping and thus bring on a clash of arms.

Recognizing as he did the possibilities of involvement in the existing conflict, Wilson tried to mediate a "peace without victory" between the two armed camps. With admirable foresight, he pre-dicted that a victor's peace could not last. But the Germans lashed back at him in January 1917 with the announcement of an unre-stricted submarine campaign. They recognized that their best hope of victory over the blockade lay in an all-out submarine attack against Great Britain and her allies, plus the supplying neutrals. Therein seemed to lie Berlin's brightest prospects, even though an unprepared United States would be forced into the war.

The British had long been taking great liberties with freedom of the seas, but to an Anglophile Wilson the German proclama-tion was intolerable. He promptly broke relations with Berlin, as he had bound himself to do at the time of the *Sussex* affair. But he could not bring himself to believe that the Germans would be so ruthless as to do what they had proclaimed. At length, in mid-March 1917, four unarmed American merchantmen were sunk on the high seas, with the loss of 36 lives. Wilson thereupon went before Congress and solemnly asked for a declaration of war which was speedily forthcoming on April 6, 1917. "The world," he proclaimed, "must be made safe for democracy."

It is evident that the United States became entangled in this frightful war because Wilson held Germany to a higher standard of conduct in operating its illegal blockade than he held the British in maintaining theirs. He seems to have been motivated primarily by his humanitarianism, the nation's honor, and his pro-British bias. Yet what he regarded as dishonorable and unthinkable in 1916–1917 was actually adopted overwhelmingly by Congress in the neutrality legislation of the mid and late 1930s. American merchant ships were forbidden to enter the declared war zones, and not one vessel legitimately flying the Stars and Stripes was sunk in these danger areas before the Japanese attack on Pearl Harbor in 1941, simply because no such ships could legally go there. Fashions change, and what had been regarded as dishonorable by the idealistic Woodrow Wilson became quite honorable under his disciple, President Franklin D. Roosevelt.

As a war leader from 1917 to 1918, the idealistic and pacifistic Wilson enjoyed great success. He keyed up an unprepared nation to an incredible spirit of self-sacrifice in fighting what was seriously called "a war to end war." The pro-German and antiwar element was largely silenced by the Espionage Act of 1917 and the Sedition Act of 1918. The Socialists were especially hard hit, and their leader, Eugene V. Debs, was sentenced to 10 years in a federal penitentiary for opposing this "capitalistic war." Wilson did not see fit to pardon him, although his successor, President Harding, did.

The belated and hurried production of war materials on an enormous scale involved considerable graft, for haste and waste, as well as conflict of interest, were an inevitable part of war production. Considerable evidence of collusion and crime developed in the Office of the Alien Property Custodian, especially in the liquidation of German assets, including chemical patents. But ignorance, error, and inefficiency were much more in evidence than actual malfeasance, especially in the frightfully costly and disappointing aircraft program. Wilson was too busy with idealistic leadership of a high level to concern himself unduly with these sordid problems of war production.

During the conflict, in a number of public addresses, the idealistic Wilson proclaimed his delusive Fourteen Points. They were designed to bring about a "soft peace" by such steps as abolishing secret treaties, establishing freedom of the seas, removing economic barriers between nations, reducing armaments, adjusting colonial claims fairly, and guaranteeing self-determination for minorities. To cap these promising points would be the yet unborn League of Nations.

In November 1918 the Germans, reeling under Allied and American onslaughts, sought a peace based on Wilson's hope-giving Fourteen Points. The Allies reluctantly agreed, but big-navy Britain entered a reservation on freedom of the seas, while despoiled France secured another that supported reparations for damages inflicted by the Germanic invaders. After receiving these solemn assurances, the Germans laid down their arms, expecting that the lenient terms of this "pre-Armistice contract" would be honored, especially by so honorable a man as President Wilson appeared to be.

At the Paris Peace Conference of 1919 Wilson found the blood-drained Allies more eager to divide the spoils and keep Germany crushed than they were in honoring the pre-Armistice agreement. He grudgingly compromised or otherwise yielded ground on a number of his points, but hoped that the League of Nations, the capstone, would iron out the inequities of the final treaty. The net result was a harsh victor's peace that, in retrospect, made inevitable a new war to undo it.

The Treaty of Versailles, with the Covenant of the League of Nations embodied as the first part, ran into stubborn resistance in the United States Senate, which was controlled by the opposition Republicans. President Wilson testified before the Senate Committee on Foreign Relations that he had never heard of the notorious treaties among the Allies for dividing the spoils of victory. This, we know, was not true, and critics concluded that he had lied because he did not want to hurt the chances of the treaty for Senate approval. Another theory is that he had been seriously ill in Paris, and that something had gone wrong with his memory. But his mind seemed exceptionally sharp in connection with other details at this same hearing. Probably he was resorting to his belief, as expressed earlier, that it was permissible to lie when a woman's honor or public policy was involved. In fact, getting the Treaty of Versailles through the Senate was public policy at the highest level.

The Republican majority in the Senate, headed by Senator Lodge, was prepared to add 14 formal reservations to the Treaty of Versailles that would safeguard the full rights of the United States, particularly those claimed under the Monroe Doctrine and the Constitution. Wilson, the stubborn and uncompromising fighter, unwisely undertook a nationwide barnstorming appeal over the heads of the obstructionist Republican Senators. His physical and nervous exhaustion were already such that he spurned the advice of physician and friends. On his return trip from the West, the weary President broke down following his fortieth speech at Pueblo, Colorado, on September 25, 1919. He was whisked back by railroad to the White House, where a massive stroke paralyzed one side of his body, including his face. He survived until 1924, a shell of his former self.

Wilson's illness, seclusion, and partisanship evidently combined to lead him astray. He flatly refused to accept the Republican [Lodge] reservations, but he was willing to permit Democratic reservations that meant about the same thing. When the time came for the critical vote, Wilson sent instructions to the Democrats in the Senate to reject the treaty with the Lodge reservations tacked on. His loyal supporters obediently followed these orders, and the treaty failed of the necessary two-thirds approval, November 19, 1919.

The country was shocked by this prolonged and fruitless disagreement. As matters stood, the Treaty of Versailles could not be ratified without the Lodge reservations, so a new vote was scheduled for March 19, 1920. A secluded Wilson again sent word to the Senate for the loyal Democrats to vote Nay, and enough of them blindly did his bidding to bring about a second and final rejection. One prominent Democratic Senator bluntly charged that the President had taken the responsibility of strangling his brainchild with his own palsied hands rather than permitting the Senate to "straighten out its crooked limbs."

Something had evidently gone wrong with Wilson's thinking processes, probably as the result of the stroke and his seclusion. Late in January 1920, before the second and final vote in the Senate, this distinguished authority on American government worked out a preposterous scheme, evidently on his sickbed. He would call upon the Republican and other Senators who opposed his League of Nations to resign. Then they could run for re-election, and if a majority of them were re-elected, he would resign. In short, he was proposing to superimpose a parliamentary form of government on the existing presidential structure. In his twisted and closeted thinking he was assuming that a Senator, even one who had four or so years of guaranteed service remaining, would leave Congress and hazard a new election.

Wilson's wildly impractical scheme was quietly shelved by those close to him. Instead he called upon the voters in the upcoming presidential election of 1920 to return a "solemn referendum" on the League of Nations, as though a presidential election can result in a clear or solemn referendum on any single issue. More than that, though broken, crippled, and confused, Wilson dreamed of being nominated for an unprecedented third term by the Democrats meeting in San Francisco in 1920. His pathetic attempts to win the nomination got nowhere. Actually his summons to make the presidential election a referendum on the League condemned that organization to death as far as the United States was concerned. The nation was fed up with Wilsonism—with altruism, idealism, humanitarianism, dogoodism, self-sacrifice, and moral overstrain. Wilson got his "solemn referendum" when the electorate arose and swept the Republican Warren G. Harding into the White House in a thundering landslide.

Wilson was not basically dishonest, but rather an upright man with Christian principles. The force of circumstances repeatedly led him to abandon, reverse, or apply these principles inconsistently, thereby leaving the impression of deviousness and duplicity. Ralph Waldo Emerson once observed that a "foolish consistency" was "the hobgoblin of little minds." By this test Wilson had an exceptionally large mind. Probably as much as anything, his humanitarian instincts sucked the nation into the bloodbath known as World War II, on the side of some nations that did not have completely clean hands.

CHAPTER 28

Warren G. Harding
1921–1923

Honesty . . . in public service will diminish public waste and extravagance.

Warren G. Harding, address,
May 17, 1923

Great wars have a way of evoking the noblest virtues of service and self-sacrifice, while creating an atmosphere favorable to selfishness, profiteering, and outright graft. Mere coincidence did not spawn the notorious Grant scandals following the Civil War, the Harding scandals following World War I, the Truman scandals following World War II and the Korean War, and the Nixon scandals following the Vietnam War.

President Harding was a small-bore Ohio politician who had ambitions to fill an office much beyond his depth. Although handsome, genial, affable, and gracious, he had mental furnishings that were not of the best. "God! What a job!" he was heard to blurt out in reference to the presidency on one occasion.

Harding, like President Grant, had little or no capacity to detect crookedness or moral halitosis in his associates. He was soon surrounded by poker-playing, nest-feathering cronies of the so-called Ohio Gang. In an era of legalized prohibition, Harding patronized a White House bootlegger, and he publicly supported the new Eighteenth Amendment while undercutting its enforcement.

"A good guy," Harding was "one of the boys." Perhaps his greatest weakness was an unwillingness to hurt people's feelings, especially those of political leeches, by saying No. A current saying claimed that George Washington could not tell a lie, but Harding could not tell a liar. He was heard to groan that he could take care of his enemies but not "my Goddamned friends."

Big business Republicans, weary of Wilsonian liberalism, wanted a "putty man" as much as a party man in the White House, and they thought they had found one in the amiable Ohioan. Harding had commended himself to wealthy conservatives by calling for a return to what he called "normalcy." He had opposed the League of Nations in his successful run for the presidency in 1920, but had advocated as a substitute a rather vague association of nations. In short, a league but not this League. Neither organization had a chance in America after the awesome anti-League landslide of 1920, and Harding, taught this impressive lesson, conveniently let his substitute drop. What he did was politically wise but he did turn his back on this nebulous promise once he had reached the White House.

Not a university graduate, Harding was painfully aware of his scanty intellectual background, so he promised to gather about him the "best minds" among the Republicans. He redeemed this pledge only in part. He chose for his Secretary of State the masterful Charles Evans Hughes, and for Secretary of Commerce the world-famous feeder of the Belgians and other hungry people, Herbert C. Hoover. But he offset these two superior minds with two of the most notorious crooks in the nation's history: Albert B. Fall as Secretary of the Interior, and Harry M. Daugherty as Attorney General. As will be noted, appointing Fall to watch over the nation's natural resources was like using a hungry wolf to guard the sheep. As for Daugherty, he was a crook who was expected to prosecute, not join, fellow crooks.

Harding was a darling of Old-Guard big business, which managed to turn back the hands of the clock to "normalcy." Such a move was perhaps not so much dishonest as illiberal and reactionary. A conservative Supreme Court, to which Harding appointed four out of nine members, handed down landmark decisions that were anti-labor, anti-children, and anti-women. Anti-trust laws were feebly upheld by the federal government, if upheld at all, while tariff rates were boosted. The giant corporations could relax, expand, and rake in the profits. Secretary of the Treasury Mellon scaled down the income tax for millionaires by about two-thirds, while reducing the national debt from about $26 billion to about $16 billion.

The assurances of future protection that Wilson had given the Allies in Paris were tossed into the ashcan, along with Wilsonian idealism. The victors were left with no choice but to build up their own armaments against possible future aggression by Germany and the Soviet Union. The Treaty of Versailles, with its League of Nations built in, was never approved by the United States. Instead, Congress ducked its responsibilities by passing a joint resolution in July 1921. It declared the war ended, while claiming all the rights and privileges conferred on the United States by the yet unratified treaty settlements.

So it was that the once-chivalrous Uncle Sam worked both sides of the street by claiming advantages without obligations and responsibilities. The war-torn Allies regarded such action as an unethical betrayal of the high hopes generated by Wilsonian idealism. Completely forgotten was Harding's vague substitute, an association of nations.

Many Republicans suffered from guilty consciences as they looked back on their role in the rejection of the League of Nations, and as they viewed the costly naval race spurting forward in the atmosphere of dangerous uncertainty. As events turned out, Harding was pressured into summoning a multipower conference on the limitation of armaments in Washington, D.C., 1921–1922. Republicans were prone to refer to this conclave as a substitute "peace conference," to some extent replacing that at Paris in 1919.

As the result of prolonged deliberations, the assembled delegates agreed to scale down their navies and place a limit on the building of capital ships. Nothing could be agreed on about cutting down armies. The Harding administration praised itself unduly for its contribution to peace, but the air-clearing was only temporary, largely because only capital ships were junked or otherwise limited. The alarming naval race in smaller vessels went merrily on, but less expensively. Uncle Sam proved to be something of a sucker as he scrapped new battleships carried over from the wartime building program, and then lagged behind in constructing cruisers and other smaller warships.

Despite the Washington Conference and other more solid achievements, the Harding administration is best remembered for the scandals that besmirched it. Most of them were exposed after the President's untimely death in August 1923, and it must be said in his defense that he was not personally involved in receiving tainted money. Mounting evidence that his trusted appointees had betrayed his confidence in them may have further undermined his health and thus hastened his demise.

Shortly before Harding died, the colossal peculations of Colonel Charles R. Forbes, director of the Veterans' Bureau, were revealed. His "take" amounted to about a quarter of a billion dollars, and an embarrassed Harding forced the resignation of this greedy "public servant" in February 1923. A more conscientious president, rising above politics, might have instituted legal prosecutions or prompted a Congressional investigation. But Harding, acting like the professional politician he was and no doubt fearing unfavorable publicity when he sought reelection the next year, tried to sweep the unsavory mess under the rug. After Harding's death, a Congressional exposé led to Forbes's being found guilty of defrauding the government. He was sentenced to two years in a federal penitentiary.

Further corruption saw the light of day after Harding's death, notably the Teapot Dome scandal. Subterranean oil reserves in the United States for the navy had been under the control of the Navy Department until Secretary of the Interior Albert B. Fall, a major custodian of national resources, persuaded Secretary of the Navy Denby and President Harding to transfer certain naval oil reserves to his jurisdiction. Both Denby and Harding, for what appear to have been valid reasons, believed that they were acting in the national interest. Private exploiters were planning to drill wells near the existing reserves and thus drain off navy oil. Also, the navy needed refined oil in storage tanks, as well as fuel tanks in strategic places, especially at Pearl Harbor.

All probably would have gone well if the financially pinched Secretary Fall, whom Harding trusted, had not turned out to be a crook. After secretly receiving some $400,000 from two millionaire oil exploiters, Harry F. Sinclair and Edward L. Doheny, Fall leased to them the priceless reserves entrusted to his care. Sinclair secured drilling rights in Wyoming at Teapot Dome; Doheny received the Elk Hill reserves in California.

If Fall had been an honest man, his actions to some degree would have been commendable. The enormous oil tanks that Doheny later built at Pearl Harbor, spared by Japanese bombs in 1941, were of crucial importance in finally overcoming Japan in 1941–1945. But the bribing of Fall resulted in one of the most notorious scandals in American history, and presents a classic case of a well-meaning president being betrayed by subordinates.

In 1929, after a series of trials, Secretary Fall was sentenced to prison for taking a bribe, while, oddly enough, the juries refused to convict the two millionaires, Sinclair and Doheny, who had paid the bribe. But Sinclair was found guilty of hiring agents to shadow the jurors, and was sentenced to prison for six months, thus giving the lie to the saying, "You can't put a millionaire in jail."

The opposition Democrats were delighted with the exposure of the Harding scandals. These partisans hammered relentlessly on Teapot Dome and related sensations until many citizens grew weary of all this excitement. Especially damaging to what was left of the good name of Harding was the role played before and after the President's death by Attorney General Harry M. Daugherty, a small-town lawyer in Ohio but a big-time crook in Washington. In two trials for financial irregularities, he refused to take the stand and testify, alleging that he had privileged information as a lawyer that presumably would incriminate both himself and Harding. This bald attempt to hide behind both the Fifth Amendment and the shroud of his old friend shocked the nation. Daugherty was finally let off when two successive juries failed to agree. Some of the key evidence had been destroyed, probably with the defendant's knowledge or connivance.

In the summer of 1923 Harding had started on a cross-country trip that took him to Alaska. On his return journey he died in San Francisco, the victim of what five reputable physicians diagnosed as pneumonia and apoplexy. An earlier report declared that he had suffered a digestive upset from eating some tainted crabmeat. This episode may have helped to prompt a popular writer to publish a book in 1930 which more than intimated that Harding had been poisoned by a jealous wife who knew of his infidelities. This interpretation was probably accepted by many persons prepared to believe the worst, but this book was a ghost-

written work, the effusion of a notorious swindler, perjurer, and
ex-convict.

One of the worst blots on Harding's reputation was the
widely accepted story that his wife had covered up for him by
burning all of his papers after his death. She actually destroyed
some trivia but the great body of his papers—some 350,000 items
—remained intact in the possession of the Harding Memorial
Association. They were made available to scholars in 1964, although a much earlier opening would have better served the dead
President's reputation.

Scandal pursued the deceased Harding even into his private
life. In 1927 a young woman from his hometown in Ohio, Miss
Nan Britton, published *The President's Daughter*. The author
charged that in 1919, while Harding was still a United States
Senator, he fathered a baby during a prolonged liaison which
lasted into his presidency. Miss Britton was unable to prove a
paternity case because, she alleged, she had burned all of Harding's love letters to her. But many readers found her tale convincing.

In 1964, 41 years after Harding's death, some two hundred
passionate love letters were discovered among the effects of a
deceased widow in Marion, Ohio. All indisputably in Harding's
writing, they provide convincing evidence of the infidelity of the
future President, who had married a woman five years his senior
in 1891. This illicit affair ran its course from 1910 to 1920. Harding's heirs brought suit to prevent the publishing of these letters,
and an agreement was reached in 1971 that they would be tightly
sealed until the year 2014.

There is no evidence that Harding's infidelities in any significant way interfered with his duties as President. They suggest
that, although a Baptist, he had human weaknesses, and that the
Sixth Commandment forbidding adultery held no great terrors
for him. Acid-tongued Alice Roosevelt Longworth said, "Harding
was not a bad man. He was just a slob."

Harding's basic problem was that he was a reasonably honest
and able politician in beyond his depth. He put in long hours on
the job, partly because his abilities were not of the highest. To be
sure, he was something of an isolationist, but if the landslide that
swept him into office meant anything, it was that American voters
were content to let Europe stew in its own juice. Harding shunned
the so-called League of Nations, as the voters evidently wanted

him to do, but he unsuccessfully favored adhering to the World Court, the judicial arm of the League of Nations.

As a humanitarian and man of good will, Harding established a record that partially offsets the dishonest doings of his appointed associates and others. As a Christmas present, he released from federal prison the fiery Socialist Eugene V. Debs, who had been jailed under Wilson for opposing the war against Germany. The Harding administration also concluded a heart-balm treaty with Colombia that provided $25 million as solace for President Theodore Roosevelt's so-called "rape of Panama." By this time American oil tycoons were interested in recently discovered Colombian petroleum.

Harding's humanitarianism was best reflected in two quite different areas. Before his presidency the steel manufacturers, rather than letting the furnaces cool off, had sweated their laborers in two twelve-hour shifts. By personal intercession Harding managed to reduce the man-killing stint to three humane eight-hour shifts.

The Soviet Bolsheviks, with their open declaration of ideological war on the capitalistic world, had few outspoken friends in the United States. Not until the days of President Franklin Roosevelt in 1933 would Washington extend to Moscow formal recognition. Yet when a frightful famine struck the Soviet Union in 1921 and millions of people were faced with starvation, Congress voted some $20 million in relief supplies. A humane Harding carried through the program under the auspices of Herbert Hoover, "the Great Humanitarian." Perhaps 10 million people were saved, many of whom lived to fight America's common foe, Adolf Hitler.

The proverb tells us that to know all is to forgive all. The opening of the Harding papers in 1964 has resulted in more favorable assessments of this scandal-ridden era and the glad-handing President who presided over it.

CHAPTER 29

Calvin Coolidge
1923–1929

Inflation is repudiation.

Calvin Coolidge, speech,
January 11, 1922

Calvin Coolidge was a dyed-in-the-wool New Englander, born at
Plymouth Notch, Vermont, appropriately on the glorious Fourth
of July 1872. He seems to have developed to a high degree the
New England virtues of honesty, morality, industry, and frugality.
His father reportedly said the youthful Calvin seemed to be able
to get more sap out of a maple sugar tree than any of the other
boys in the neighborhood.

After studying and practicing law in Massachusetts, Coolidge
cautiously put his hand on the political escalator and rose by
gradual degrees through a succession of offices until he became
governor of the state. "Cautious Cal" burst into the nation's headlines in September 1919 when he somewhat belatedly called out
the state militia to end the looting in Boston following a walkout
by the police. After the disturbance was in hand he fired off a
defiant telegram to the labor leader, Samuel Gompers, denying

the right to strike against the public safety. From then on Coolidge was a national hero, at least with the law-and-order citizens, and he was overwhelmingly put on the winning Harding ticket in 1920 as the candidate for vice president.

Coolidge seemed to be a crystallization of the commonplace. A conspicuously shy individual, he exercised only unspectacular powers of leadership, and his speeches were usually boring, delivered as they were in a nasal New England twang. A conservative dedicated to the status quo, he was no knight in shining armor riding forth to tilt at assorted wrongs. Indeed, the only horse he kept at the White House was an electric-powered steed for purposes of exercise. Faithful to his Republican philosophy, he became as was said, a kind of "high priest of the great god Business." He believed that "the man who builds a factory builds a temple" and "the man who works there worships there."

Coolidge was not one to pummel big business with a big stick from the White House. No foe of huge corporations, he preferred to stay off their backs during his five and one-half years of national prosperity—the lull before the Great Depression. As he pontificated in 1925, "The business of America is business." His thrifty, cheeseparing temperament led him to sympathize fully with the efforts of Secretary of the Treasury Mellon to reduce the national debt and taxes, chiefly for the rich, including the multi-millionaire Andrew Mellon.

As a vice president overshadowed by the robust Harding, Coolidge expected to rise no higher. His caution, thrift, shrewdness, and taciturnity contrasted sharply with Harding's volubility, gullibility, and good fellowship. Suspicious by nature, Coolidge was evidently bored by his job as Vice President. He probably sensed that Harding was being taken advantage of by designing cronies, but he certainly managed to keep quiet about what he did know, if anything. He could have done little or nothing to stop the swindles, and he certainly did not feel that a part of his job as vice president was to blow the whistle of disloyalty on the President. He evidently did not believe that he would become a partner in crime if he failed to cry out whenever one was being committed.

Harding died as various scandals were breaking, and Coolidge came as a godsend to the blackened Republican party. Few critics suspected this shrewd and frugal New Englander of being in league with the "Ohio Gang" or Wall Street. More than that,

Coolidge revealed an almost unaccountable reluctance to clean house in a hurry, if at all, as the unfolding events reveal.

Coolidge's stand on the oil scandals has been described as one of "cautious immobility." But he did go so far as to relieve the corrupt Attorney General, Harry Micajah Daugherty, of his responsibilities, and early in 1924 the President appointed two men to investigate the illicit oil leases and prosecute malefactors. Secretary of the Navy Denby, who had unwisely transferred the government's petroleum properties to Secretary of the Interior Fall, came to feel that he was a continuing embarrassment to Coolidge. He resigned on February 18, 1924.

We recall that about six months before Harding died, Charles R. Forbes, director of the Veterans' Bureau, also resigned under charges of mismanagement. On February 29, 1924, some seven months after Harding's death, Forbes was indicted for defrauding the government of $250 million in corrupt contracts and construction abuses. Nearly a year later, February 4, 1925, Forbes was fined $10,000 and sentenced to two years in prison.

Not until March 1924, about eight months after Coolidge's accession, did the federal government formally institute proceedings to cancel the Teapot Dome leases of Harry F. Sinclair and the Elk Hills leases of Edward L. Doheny. Not until 1927 did the Supreme Court declare both of those transactions invalid, and not until 1929 were the two big oil bribers acquitted of conspiracy to defraud. As we have seen, only Secretary of the Interior Fall, the bribe-taker, was sentenced to a prison term of one year. At all events, no one could properly accuse "Cautious Cal" of undue haste in cleaning up the oil mess.

On other fronts, Coolidge was hardly a spectacular success. He urged on Congress at the outset a program of thirty legislative items, only a few of which were passed. He honored Wilson's assurances to the other powers to the extent of urging America's adherence to the World Court, the judicial branch of the League of Nations. The United States Senate, now addicted to safeguarding reservations, tacked on unwanted stipulations, allegedly unworthy of America, and the issue of formally joining the World Court was passed on to succeeding administrations.

The opposition Democratic Party had continued to make angry noises about the Harding scandals. But Coolidge, the honest New Englander, had brought a comforting degree of respectability to the blackened White House. At the Republican national convention in Cleveland, Ohio, "Cautious Cal" was nominated for President by the overwhelming vote of 1,065, as compared with 34 ballots for his nearest rival.

The presidential election of 1924 was fiercely fought. Favorite Democratic slogans included "Honesty at Home—Honor Abroad," presumably a reference to the Republicans' forsaking of the League of Nations and its supporting Allies. Another ran, "Remember the Teapot Dome." But America of the Roaring Twenties was drugged by prosperity and oriented toward big business, which Coolidge was content to leave alone. At the same time, the masses seemed to be impressed with the President's frugality, caution, honesty, industry, and sagacity. He was to continue to show little sympathy for the depressed farmers, miners, and textile workers.

Content to mark time, Coolidge had not displayed, nor was he ever to display, two-fisted leadership. He temporized, all the while hoping that oncoming problems would solve themselves by running into the ditch before they reached the White House. Yet so comfortably did he fit into the mood of the times that he received an overwhelming endorsement by the voters in the election of 1924, despite the scandals, both revealed and unrevealed, of the Harding administration. Democratic cynics claimed that the election results were a mandate for the Republicans to keep on stealing.

Honest "Cal" Coolidge had been reared in a New England farming community, where the payment of a debt on schedule and in full came close to being a religious principle. He had scant sympathy for those who defaulted on their obligations. His tight-fisted attitude toward the Allied debts of World War I related directly to the rise of that great debt flouter, Adolf Hitler.

The background of this vexatious problem was relatively simple, though the problem was complex. America plunged into the Great War of 1914–1918 on the side of the Allies as a belated arrival in 1917. The nation's gigantic task was to raise, train, and equip an army while there was yet time to throw it into the fray. Meanwhile each of the Allies was contributing its money and manpower in an effort to hold back the enemy. The United States itself advanced to its associates about $10 billion.

The British were willing to cancel the debt owed them by France, provided that the United States cancelled the debts owed to it by both Britain and France. Thus the Allies would not have to collect back-breaking reparations from postwar Germany. The catch was that the American taxpayers, already disillusioned with the imperialistic greed of the Allies, would have to dig down into their own pockets and reimburse their own Treasury. In such circumstances Uncle Sam would look more like Uncle Sucker.

Another bothersome phase of the debt problem persisted. There were only three ways the ex-Allies could use to pay off their obligation: and these were in gold, goods, or services such as shipping. But the debtors did not have enough gold; American tariffs had built a forbidding wall against their goods; and services could not possibly amount to enough dollars. The American response was "pay anyhow" over a period of 62 years. As tight-fisted Calvin Coolidge insisted, "They hired the money, didn't they?"

Under Presidents Harding, Coolidge, and Hoover, agreements for repayment were wrung from all of the 17 debtors by May 1930. On the basis of presumed ability to pay, the going interest rate of World War I was renegotiated downward in all cases save one, so that the total obligation was reduced by about 50 percent. Actually, only about $2.75 billion was ever collected of the $10 billion or so owed. This haul was largely interest, and it came wrapped in great bitterness. Honesty may be the best policy in the payment of debts, as a general rule, but forgiveness of wartime debts might have cooled the reparations problem to such a point that Hitler could never have emerged from obscurity. If so, a grasping Uncle Sam outsmarted himself, and penny-pinching Calvin Coolidge looks less statesmanlike.

President Harding had resolutely declared, no doubt thinking of his anti-League landslide, that the nation would not enter the League of Nations trap "by the side door, or the back door, or the cellar door." But the League was much too important to be ignored, so America gradually sidled toward the back door, and gradually became involved in many of the non-political functions of "The League of Hallucinations." Nobody much in America seemed to realize that a viable League of Nations, with the United States exercising appropriate leadership, might conceivably have headed off the great explosion known as World War II in 1939.

Following the Washington Conference on Arms Limitation in 1921–1922, the naval race in smaller vessels, below the battleship class, went busily forward. Concurrently, a tidal wave of sentiment for the "outlawry of war" had been building up in

America. The basic concept was that the nations of the world would swear off war, somewhat as a nation such as the United States would swear off drinking by making the possession of alcohol illegal.

Neither Coolidge nor his Secretary of State, Frank B. Kellogg, displayed any enthusiasm for the outlawry-of-war idea, but public pressures finally became so overwhelming in America that both men climbed onto the bandwagon. The overborne Secretary signed the Kellogg-Briand Pact in Paris, August 27, 1928, together with the French Foreign Minister and 14 other nations. Others adhered later.

The Pact of Paris was grossly misleading, and Coolidge must have had some qualms about lending his support to it. The loophole was that although 63 nations formally outlawed war as an instrument of national policy, defensive wars were still permitted. And what scheming dictator could not trump up some excuse for offensive self-defense, as Hitler did in 1939 before attacking Poland. As events turned out, the new Pact of Paris did not abolish war, but it did make declarations of war unfashionable, while lulling potential victims into a false sense of security. American critics branded the Kellogg-Briand Pact as "an international kiss" and "a letter to Santa Claus."

During the Coolidge years, from 1923 to 1929, the enforcement of the Eighteenth Amendment against alcohol broke down, primarily because there were vastly more drinkers than enforcement agents. Unlike Harding, Coolidge was not a drinking man and not under the same pressures to uphold the law with one hand and lift a glass with the other.

The "Coolidge luck" held, prosperity continued, and the New Englander's administration was generally judged, particularly by fellow Republicans, as a resounding success. It certainly contrasted favorably with the orgy of scandal under President Harding and the withering depression under President Hoover, who came next. If Coolidge had only lifted an acquiescent finger in 1928, he almost certainly could have won renomination and reelection in a walk. Instead, he issued a terse statement in New Englandese: "I do not choose to run for President in 1928."

What did this mean? Was Coolidge definitely taking himself out of the race or was he waiting for a "draft" movement that would cause him to change his mind and "choose" to run? The consensus among researchers seems to be that because of weariness, failing health, and other motivations, Coolidge had no intention whatever of running again. Then why did he not end all uncertainty and speculation by coming out flatly and saying so, with complete candor and forthrightness? He apparently enjoyed playing the game of hard-to-get with no intention of being caught, and if this conclusion is correct it does not speak well for his basic candor.

This frugal Yankee with high ethical standards became involved in a transaction that may have bothered his conscience. But the incident came after he had left the White House. Taking advantage of an "insider's" opportunity, he bought 3,000 shares of Standard Brands stock at $32 a share. The same stock was priced at $40 a share when it reached the open market, for a paper profit to Coolidge of $24,000, if sold promptly and before the great crash of October 1929.

Despite some deviousness and considerable delay as a housecleaner, Calvin Coolidge, the New England Calvinist, deserves honorable mention as an upright man. He did for the Republican party of Harding what Gerald Ford was to do for the Republican party of Richard Nixon: he restored it to respectability.

CHAPTER 30

Herbert Clark Hoover 1929–1933

When there is a lack of honor in government, the morals of the whole people are poisoned.

Herbert Hoover, 1951

Herbert Hoover was the living embodiment of the American success story. Born in Iowa and early orphaned, he graduated from Stanford University and embarked upon a spectacularly successful career as a mining engineer and as a special consultant in foreign lands, first in Australia and then in China and elsewhere. Happening to be in Europe when World War I erupted in 1914, he was eventually named chairman of the Commission for Relief in Belgium, in which capacity he became known as "The Great Humanitarian." During America's years in the great war, he was made Food Administrator, and as "The Knight of the Lean Garbage Can" taught America to "Hooverize" on its intake of food. After the war this "Friend of Helpless Children" had a large hand in the economic rehabilitation of Europe, including extensive food shipments to the Soviet Union during the frightful famine of 1921–1923. In 1921 President Harding appointed Hoover

Secretary of Commerce, and he continued in that office until early 1929, the year after he was triumphantly elected President over the Democrat Al Smith of New York.

Herbert Hoover was undeniably an administrative genius of international fame. If he had occupied the White House during the prosperous Coolidge years, he almost certainly would be ranked high on the roster of Presidents. But the pall of the Great Depression descended in 1929, about eight months after his inauguration, and increasingly overwhelmed him with oppressive problems that defied solution. Not only was Hoover roundly booed by disappointed citizens, but cynics said that "The Great Engineer" had "ditched, drained, and damned the country" in less than four years.

President Hoover liked to make a distinction between people who were "money honest" but otherwise dishonest. There were many politicians who would not steal a dime from a child's piggy bank but who would dishonestly distort, deceive, or misrepresent to gain their own ends, whether financial or political.

As for his personal and political finances, Hoover shines forth as a scrupulously honest man. His private fortune was thought to be about four million dollars, so he kept none of his annual salary as Secretary of Commerce or President. All such payments were returned to the Treasury, donated to charity, or used in some way to serve the public interest. No doubt he was basically money-honest, but it is easier for a millionaire to be money-honest than the starving man who steals a loaf of bread from a grocery store.

President Hoover came under some fire when he established a summer camp during 1929 in the mountains of adjoining Virginia. Certain newspapers charged that he had improperly used public funds to pay for this private recreational hideout. Hoover countered by making public a letter in which he explained that his personal contribution had been "the purchase and preparation of the building materials, plus some labor costs." In addition, the Marine Corps provided the labor that constructed the cabins, which in themselves involved an indirect use of public money. Hoover finally removed any possible taint by deeding this property to the Shenandoah National Park for the recreational use of his successors. The estimate was that Hoover had poured about $114,000 of his own money into the camp.

A Senate committee investigating lobbyists for the sugar interests came up with letters, in December 1929, that seemingly implicated Hoover in the machinations of Cuban lobbyists for a lower American tariff. After about a month of inquiry the Congressional probers found "no impropriety or anything open to censure or criticism."

In September 1930 a veteran member of the Interior Department, Ralph S. Kelley, alleged in a published letter that an oil scandal comparable to Teapot Dome of the Harding years was in the making. He charged that the petroleum interests were planning "by fraud" to secure title to some 800,000 acres of shale oil reserves in western Colorado. Allegedly involved were 40 billion barrels of petroleum worth $400 billion.

After a careful investigation the Department of Justice branded Kelley's charges as baseless. Only three percent of all public land containing shale had been patented by private interests. At that time, and for many years to come, shale oil was of scant interest to producers of petroleum; the cost of extracting the oil was considerably in excess of the monetary value of the product. The case was closed when Kelley, the false whistleblower, was dismissed from the Interior Department. President Hoover issued a statement declaring that such "reckless, baseless, and infamous charges" could "only be damaging to public service as a whole."

Accusations that Hoover was remiss in his efforts to check the illegal use of alcohol are without substance. It is true that the Eighteenth Amendment of 1919, as implemented by the Volstead Act of the same year, was being widely flouted—and continued to be. Yet Hoover, far from winking at widespread rum-running and bootlegging, made a sustained effort to enforce an unenforceable law. He managed to transfer the implementing agency from the Prohibition Bureau of the Treasury Department to the Justice Department. The number of convictions and jail sentences increased sharply, though futilely.

In the depths of the Depression, the Reconstruction Finance Corporation (RFC) was established by Congress in 1932. It was a government lending agency recommended by Hoover and specifically designed to bail out big banks, railroads, and other corporations suffering from the financial pinch. It proved to be a monetary success. The head of the Reconstruction Finance Corporation was Charles Gates Dawes, a lawyer-banker of high repute, who had served as vice president under Coolidge, and who became co-winner of the Nobel Peace Prize in 1925 for his part in the Dawes Plan for collecting Allied reparations from Germany.

Early in June 1932 Dawes resigned his position as head of the RFC to take charge of the financially distressed Central Republic Bank of Chicago. On June 27, 1932, only three weeks after his resignation, he announced that he had received large loans from the RFC to keep his own bank solvent. The sum turned out to be $90 million. Critics, especially opposition Democrats, were quick to point out that this kind of "buddy deal" did not look right, especially when smaller banks were having difficulty staying afloat.

When the Dawes loan was brought up during Hoover's campaign for reelection, the President explained (November 4, 1932) that two Democratic members of the governing board of the RFC, as well as other bankers, had suggested the loan almost three weeks after Dawes's retirement. Even so, not all of Hoover's critics were satisfied.

If Hoover's record as a money-honest millionaire is above reproach, the same cannot be said of his conduct in other areas, particularly in his deliberate deception of the public. The most conspicuous examples of this species of deceitfulness should be mentioned, even though some of them were forced on him by circumstances over which he had little or no control.

As an amateur politician, presidential nominee Hoover had been pressured during his 1928 campaign into promising to summon Congress into special session to consider agricultural relief and to bring about "limited changes" in the tariff. Yet seasoned politicians, better than Hoover, knew that traditionally "tariff tinkering" had usually hurt the party in power at the next general elections.

The outcome was the bitterly controversial Hawley-Smoot Tariff of May 1930. By the time the high-pressure lobbyists got through with it, this measure had acquired about a thousand amendments and thus turned out to be the highest protective tariff thus far in the nation's peacetime history. The average duty on non-free goods was raised from 38.5 percent to nearly 60 percent.

Hoover was reluctant to sign the measure, so far was it from what he had envisaged and advocated, but he was loath to split his own party. He also found some solace in the flexible-rate provision, which would enable him, upon recommendation of the

Tariff Commission, to adjust rates up or down by as much as 50 percent. In the face of a storm of protests, spearheaded by hundreds of economists or would-be economists, he appended his signature to the Hawley-Smoot Tariff Bill.

As anticipated by experts, this highest protective tariff in the nation's peacetime history proved to be disastrous. It brought on reprisals from 25 exporting nations, promoted economic isolationism abroad, and deepened the depression, among other drawbacks. But Hoover, who believed in tariff protection, resolutely defended the maligned law, without pointing out that the new measure hurt rather than helped agriculture. He went so far as to argue disingenuously that the new tariff was really moderate, and he reached this astonishing conclusion by juggling statistics.

The customary way of reckoning tariff levels was to compute them on goods that are charged customs duties, exclusive of those on the free list, and by this way of reckoning the Hawley-Smoot rates rose to about a towering 59 percent. But if one lumps together the items on the free list with those requiring tariff duties, one comes out with the modest overall figure of 16 percent. This was the circumvention that Hoover employed.

As the Great Depression worsened, Hoover periodically issued cheery statements about impending recovery, all designed to boost drooping morale, especially among victims at the soup kitchens or standing in the unemployment lines. Some shivering citizens in the largest cities sold apples on the street corners at five cents each. Hoover states in his memoirs, with obvious exaggeration, that the apple-growers shrewdly and profitably capitalized on "the sympathy of the public for the unemployed." He further says, "Many persons left their jobs for the more profitable one of selling apples." Hoover indeed found himself in the uncomfortable but justifiable position of the doctor who is treating a patient in the throes of an incurable or near-incurable disease. The continued ravages of the depression prompted cynics to say that prosperity was "Hoovering" around the corner.

Hoover's false optimism was glaringly evident in his reaction to the work of the five-power naval conference in London in 1930. Only three of the powers—Britain, the United States, and Japan—signed the final treaty. The United States was finally granted parity with Great Britain in all categories of ships, not just capital ships. But in order to build up to paper parity with

Britain the United States would have to spend about a billion dollars on cruisers and other smaller warships. Ever resourceful with figures, Hoover argued that the United States would save a huge sum—that is if one reckoned from the higher standards that had been rejected by the abortive Geneva Conference of 1927.

As a peace-loving Quaker, Hoover enjoyed even less success when he tried to inject life into the World Disarmament Conference, then meeting in Geneva in 1932. He sensationally but unrealistically proposed that existing land armaments be reduced by about one-third, and that certain offensive weapons be abolished. A cut of one-third was certain to be rejected, partly because the defensive-weapons concept was unworkable. Hoover must have known, or at least suspected, that most so-called offensive weapons, in certain circumstances, can be used defensively. An armored tank is usually used to attack, but an immobile tank can sometimes be used defensively with lethal effect.

We recall that in the 1920s the Allied war debts owed to the United States had been adjusted substantially downward on the basis of a presumed capacity to pay. Using the inflow of reparations extorted from a defeated Germany, the debtor nations had barely managed to meet their obligations until 1931, when the worldwide depression sank into an acute phase. All along Hoover had taken the position that the debts and reparations were not or should not be interconnected, although a man of his intelligence and experience must have perceived considerable connection.

In June 1931, when it became evident that the debtors could no longer meet their obligations, President Hoover proposed a year-long moratorium on the payment of reparations and intergovernmental debts. Simultaneously he proclaimed anew his opposition to the cancellation of the war debts or to any linkage of German reparations with them. At the end of the one year moratorium, as could have been expected, six of the heaviest debtors defaulted outright. After another year all of the remaining group had done likewise, except "brave little Finland," a non-Associate of the United States in World War I.

In June and July of 1932, representatives of the European debtors, meeting at Lausanne (Switzerland), agreed on a virtual cancellation of German reparations, thus reducing the initial indemnity from about $33 billion to $714 million. The catch was that an equivalent cancellation of Allied debts to the United States would have to be arranged. But Hoover and American public opinion would never acknowledge the obvious debt-reparations connection. The problem then became one of facing up to reality and getting some money or refusing to recognize reality and get none. Clinging to his obviously unrealistic notions, Hoover and his successors wound up with some worthless IOUs, except the one for lone-wolf Finland, a minor borrower.

In the summer of 1932 a "bonus army" of some 20,000 or so men, mostly depression-cursed veterans of World War I, descended on Washington. Their aim was to persuade Congress to pay them prematurely the bonus ("adjusted compensation") that was due them in 1945, thirteen years in the uncertain future. Congress declined to pass the desired legislation, and several thousand of the "army" departed, some with loans granted by Congress against their future bonus payments. The remainder camped in vacant buildings and in a shantytown "Hooverville" on the Anacostia mud flats.

This throng of people, trapped as they were in unsanitary surroundings, presented a menace to the public health. Various disturbances created confrontations with the police, who finally reacted to brickbats by killing two of the intruders. Officials of the District of Columbia then called upon the President for assistance, and Hoover authorized General Douglas MacArthur to disperse the bonus army. The military responded with 600 troops, supported by a machine gun squadron and six tanks, clearly a case of overkill. During the rout of the unarmed invaders, the vacant buildings were cleared and the encampment at Anacostia was put to the torch.

Hoover indicates in his memoirs—or whoever wrote them so alleged—that the federal troops used more force than he had wanted or anticipated. He evidently had not contemplated wiping out the Anacostia encampment. He further declares that "not a single person" was injured, even though some of MacArthur's soldiers were hurt by brickbats, and many of the bonus veterans (and U.S. soldiers) were gassed or burned by the gas bombs. Hoover also alleges that the riffraff thus evacuated included relatively few genuine veterans but a large number of Communists, criminals, and ex-convicts. This is obviously an exaggeration, although there were some undesirable characters present.

Clearly the bonus army should have been disbanded, either by persuasion or a modest show of force. Congress should not have to deliberate under pressure from a mob, and dangerously unhealthful conditions should not be allowed to develop in a large city, vulnerable to an epidemic of disease. But Hoover's image as the "Great Humanitarian" suffered irreparably, and he did not help matters much by stressing unduly the threat posed by so-called Communist leaders.

Clearly Hoover was money-honest but he was not above mis-representing the facts, for this is what politicians routinely do. Until he ran for the presidency in 1928 he had been above poli-tics, and the unfortunate circumstances into which he was forced more or less compelled him to explain away a number of distress-ing events without a meticulous regard for the whole truth.

The much-booed Hoover, a Republican, was soundly beaten by Franklin D. Roosevelt, a Democrat, in the election of 1932, 472 electoral votes to 59. Much to his distaste, Hoover had finally supported relatively heavy outlays from the Treasury to sustain farmers, bankers and other groups affected by the withering depression. An ironical slogan of the incoming but free-spending Democrats was "Throw the spenders out."

Although overwhelmingly elected on November 8, 1932, Roosevelt could not take office until March 4, 1933, nearly four months later. During this critical lame-duck period, as the depres-sion was worsening, Roosevelt and Hoover had two tense meet-ings. No agreement emerged on critical issues, presumably because the incoming President would have no immediate au-thority to implement decisions made by the outgoing lame-duck administration. Hoover and many Republican leaders believed that Roosevelt was simply dragging his feet and waiting for the depressed conditions to become worse. Then he would spring forward, seize the helm, and emerge as a popular hero by saving the country from complete disaster.

On February 17, 1933, about two weeks before inauguration day, President Hoover sent President-elect Roosevelt a letter urg-ing his rival to give "prompt assurance" that he would balance the unbalanced budget, preserve government credit, and not tamper with or inflate the currency. Roosevelt failed to respond affirma-tively, and Hoover wrote in a "confidential" memorandum: "I realize that if these declarations be made by the President-elect, he will have ratified the whole major program of the Republican Administration; that is, it means the abandonment of 90 per cent of the so-called new deal."

This memorandum reveals clearly that Hoover had tried unsuccessfully to trick his rival into abandoning the proposed New Deal. The outgoing President was so inexperienced a politician as not to realize fully that the winner, not the loser, should be allowed to call the tune. Hoover was less than candid in accusing Roosevelt of non-cooperation, and this was only one of the specious charges that the floundering President leveled against his rival in the electoral campaign of 1932.

Hoover left the presidency as a weary, disheartened, and beaten man who sustained to the end his criticism that Franklin Roosevelt's New Deal undermined character. Hoover abhorred a dole, but within the limits of his "rugged individualism" he had supported limited help for financially distressed farmers, bankers, and other worthy citizens. Yet at times he gave the unfortunate impression that he was more willing, like a Grover Cleveland, to support hungry pigs than hungry people. Pigs had no character to undermine with government handouts. Yet people cannot pull themselves up by their bootstraps when they have neither boots nor straps.

Franklin Roosevelt, with enormous financial outlays, did not conquer the Great Depression. The outbreak of World War II in 1939, with an accompanying production of war materials for use at home and abroad, succeeded where both Hoover and Roosevelt had failed. And the nation still has the problem of Roosevelt's Social Security and other benefactions of the welfare state. Contemporary critics of the New Deal complained that it was more likely to strengthen the wishbone than the backbone.

CHAPTER 31

Franklin Delano Roosevelt 1933–1945

We have earned the hatred of entrenched greed.

Franklin D. Roosevelt, message to
Congress, January 3, 1936

As far as money-honesty went, Franklin Roosevelt could not be fairly accused of having used the White House to feather his own nest. That nest had already been well feathered by the wealthy family into which he had been born, and he was commonly known as "the Squire of Hyde Park," after his princely estate in New York state. As President he once claimed that he was also a businessman in the lumber business, and this boast was true only if one can categorize the marketing of a considerable number of Christmas trees as the "lumber business."

While running for reelection in 1936, Roosevelt alleged that despite his lavish outpouring of billions of dollars in relief funds for the needy, there had been no public scandal comparable to Teapot Dome. This claim held generally true not only for his first four years but also for the unprecedented four terms to which he was elected. The Republican party of the "outs" went sniffing around for any possible evidence of graft, but these critics came up empty-handed as far as a headline scandal was concerned. No charges appear to have resulted in the indictment, conviction, or forced resignation of any member of the White House staff or even of any major New Deal administrator.

This record seems incredible in view of the vast sums of relief money being thrown around, seemingly with careless abandon. Fortunately for honesty, the beneficiaries were so numerous and the sums disbursed to them were relatively so small that the opportunities for wholesale graft were greatly lessened. Also, the nation was deeply mired in an unprecedented economic and social bog, and the time had come for all high-minded men, especially those dedicated to public service, to come to the aid of their country.

When the war years followed, and enormous sums were poured into munitions contracts and other expenditures, there was more of a tendency for dollars to cling to sticky fingers at the lower levels of the Washington administration. Even so, the Roosevelt administration appears to have escaped all taint of major graft at the upper echelons. The famous watchdog committee under Senator Harry S. Truman in 1941 turned up abundant evidence of fraud by private companies in connection with the defense program but found only two cases of official misconduct. Neither of the two implicated the executive branch of the federal government.

Oddly enough, among the first pressing problems confronting Roosevelt was a hangover from the relatively clean Hoover administration. In September 1933, some six months after Roosevelt's inauguration, information came to the White House that certain mail contracts awarded by Hoover's postmaster general, Walter F. Brown, had been secured by collusion. Roosevelt moved slowly, for not until February 1934 did he cancel the contracts in question and order the Army Air Corps to fly the mail on an emergency basis. Yet the President paid dearly in public esteem for his effort to wipe out corruption in this area. The Air Corps, evidently unused to flying in stormy weather, lost six planes and five pilots in one week. The resulting public outcry forced Roosevelt to return the carrying of air mail to commercial lines.

Louis M. Howe, an intimate adviser of Roosevelt and a veteran member of his official family, was given the task of overseeing the Civilian Conservation Corps, which employed young men to plant young trees, among other outdoor chores. After an earlier charge had been quashed, Howe again got into trouble over the awarding of contracts. He tried to have some business awarded to an ironworks in Maine, evidently in the expectation that such a deal would redound to the advantage of the Democratic administration in the upcoming midterm elections in the state. This political ploy would have raised fewer eyebrows if the company in question had been the low bidder, but it was not. Roosevelt had been alerted to such ill-concealed bribery while Assistant Secretary of the Navy during World War I, so he squelched the transaction by warning Howe that awarding the contract to the high bidder would be "indefensible."

In 1935 Roosevelt's rivalry with Senator Huey P. Long, the colorful Louisiana demagogue, resulted in a bitter feud in which Roosevelt questionably used the powers of his high office for political ends. First, the President blunted the Senator's vicious attack on Postmaster General Farley. After Long was slain by an assassin in September 1935, Roosevelt launched a sweeping investigation of the income taxes of Long and his associates. Twenty-five indictments were handed up, but early in 1936 the Washington government moved to dismiss most of these criminal charges and to employ only civil suits to collect taxes in arrears.

Rumor had it that Roosevelt called off the hounds in Louisiana so as to win the allegiance of the Long political machine. This charge is improbable because political experts were certain that this state would vote Democratic anyhow in 1936, as it indeed did overwhelmingly. Even so, the suspicion lingered that Roosevelt's blistering attack through the Bureau of Internal Revenue was motivated by the kind of dirty politics that a President would do well to avoid.

The major relief agencies of the Rooseveltian era could hardly escape all charges of wrongdoing. Their goal was to place assistance in the hands of the unemployed sufferers and others as expeditiously as possible, not to prolong investigations and pinch pennies. Democratic politicians charged with administering these funds were accused of extorting political contributions from favored recipients, and in other ways using public means and private misery for improper ends. Indeed, checks for relief seemed to have a curious way of coming in bunches shortly before elections. There appears to have been some lower-level substance to such accusations, although probably such charges were exaggerated by Republican partisans.

Where did Roosevelt stand amid all of this outpouring of dollars from the Treasury? His commitment was to get relief to the needy, not to the greedy, but as a professional politician he felt no pressing obligation to tear his own Democratic party to pieces by exposing Republican charges of misconduct. He knew a lot about human nature and realized that immense outlays of federal money would inevitably spawn some corruption. Accordingly, he left to Congress the responsibility of passing reform legislation, which in fact he did not find completely satisfactory. Historians are not prone to blame Roosevelt unduly for lower-level irregularities in the relief program, especially when these scholars consider its size, achievements, and the desperate need for speed.

During America's involvement in World War II and its preliminaries, as we have seen, federal money was dispensed with prodigal hand, and there was abundant opportunity for fraud. Human nature being what it is, there was some irregularity but no major scandal blackened the White House. Members of the President's family may have traded on his name, but without his permission or encouragement. Attention was focused on Mrs. Roosevelt's lucrative earnings as a lecturer, radio commentator, and author of a newspaper column, "My Day." Suspicious Republicans caused a Congressional investigation to be launched, including a close examination of the income tax returns of both the President and his wife. The result was a clean bill of health, accompanied by the judgment of the ranking Republican member of the probing committee that Roosevelt's returns were "eminently fair."

If Roosevelt comes off well by the test of money-honesty, other troublesome questions arise in connection with his attempts to deceive the public. Here he is more vulnerable, for we must remember that he was a professional politician, and an eminently successful one at that. Few aspirants have ever gone far in public life by blurting out on all occasions "the truth, the whole truth, and nothing but the truth." Politics has been described as the art of the possible, and like the doctor who tells his patient white lies for the patient's good, the professional politician on occasion will ignore the truth or twist it for what he regards as the public good. On such occasions he is often able to rise above principle and equate the public good with his own political good.

In 1920 Franklin Roosevelt, as the Democratic nominee for Vice President, toured the country making speeches for the head of the ticket and Wilson's League of Nations. He stressed the point that the United States could count on the vote of Latin American satellites in the Assembly of the League of Nations, and he even departed from his prepared text to boast that Haiti, for example, could be counted on. "The facts are," he said, "that I wrote Haiti's constitution myself and, if I do say it, I think it a pretty good constitution."

This ad-libbing was not only untrue but also indiscreet, and the opposing Republicans exploited the indiscretion for all it was worth. As a professional politician loyal to the Democratic ticket, Roosevelt had no choice but to foreswear himself like a gentleman and deny that he had ever made this statement. In short, he denied and lied.

As President, Roosevelt gave out an extraordinary amount of information in public speeches, in messages to Congress, in fireside chats, and, above all, in the weekly news conferences, in which he gladly answered or parried questions at great length from the gentlemen of the press. Often he was surprisingly candid, but from time to time he would give the reporters information that was strictly off the record, and as such not usable by them.

One of Roosevelt's ablest biographers regarded the President as a combination of the lion and the fox. At times Roosevelt would courageously meet problems head on; at others he would slink around them with deceptive language or beat a hasty retreat. In 1937 he made a famous speech in Chicago in which he proposed quarantining the rampaging aggressors. When the isolationists in the country raised a fearsome outcry, he wisely backed down and resorted to less direct strategy. When the production of arms was lagging he would deliver a fireside chat saying that a large number of arms, say 1,000 aircraft, were "on hand or on order." This might mean that 5 were "on hand" and 995 were "on order."

Roosevelt was bitterly assailed, especially by Republicans, for "treacherously" breaking the promises set forth in the several platforms on which he ran. That of 1932, on which he first took his stand, strongly advocated a "drastic reduction of governmental expenditures," a balancing of the federal budget, and the preservation of a sound currency. The depression turned out to be so overwhelming that all these promises had to go out the window, as federal money poured out like water and the nation forsook the gold standard.

The Democratic platform of 1940 stated categorically, "We will not participate in foreign wars, and we will not send our army, naval or air forces to fight in foreign lands outside of the Americas except in case of attack." In a memorable campaign speech in Boston, delivered during the ensuing campaign, Roosevelt repeated this pledge more emphatically, though indiscreetly leaving out "except in case of attack." The next year, 1941, came Pearl Harbor and the United States itself was deeply involved in a "foreign" war.

Every politician worth his salt knows that campaign promises and platform promises are not covenants sealed in heaven, and that most of the voters have the same view. There is an old saying among politicians that platforms are not made to stand on but to get in on. The aspirant for public office means when he makes or backs such pledges that he will try to achieve certain goals, provided that Congress is cooperative and such aims are possible of realization in the light of unforeseen circumstances. Also, their attainment under these changed circumstances should be in the national interest. Such qualifications are implicit in campaign promises, though seldom specifically spelled out. As for Roosevelt's pledge to stay out of foreign wars, the great conflict did become an American war as well as a "foreign" war after the Japanese attacked Pearl Harbor.

In dealing with the neutrality furor that developed in the mid 1930s and later, President Roosevelt appears most devious. During these years the conviction had seized many people that the nation had been sucked into World War I in 1917 as a result of the enormous loans and mountainous munitions advanced or sold to the embattled Allies. This outpouring had been completely legal but in spirit unneutral because the British blockade had prevented American war material from going to Germany.

Responding to the clamor from American isolationists, Congress passed the hand-tying neutrality laws of 1935, 1936, and 1937. As finally perfected, these statutes prohibited loans or credits to belligerents, embargoed direct or indirect shipments of weapons or ammunition to them, and prohibited American citizens from traveling on belligerent ships, such as the ill-starred *Lusitania* of 1915. The act of 1937 was so modified as to permit the sale of commodities, such as oil, lead, and copper, that could be used to make munitions, provided that the purchaser paid for them on the spot and took them away in his own ships on a cash-and-carry basis.

President Roosevelt harbored no enthusiasm for the first three neutrality acts, for to him they denied to the Chief Executive the right to distinguish between the aggressor and the victim in the event of another global conflict. But he did issue a routine proclamation of neutrality, calling upon the American people to remain on the sidelines. Yet from the beginning he was personally a partisan of the Allied cause because he believed that in the interests of the United States the rampaging dictators should be defeated. From near the outset he secretly ordered American warships to broadcast by wireless the position of German merchant ships so that they might be intercepted and captured by British patrols.

On September 1, 1939, Hitler's armed forces crashed into Poland and knocked this neighboring nation out of the war in about six weeks. On September 21, 1939, Roosevelt went before Congress and in a rather specious appeal urged a repeal of the arms embargo so as to help the victims of aggression. He pleaded for "a return to international law," even though the United States had never abandoned international law. The nation had merely embarked upon a temporary program of not exercising to the full its rights under international law. Roosevelt further argued that traditional "neutrality" had served the nation well, and that the one "disastrous" departure from that policy under Presidents Jefferson and Madison had been a "major cause" of the War of 1812. This conflict, the speaker noted, had resulted in the burning of the capitol building which had preceded the structure in which the Congress then sat. Roosevelt's resort to these scare tactics evidently was the result of his having misread history, whether deliberately or not. Actually the embargo of 1807 to 1809, followed by the Non-intercourse Act, had forced the British to revoke their odious Orders in Council in 1812. If there had then been a cable to inform the United States of this concession in time, Congress probably would not have declared war in 1812.

In any event, Roosevelt's Congress finally responded with a trade-off in November 1939. The embargo on arms was lifted, but the Allied purchasers would have to come and get them on a cash-and-carry basis. As a concession to the homegrown isolationists, American merchant ships were forbidden to enter the proclaimed war zones established by the contending belligerents on the high seas. The preamble of the new revision declared specifically that the United States was not abandoning its "rights and privileges," but was merely declining to exercise them.

After France collapsed under Hitler's might in June 1940, the pretense of neutrality was largely abandoned by Roosevelt. Various undercover schemes were employed to send surplus arms and even new airplanes to the beleaguered British. Among various breaches of neutrality was the training of large numbers of British pilots in balmy Florida rather than in wintry Canada, as well as the repairing of damaged British warships in American shipyards.

A realistic Roosevelt was well aware that in an era when the dictators were flouting international law nothing would be more foolish than to permit the President to be shackled by ancient rules. The British were in desperate need of more destroyers to fend off an expected invasion by Hitler's victorious forces, and the upshot was the destroyers-for-bases deal of September 2, 1940. Roosevelt arranged to transfer to Great Britain 50 over-age but still usable destroyers from the U.S. Navy. In return the British agreed to grant to the Americans for 99 years rent-free base sites on six islands stretching from the Bahamas to British Guiana. In addition, Great Britain made an outright gift of base sites for 99 years on Newfoundland and Bermuda.

To transfer 50 warships from the navy of a nominally "neutral" nation to that of a belligerent power was clearly a violation of international law, especially after neutrality had been officially enjoined by the President of the neutral country. But the Attorney General, who is prone to tell the President what he wants to hear, produced a labored defense of the legality of the transaction.

Roosevelt himself defended the destroyers-for-bases deal as a means of protecting the Atlantic shores and outposts of the United States. In a regular press conference he likened the acquisition of the eight offshore base sites as comparable, from the standpoint of defense, to the Louisiana Purchase of 1803. Actually there was some parallelism but the historical background that Roosevelt fed to the reporters was riddled with factual errors. His memory may have been faulty, but one is less sure that it was when one notes that the erroneous statements were supportive of the destroyers-for-bases deal.

Members of Congress, especially the highly vocal isolationists, were outraged to learn of the destroyers deal only after it was accomplished. But Britain was in dire peril and the debate might have dragged on for months. Ultimately, Congress indirectly approved the destroyers-for-bases exchange by voting funds for the development of the sites thus acquired.

This momentous swap was merely a curtain raiser for the enormous lend-lease program. The British were about to exhaust their capacity to purchase more war material from the United States, and the danger loomed that Britain would collapse in the face of Hitler. Lending money would merely generate the old unpleasantness of trying to collect a war debt from exhausted Allies, which Roosevelt well remembered. After he was safely reelected in 1940, he came up with a clever scheme known as lendlease. He unveiled it at a press conference, where he used the analogy of lending one's garden hose to a neighbor whose burning house endangers one's own. When the fire is extinguished, the hose is returned. Similarly, the United States could lend arms to those nations resisting aggression and expect the return of this equipment, or replacements for it, when the fire was extinguished.

After prolonged debate throughout the country and in Congress, lend-lease was formally approved and the necessary appropriations were voted. Some deception inevitably accompanied the scheme. The lend-lease bill was given the symbolic and patriotic number 1776. The measure had the reassuring name, "An Act Further to Promote the Defense of the United States." The implication was that the British and their allies would continue to shed their blood, using American weapons, while the Americans stood with folded arms on the sidelines.

Roosevelt's clever analogy of the garden hose was not completely convincing or candid. Suppose that the ruptured hose came back with holes burned in it? Tanks and airplanes sent to Europe would be either battered, obsolescent, or obsolete when the war ended. Then there would surely be a period of peace when outmoded arms would become increasingly worthless. Republican Senator Taft, a leading isolationist, scoffed, "Lending war equipment is a good deal like lending chewing gum. You don't want it back." Isolationist Senator Wheeler of Montana branded lend-lease as the "New Deal's 'triple A' foreign policy— to plow under every fourth American boy." Stung to the quick,

Roosevelt told his press conference two days later, "That really is the rottenest thing that has been said in pubic life in my generation."

Despite a certain amount of adroitness, lend-lease can hardly be categorized as a scheme that Roosevelt "put over" on the American people in the dead of night. This historic bill was introduced in Congress in January 1941 but not signed by the President until March 11, 1941, after prolonged debate. The measure was discussed in the press at great length and dissected in the public opinion polls, which registered a strong vote in favor of lend-lease.

The final cost of lend-lease aid to the Allies amounted to some $50 billion, mostly to Britain and the Soviet Union, and it was spent on the winning side. The act was in effect an economic declaration of war on the dictator powers, or rather a counter declaration of war on them, and it was recognized as such. Roosevelt can hardly be accused of having deceived the people when he proposed this legislation, without which the Allies almost certainly would not have won. As for his breaching neutrality, the President had already done so spectacularly with the destroyers deal, if not before.

It was evident to Roosevelt, as to many of his critics in Congress, that German submarines would sink or attempt to sink cargoes of lend-lease supplies destined for Great Britain. Would the President then order American warships to intercede or would he allow the German submarines to send valuable lend-lease shipments to the bottom rather than to Britain? In short, would he get involved in a shooting war with Hitler's Germany by escorting carriers of lend-lease assistance?

In his press conferences and elsewhere Roosevelt was evasive on the issue of escorting convoys. He knew that the question would come up sooner or later, but he saw no point in raising objections himself that would soon be voiced by others. After weeks of debate Congress passed lend-lease by wide margins, but tacked on a meaningless clause that "Nothing in this Act shall be construed to authorize or permit the authorization of convoying [escorting] vessels by naval vessels of the United States." Roosevelt recognized this proviso as a sop to the isolationists, for he already had constitutional authority as Commander-in-Chief to deploy the warships under his command as he saw fit.

At first Roosevelt ordered American destroyers to alert by

radio nearby British and Canadian warships that were involved in escorting lend-lease shipments. But the sinking of these cargoes increased, and by July 1941, American destroyers, under orders from Washington, were fighting off German U-boats in an undeclared shooting war. Irate isolationists in particular charged that Franklin Roosevelt was deliberately dragging the United States into war by stealth. Congresswomen Clare Boothe Luce charged in a campaign speech in 1944 that Roosevelt "lied us into a war because he did not have the political courage to lead us into it."

Clearly an informal and undeclared shooting war developed in the North Atlantic between German submarines and American destroyers before the Japanese attacked Pearl Harbor in December 1941. The truth is that Hitler, bogged down in Russia, did not declare war on the United States as a result of these occasional brushes in the Atlantic. Another reason for his hesitancy was his desire to win the cooperation of his reluctant Japanese ally in the widening conflict.

The United States is a democracy in which the majority is supposed to prevail. A strong majority of citizens in the country and in Congress favored the Lend-lease Act because they wanted this wholesale assistance to go to Great Britain and not be pushed off the pier or sunk en route by German submarines. Because this objective was the wish of the people and of Congress, Roosevelt felt that he had a kind of mandate, despite the noisy isolationist minority, to use force to ensure that the lend-lease cargoes reached their destination, usually Iceland, where they were further shepherded by British escorts through the German war zone.

A series of clashes between U.S. destroyers and German U-boats southwest of Iceland occurred in September and October of 1941. The destroyer *Greer* provoked an attack but came off unscathed, the destroyer *Kearny* suffered serious damage and the loss of 11 lives, and the destroyer *Reuben James* was sunk with the loss of more than 100 officers and men.

The *Greer* incident of September 11, 1941, was the only one of the three clashes that raised grave doubts as to Roosevelt's basic honesty. This destroyer was not engaged in escort duty but was carrying passengers, mail, and freight to the American outpost on Iceland that had been rather irregularly acquired by the United States in July 1941. The *Greer* had been trailing a German submarine for about three and one-half hours, all the while broadcasting its position to British aircraft and warships operating nearby. These enemy aviators managed to drop several bombs near the U-boat, without inflicting damage. The submarine commander, believing with good reason that he was under attack, finally fired two torpedoes at his American tormentor, which retaliated with numerous depth bombs. No hits were registered by either side, but the engagement lasted about nine hours altogether.

President Roosevelt, though promptly provided with official information as to what had happened, chose to represent this incident as a clear-cut attack on an innocent American warship merely engaged in peaceful transport service. The truth is that the *Greer* was obviously the aggressor, and that the U-boat commander had every reason to believe that he was under an unprovoked attack. A week later Roosevelt delivered a shoot-on-sight radio message to his countrymen, September 11, 1941. He declared that henceforth American warships, not content with repelling attacks, would defend freedom of the seas by striking first at Axis raiders found within American defensive areas.

Again Roosevelt was practicing deception so as to rally American opinion behind an offensively warlike course of action. Because the U.S.S. *Greer* had obviously been the aggressor, the U-boat had been fully justified in striking back. As for freedom of the seas, which Roosevelt often invoked during these weeks, it had no relevance whatever in wartime to the armed convoying of lend-lease gifts through German-proclaimed war zones to the enemies of Germany. But freedom of the seas was so deeply embedded in the American tradition that its invocation, whether relevant or not, was bound to have an electrifying appeal.

On December 4, 1941, three days before the Pearl Harbor attack, the *Chicago Daily Tribune* published what its headline correctly claimed to be "FDR's War Plans!" The President's top-secret goal was declared to be ten million armed men, half of them to fight in Europe. Does this prove that Roosevelt was diabolically planning to drag his nation into the Hitlerian bloodbath? The plain truth is that all major powers likely to be involved in war have their contingency plans; indeed they would be foolish not to fashion them well before the shooting starts. Early in 1941 British and American military experts had met in Washington and concocted plans for joint cooperation in the event of war. One farsighted decision, which may have spelled the difference between victory and defeat, was to crush Hitler, not Hirohito, first.

The blunt truth is that in the months before the Japanese attack on Pearl Harbor, December 7, 1941, Roosevelt and Hitler were involved in an undeclared war on the high seas. The available evidence supports the view that neither antagonist really wanted more than informal hostilities at this time. Hitler was deeply enmeshed in Russia; Roosevelt had no way of extorting a declaration of war from Congress, and to him the destroyer-versus-submarine war in the North Atlantic was the most effective means available to get the lend-lease shipments to Great Britain (and Russia) and keep that potential ally afloat.

The Japanese attack on Pearl Harbor brought into being overnight a new and radically different lineup. Japan, Germany, and Italy all promptly declared war on the United States, which in each case formally recognized the existence of hostilities by overwhelming votes in Congress. As a consequence, Roosevelt did not have to lead a divided nation into war, whatever may have been his personal desires to curb the aggressions of the dictators. Even the most rabid isolationists had to concede that the only thing left to do was to "lick hell" out of the enemy.

The devastating surprise attack at Pearl Harbor by the Japanese in December 1941 neatly wiped out the opposition of American isolationists to war resolutions. Some rabid critics of the President charged that he had planned things that way. Allegedly, he had deliberately exposed the American fleet at Pearl Harbor so as to lure the Japanese into an attack that would substantially destroy America's formidable force. Such a scheme, if successful, would rank Roosevelt in the American hall of infamy with Benedict Arnold.

No proof has ever surfaced to convict Roosevelt of such Machiavellianism. If a president takes his country into an armed conflict, he wants to go down in history as the leader who emerged victorious. How does a statesman win a contest against powerful adversaries by contriving to have the Pacific fleet, already weakened by transfers to the Atlantic, essentially destroyed on the first day of a war? Roosevelt had his faults, but he was not crazy.

Once Roosevelt was deep in the conflict against the dictators, his severest critics were inclined to shift their attacks from his deviousness to his favorable treatment of unfriendly neutrals and suspicious allies. Actually the pressure of wartime events caused the President to shortchange China, conciliate dictator Franco in Spain, postpone the opening of a second front, defer to the Soviet

Union, and continue to send enormous quantities of lend-lease to Stalin after this Man of Steel had amply demonstrated anew that he would go his own Communist way. Roosevelt yielded much ground to this ruthless dictator in his determination to bring into being a viable United Nations Organization after World War II.

The war was still unwon and the peace yet unmade when the presidential election of November 1944 intervened. Though obviously aging and no doubt weary, Roosevelt agreed to run again for an unprecedented fourth term, and again swept to an unprecedented victory. When he died unexpectedly about four weeks later his critics claimed that a dying man had deliberately deceived the American voters. Actually, he expired at age 63, after displaying unusual vigor in the recent campaign. A president may die at any age, and this one had taken pains to secure Harry Truman as his running mate, after ridding himself of the ultraliberal incumbent, Henry A. Wallace.

Early in February 1945 Roosevelt met with Winston Churchill and Joseph Stalin at Yalta, in the Russian Crimea. Roosevelt was bitterly criticized for some of the decisions that he agreed upon at this conference. But in the main these judgments were reached in an effort to conciliate Stalin and were aboveboard. Roosevelt managed to extract from the Soviet dictator a pledge to facilitate "free elections" in the satellite countries of Eastern Europe. When Stalin failed to honor this commitment, or what Roosevelt regarded as a commitment, charges of betrayal by the Soviets were widely voiced.

Roosevelt was no doubt too trusting of the Soviets at Yalta, but he did not have an acceptable alternative. The Red Army was on the ground in Eastern Europe, and Stalin was in a position to take and hold what he wanted. In a further effort to induce Stalin to back the United Nations Organization and to enter the war against Japan, the Soviets at Yalta were permitted to partition unfortunate Poland and wrest concessions from prostrate China. The taint of deviousness, not to say misjudgment, arose when a secret agreement that Roosevelt had made with Stalin at Yalta finally leaked out. The Soviets would be allowed to have three votes in the yet unborn United Nations, and the United States might ask for as many for itself. But this option was never implemented, and it would have been inconsequential if adopted. The one veto vote in the Security Council of the United Nations was all that the Soviet Union needed to paralyze official action.

Returning from Yalta in February 1945, Roosevelt appeared before Congress on March 1 to deliver an address on his recent trip to Yalta. For the first time in presenting such a message, he announced at the outset that his leg braces were bothering him to such a degree that he was sitting down. A phonograph record of this message has been preserved, and the golden voice has much the same vibrancy that it had on similar records recorded several years earlier.

In his public and political life Roosevelt resorted to considerable deviousness and deception, usually in what he regarded as the public interest, notably in dealing with a balky Congress. His sympathizers would say that the ends justified the means; his isolationist critics would judge otherwise. Historians, with the menace of the dictators in retrospect, are inclined to be more charitable than many of his critics.

In private life Roosevelt appears to have been a man of integrity, except notably for a prolonged and clandestine love affair with a former social secretary, Lucy Mercer. This attractive woman was with him at Warm Springs, Georgia, the day he died unexpectedly, and Mrs. Eleanor Roosevelt was then profoundly shocked to learn of the relationship. What effect, if any, this affair had on the President's discharge of his official duties is a matter of conjecture.

CHAPTER 32

Harry S. Truman
1945–1953

To me, party platforms are contracts with the people.

Harry Truman, 1956

Feisty Harry Truman inherited the crushing burdens that developed in the closing days and aftermath of World War II. After President Roosevelt died unexpectedly and left his vice president unbriefed, Truman told reporters, "When they told me yesterday what had happened, I felt like the moon, the stars and all the planets had fallen on me."

Truman became one of the most controversial of all the presidents, primarily because his "great decisions" all encountered bitter criticism. Prominent among them were the decision to drop the atomic bombs on Japan; the "get tough with Russia" policy that led to the enunciation of the sweeping Truman Doctrine in 1947; the Marshall Plan of 1947 to rehabilitate Europe in the teeth of Moscow; the challenging of the Soviet blockade of Berlin in 1948; the creation and overhasty recognition of the new state of Israel in 1948; the decision in 1950 to go ahead with the hydrogen bomb; the leadership of the U.N.-U.S. intervention in the

Korean War in 1950; and the sacking of General Douglas Mac-Arthur in 1951.

In every one of these major decisions Truman could have pursued a different and possibly better course of action. But in no one of these instances could he be accused of deliberately attempting to line his own pockets or even promote his popularity at the polls. A possible exception would be Truman's key role in the creation of Israel in 1948, on the eve of his supposedly hopeless bid for election to the presidency in his own right. Whether he was purposely bidding for the Jewish vote or not, he got enough of it to boost him again into the White House. Truman was an exceptionally clever politician.

The most damaging charges against Truman's money-honesty have grown out of the misbehavior of many of his appointees and close associates ("cronies"), followed by his reluctance, like that of General Grant, to clean house as quickly and as thoroughly as the opposition party desired. Traditionally the President takes credit for the accomplishments of his nominees, while having to suffer the blame for their shortcomings. His nostrils should be delicately attuned to the odor of wrongdoing.

After the enormous outlays of money during World War II, the Truman years were blackened by the misconduct in public office of a number of Truman's appointees or "cronies," sometimes called "the Missouri Gang." In theory the President was responsible for their behavior, and although he generally opposed their questionable practices, he was all too prone to stand behind them as individuals. Accusatory Republicans had much to say about "government by crony" and "the mess in Washington," all of which contributed to the landslide election of General Eisenhower over Adlai Stevenson in 1952. The irony is that Senator Truman had made his nationwide reputation in World War II by heading a committee that saved millions of dollars by probing into mismanagement, extravagance, "influence peddling," and fraud in connection with contracts for war production.

Early in his troubled administration, President Truman chose as his Undersecretary of the Navy Edwin W. Pauley, former treasurer of the Democratic National Committee. At first glance, this appointment seemed like the customary reward for a deserving Democrat and hence simply a political deal. But Pauley was prominently connected with the oil business, and his new post would enable him to administer the nation's oil reserves—another classic case of the wolf being asked to guard the sheep.

Pauley was already conspicuous for his opposition to federal designs on tidelands oil fields that had previously been claimed by the ocean-fronting states. During the hearings on his confirmation as Undersecretary of the Navy, critics charged that Pauley opposed federal jurisdiction over the tide-lands because of political contributions from oil interests in the states involved.

President Truman had already gone on record as favoring the claims of the federal government to the tidelands oil deposits then under state jurisdiction. He remained true to this policy to the end, but oddly enough he also remained true to Pauley, who opposed him on this issue. The Secretary of the Interior, "Honest Harold" Ickes, carried the fight all the way to President Truman, who indicated that Ickes was mistaken. Ickes hotly resigned in a letter that impugned Truman's truthfulness and warned of a scandal comparable to Teapot Dome. Truman accepted this indignant resignation, and stood squarely behind Pauley until the embattled nominee, certain of not receiving confirmation, withdrew his name. In this battle of the three clashing personalities there appear to have been no real winners.

The President of the United States should be above reproach, but Truman was unable to shake off entirely the taint of his connection with the allegedly corrupt political machine in Missouri of Tom Pendergast. This relationship appears to have been no more than a marginal connection, but the facts are that under the aegis of the notorious Pendergast machine Harry Truman became administrative judge of Jackson County, Missouri, in 1922–1924, and a presiding judge from 1926 to 1934. In 1945, while vice-president of the United States, Truman braved the uproar and journeyed back to Missouri to be present at Tom Pendergast's funeral.

As President, Truman became involved to some extent in Missouri politics. In combination with the Pendergast machine, he attempted to oust a Democratic Congressman, Roger S. Slaughter, who had not satisfactorily supported the policies of the Democratic Truman administration. Enos Axtell, endorsed by both the President and the Pendergast machine, won by a margin of five to one in the Pendergast-controlled wards, but his Republican rival triumphed in the later general election.

Suspicions were promptly voiced that there had been grave

irregularities in the Missouri voting. The Department of Justice, including the Federal Bureau of Investigation, dragged its feet in the subsequent inquiry, and then declared the case closed. Critics were quick to conclude that Truman, former beneficiary of the Pendergast machine, had called off the dogs.

Under Republican auspices, a committee of the House of Representatives undertook an investigation of these alleged Democratic misdoings in Missouri. Yet on the day before the public hearings were scheduled, the relevant ballots and related records mysteriously disappeared from the files of the Kansas City board of elections. Two federal grand juries produced 24 indictments, but by then convicting proof was unavailable.

The feet-dragging of Truman's Department of Justice generated further inquiries of a damaging nature. Theron Caudle, a responsible official in the Department later conceded that the initial investigation by the FBI had been severely limited and had received "top-level attention," a phrase that strongly suggested President Truman's intervention. Unfriendly Republicans in Congress pointed to the damaging fact that those officials in the Department of Justice who had fallen in with White House wishes were subsequently singled out for favored treatment in their promotions. Theron Caudle, who had been in charge of the criminal division of the Department of Justice, was moved up into a new position in the tax division.

We do know that the Democratic White House was out to get the Democratic Representative Slaughter, and that the President had long profited from his association with the Pendergast machine. He evidently had nothing to do with ballot-box stuffing or with stealing records. But he probably had the Justice Department move with conspicuous slowness, for Democrats, no less than Republicans, dislike washing their dirty linen in public. As for seeking to purge Congress of a Democrat like Slaughter who did not follow the party line, this move was a common ploy in politics. Truman's predecessor, Franklin Roosevelt, had tried publicly to "purge" Congress of three Republican Senators in the midterm elections of 1938, and this effort evoked charges of dictatorship but little was said about criminality. (Incidentally, the three potential victims were all triumphantly re-elected.)

A major source of Truman's embarrassment was his military aide, Brigadier General Harry H. Vaughan, an old crony of the Missouri Gang. He gave some unwelcome notoriety to the refrigerator known as the "deep-freeze" after he told a prominent Milwaukee manufacturer that such a convenience would be welcome in the Vaughan home and in Truman's Little White House in Missouri. The giver of gifts no doubt realized what he was doing when he sent a deep-freeze to Vaughan and to Mrs. Truman, and to four other prominent officials of the administration, only one of whom returned this handout. Of course, the Constitution forbids the President (and other officials) to accept valuable presents only from foreign states or potentates. The official who receives such favors is often expected to do something, perhaps questionable, in return.

General Vaughan was guilty of other improprieties as well, including influence-peddling through "five-percenters." These were free-lance agents who arranged for interested manufacturers to negotiate lucrative government contracts for a "finder's fee" of five percent. A number of such helpful gentry were alleged to be on the loose in Washington. The most sensational case appears to have implicated a New England manufacturer of furniture who involved not only General Vaughan but several other persons prominent in Washington. In this instance General Vaughan appears not to have accepted any of the standard five percent, altough he allegedly had collected campaign contributions from such sources for the Democratic party.

The Reconstruction Finance Corporation (RFC) had been set up during the Hoover administration as a pump-priming agency designed to bail out big banks and giant industrial corporations, but not to help individuals. In the days of President Roosevelt this institution had disbursed about $11 billion in loans, and before its termination in 1956 it had proved to be the most successful financially of the anti-depression agencies. But where so much money is being disbursed, opportunities abound for improper influence and other irregularities.

In 1950, following a default on a multimillion dollar loan, the Senate launched an investigation into favoritism and influence. Directors of the Reconstruction Finance Corporation (RFC) were found to have been swayed by influence-peddlers, by officials of the incumbent Democratic party, and by at least one minor member of Truman's staff. The husband of a White House secretary managed to have his wife made the recipient of a royal pastel mink coat valued at a discounted $1,000. Cynics jeered that although President Truman might have no relationship with the

Chinese Ming dynasty he was obviously reigning during the Truman "mink dynasty."

What followed was a can of tangled worms. Truman's first response to the Congressional investigators was to reappoint as directors the two men most tarred with suspicion. He also refused to permit his personnel adviser, Donald Dawson, to testify. After two months Truman relented, and Dawson denied that the President had used his influence to support certain loans by the RFC. But Dawson did admit that he had accepted free accommodations from a hotel in Florida that had received a loan of $1.5 million.

Despite such a damaging admission and other revelations, Truman stubbornly kept this black sheep on the White House staff. One is reminded of the scandals during the Grant administration, when the gullible general stood strongly behind embarrassing appointees. A reasonable verdict in the present case is that Truman finally made salutary moves to clean house in the RFC, but he was unaccountably slow in removing promptly those compromised officials who had brought about the need for reform.

Partly as an aftermath of World War II and its enormous expenditures, the Bureau of Internal Revenue was reeking with corruption during the early Truman years. The commonest offenses were the evading of personal taxes by the collectors themselves, the acceptance of bribes from taxpayers who were seeking to pay less than their fair share, and the extortion of money by collectors from those citizens who wanted special favors in escaping taxation.

A total of 64 district collectors, customarily political appointees, headed Internal Revenue. As a result of the Congressional investigation of 1951–1952, nine of these officials were removed. All told, 166 Internal Revenue employees were forced to resign in 1951 alone, some of them to enter jail. The only member of the White House staff to become involved in a criminal charge was Matthew Connelly, presidential appointments secretary. He was convicted and sent to a federal prison.

As in the RFC investigation, President Truman revealed a willingness to make organizational changes, while displaying a reluctance to acknowledge fault in guilty appointees. Early in 1952 he submitted a plan to Congress for reorganization that included desirable reforms. His purpose, he explained, was "to prevent improper conduct in the public service, to protect the government from the insidious influence of peddlers and favor seekers, and to expose and punish any wrong doers." Congress accepted his plan, which ended the jobs of the 64 collectors and substituted the appointment by the President of a single commissioner. All other positions were to be filled by the Civil Service.

Truman was severely criticized, especially by Republicans, for not having been more zealous in rooting out offenders and cleaning house. Professional politician that he was, he seems to have dragged his feet in his exposure of the shortcomings of his Democratic administration. He recommended the reforms finally accepted only in response to a public outcry about "the mess in Washington," much of it voiced by Republicans. But at least Truman himself appears not to have been corruptly involved in this orgy of criminality.

After nearly eight years in office, "Honest Harry" Truman was eligible for re-election in 1952, and if he had been nominated and elected he might have served another full term. But he had the good sense to bow out and pass the Democratic torch on to Adlai Stevenson, who was soundly beaten by the glamorous General Dwight D. Eisenhower, the Republican nominee.

Candidate Stevenson suffered to some extent from the corruption that had been only partially uncovered in the days of Truman. The Republican platform on which "Ike" ran detailed in partisan fashion the shortcomings of the previous administration. Although Democrats were prepared to argue about some of the specific charges, the overall picture contained considerable truth. The Republican platform writers blasted away in this partisan fashion:

"The present Administration's sordid record of corruption has shocked and sickened the American people. Its leaders have forfeited any right to public faith by the way they transact the Federal Government's business.

"Fraud, bribery, graft, favoritism and influence-peddling have come to light. Immorality and unethical behavior have been found to exist among some who were entrusted with high policy-making positions, and there have been disclosures of close alliances between the present Government and underworld characters.

"Republicans exposed cases of questionable and criminal conduct and relentlessly pressed for full investigations into the cancer-like spread of corruption in the Administration. These investigations uncovered a double standard in Federal tax law enforcement—lenient treatment to political favorites including even some gangsters and crooks, but harassment and threats of prosecution for many honest taxpayers over minor discrepancies.

"Besides tax fixes and scandals in the Internal Revenue Bureau, investigations have disclosed links between high officials and crime, favoritism and influence in the RFC, profiteering in grain, sale of postmasterships, tanker-ship deals in the Maritime Commission, ballot-box stuffing and thievery, and bribes and payoffs in contract awards by officials in agencies exercising extraordinary powers and disbursing billions of dollars.

"Under public pressure, the Administration took reluctant steps to clean house. But it was so eager to cover up and block more revelations that its clean-up drive launched with much fanfare ended in a farce.

"The Republican Party pledges to put an end to corruption, to oust the crooks and grafters, to administer tax laws fairly and impartially, and to restore honest government to the people."

One of the favorite Republican slogans in the Eisenhower-Stevenson campaign of 1952 lambasted the Democratic Party of Honest Harry Truman in four damning areas: "Crime, Corruption, Communism, and Korea." Truman had indeed taken the nation into war in Korea in 1950, but that involvement was primarily to combat Communism and save the United Nations. He had indeed been accused by Senator McCarthy of being too "soft" on Communism, when in fact he had stood up to Communism with his Truman Doctrine and the Marshall Plan. But there was a great deal of crime and corruption in the days of Truman, and although the President seems not to have been personally involved in it, there was no doubt much wrongdoing among his cronies and subordinates of the "mink dynasty."

CHAPTER 33

Dwight David Eisenhower
1953–1961

I don't believe that criticism that is honest and fair hurts anybody. . . . Criticism of public figures is a good thing.

Dwight D. Eisenhower, press
conference, April 10, 1957

Except for President Grant, Eisenhower was the only West Pointer ever to occupy the Presidential chair. As in the case of Grant, his reputation as a war hero was primarily responsible for his elevation to the White House. Also like Grant he was inclined to shield misbehaving subordinates, but he learned a good deal while on the job. He finally made a better President, despite serious handicaps, than the voters of the country deserved for electing to high political office a man whose chief assets were a highly successful military record and a glamorous grin.

Soldier that he was, Eisenhower was prone to pass on to politically experienced advisers much of the responsibility for major decisions. Conspicuous among his Cabinet members was Secretary of State John Foster Dulles, who set new records in flying enormous distances to foreign countries. General Eisenhower, long in the public eye, evidently did not relish any more of center stage than he already occupied, with the result that much of his decision-making consisted of ratifying the recommendations of lieutenants.

When Senator Joseph McCarthy launched his wild attacks on alleged Communists in government, Eisenhower was reluctant to rush to the defense of those falsely accused. He remarked that he did not want to get "into the gutter with that guy." When one fights with a skunk one will come out smelling like one's adversary, even if triumphant.

In July 1956 Secretary Dulles abruptly withdrew American financial support for the proposed high dam on the upper Nile, and in retaliation, President Nasser of Egypt seized the Suez Canal. Britain and France attacked Egypt, but Eisenhower, loyally supporting America's commitment to the United Nations, turned against his NATO allies. When the Soviet Union sided with the United States, the crestfallen invaders were forced to withdraw. The White House warrior won a victory for peace but at the cost of temporarily rupturing the NATO alliance. At least he was on the side of his nation's solemn obligations to the United Nations Organization.

Eisenhower also won credit for belated honorable conduct, but not much else, in his handling or mishandling of the affair involving America's U-2 spy plane over the Soviet Union. This airplane was specially designed to fly higher than the range of enemy anti-aircraft fire. Such aerial surveillance had been going on for about four years, to the deep annoyance of the Soviets, when, on May 1, 1960, one of the intruders was shot down and its lone American pilot was captured some 1,200 miles inside the Soviet Union.

A series of lying denials was quickly forthcoming from various underlings in Washington. These reactions were so obviously clumsy attempts to cover up the truth that "Honest Ike" Eisenhower finally decided to assume in public all responsibility for the spy flights. His candor was unprecedented in diplomacy, for although all major nations and some minor ones engage in espionage, they do not talk about it in public.

Eisenhower could have sacked some underling or underlings, or he could have said "regrettable, if true." In this way he could have cast some doubt on the Soviets, who were notorious for twisting the truth. The Soviets had offered Eisenhower a face-saving "out" by saying that they could not believe that he had ordered the incursions. But for the President to proclaim that he had not known what was going on in his own administration would have reflected unfavorably on his leadership. So he gallantly came clean, with the result that a summit conference in Paris, including Soviet Premier Khrushchev, turned into a kind of bull ring in which the Russian upbraided a red-faced Eisenhower. The returning war hero, having kept his legendary temper, was greeted by American crowds carrying banners, "Thank you, Mr. President." Actually, there was little to thank him for except his having preserved his dignity in the face of extreme provocation.

As for money-honesty, Eisenhower suffered great embarrassment during the presidential election of 1952 from charges that his vice presidential running mate, Richard M. Nixon, had been receiving about $18,000 a year from a group of California businessmen since his election as United States Senator in 1950. This revelation was especially embarrassing to Eisenhower, for his campaigners had stressed the widespread payola in Washington during the "mink dynasty" of President Truman.

Nixon, though a scared man, saved his skin by a virtuoso performance on nationwide television. In his famous "Checkers speech," he insisted that the money in question had been used only to meet political expenses, and he endeavored to prove that he had not profited personally. He further stated that his wife wore only a respectable Republican cloth coat (a slap at Truman's "mink dynasty"), and that his six-year-old daughter had received the gift of a cocker spaniel (named "Checkers") from a Nixon admirer in Texas. The family loved the little pet and was not going to give it back—a surefire appeal to the large dog-lover vote.

The response to this tear-jerking "Checkers speech" was so overwhelmingly favorable as to save Nixon's skin. Eisenhower met him at the airport, held out a friendly hand, and declared "You're my boy." Thus ended all serious talk of throwing Nixon off the Republican ticket.

Eisenhower was preeminently the candidate of the businessmen, but their employment in government was bound to involve serious conflicts of interest, especially in the awarding of contracts. The Senate Armed Services Committee held up the confirmation of the five nominees slated to head the various armed services until each man agreed to dispose of any business holdings that might create a conflict of interest.

These new standards of financial behavior forced Eisenhower to accept the resignation of a half-dozen or so second-drawer appointees. They were involved in such questionable activities as steering business toward their own firms; concluding contracts with businesses controlled by their wives or in-laws; displaying political favoritism in handling insurance business; and accepting loans and other favors from applicants for licenses. Most of these cases raised questions of propriety rather than outright illegality.

Of special embarrassment to Eisenhower was the Secretary of the Air Force, Harold E. Talbott. He was not a close friend but on occasion had played bridge at the White House. The roof fell in during the summer of 1955 when a Senate committee discovered that Talbott had used both his position and Air Force stationery to drum up business for a company in which he had a half-interest. Eisenhower forced Talbott's resignation by insisting that the conduct of a public servant had to be impeccable on both legal and ethical grounds. Democratic critics complained loudly that the wrongdoer had been let off with a mere slap on the wrist.

In 1955 a different issue was raised by the House Judiciary Committee, which was probing charges that officials within the Department of Commerce were influencing government policy in such a way as to enrich their own firms. A demand by the Judiciary Committee for official files was met with the reply "executive privilege" would prevent these records from being turned over and used by Congress for a "fishing expedition." Eisenhower, seeking to protect his executive branch of the government, ruled that the individual departments concerned were free to determine whether or not they would submit private papers to Congressional scrutiny. This same issue was to make headlines again during the impeachment proceedings against President Nixon in the 1970s.

As a rock-ribbed conservative, Eisenhower instinctively had taken a dislike to the enormous power project established by the federal government under the Tennessee Valley Authority. To him, this agency exemplified "creeping socialism." In 1953 he declared in a cabinet meeting that, "by God," he would like to see the TVA sold to private enterprise. Some months later, when the city of Memphis required increasing amounts of public power, he favored having private enterprise fill this need, rather than going to the expense of increasing the output of the already colossal TVA.

In due season Eisenhower authorized the appropriate federal officials to enter into negotiations with two private power companies, headed respectively by Edgar Dixon and Eugene Yates, to supply the electrical needs of Memphis. Thus was born the abortive Dixon-Yates power syndicate. Soon thereafter Eisenhower was accused of "cronyism," because the chief adviser of the government on the Dixon-Yates contract, Adolphe Wenzell, had, among other improprieties, been vice president of the company that stood to gain by financing the proposed costly operation.

Eisenhower offered to open to the public the official records of the government relating to the transaction in question. But the documentation thus made available apparently was not complete, notably in omitting the name of the key outside adviser, Wenzell, and it contained other excisions and falsifications. From the Democrats in Congress came charges of a cover-up and the improper invocation of executive privilege. The President's own explanations at press conferences were neither complete nor completely accurate, but such shortcomings appear to have been primarily the result of ignorance and innocence. His staff seems to have been much more blameworthy in this area than the President himself.

Eisenhower took himself off the hot seat when he ordered the Atomic Energy Commission (AEC) to cancel its formal agreement with the Dixon-Yates firm. He acted thus in response to the decision of Memphis promoters to build a municipal power plant of their own. This solution fell in so neatly with the President's own preference for local ownership that he felt fully justified in having supported private enterprise in the Dixon-Yates controversy. Eisenhower's reputation for honesty came out slightly bruised but he could properly be charged with only a certain amount of ignorance and naiveté.

After the prolonged outcry of the Republicans against the cronyism, conflict of interest, and influence-peddling under the Democratic President Truman, the Sherman Adams scandal under President Eisenhower brought in its train an acutely embarrassing uproar. Adams was Chief of the White House staff and assistant to the President, and highly valued for his no-nonsense efficiency and sterling integrity. As a former governor of

New Hampshire and onetime member of the New Hampshire legislature and the United States Congress, Adams was no greenhorn in politics or business. He should have known better than to become involved in even the appearance of evil. President Eisenhower retained the highest regard for him as a topnotch adviser and as a paragon of honesty—as cold, hard, and clean as the granite from Adams's New Hampshire hills.

Sherman Adams came to the White House in 1953, but not until early in 1958 did troublesome allegations against him begin to leak out. A sub-committee of Congress then heard that Adams, at the request of a prominent Republican attorney, had earlier discussed a pending case with the acting chairman of the Civil Aeronautics Board. In one letter to the attorney, Adams had passed on some advice as to legal strategy that had been given to him by the chairman in question. Such a backdoor approach to the Board violated its rules, but this irregularity made little stir at the time.

Worse was yet to come. In June of 1958 Congressional investigators turned up evidence proving that a prominent New England industrialist, Bernard Goldfine, had paid some $1,600 in hotel bills at a prominent Boston hotel for Sherman Adams late in 1955 and early in 1958. The official probers further claimed that Goldfine had received preferential treatment by both the Federal Trade Commission and the Securities and Exchange Commission because of the industrialist's connection with Adams.

Adams promptly branded these charges as "unwarranted and unfair." Freely admitting that Goldfine had paid his large bills at the Boston hotel, he also conceded that he had made brief and routine inquiries at the two federal agencies concerned on behalf of the industrialist. But he denied that his telephone calls had any effect one way or the other on any favors extended to or denied Goldfine. Neither Goldfine nor Eisenhower seemed ever to realize that a call or note from the White House to a federal agency on behalf of an interested party carried with it the subtle implication that the applicant should receive, if not favorable, at least sympathetic treatment.

Goldfine's denials were greatly weakened by new revelations in the press. These showed that Adams had received valuable gifts from Goldfine, including a $2,400 oriental rug and a $700 vicuna coat. Adams insisted that the rug was only a loan, and the vicuna coat was worth only $69 at Goldfine's mills. The two men, so the beneficiary declared, were intimate friends who regularly exchanged expensive gifts. But further probing revealed that Goldfine had also given expensive gifts to a number of other persons, including several Senators and 23 governors, in a position to help him in his business. More than that, he had charged these outlays off as legitimate expenses on his income tax returns, including the "loaned" oriental rug. The investigators also found that Goldfine had paid one of Adams's bills at a New York hotel in 1954, a revelation that undermined Adams's contention that the industrialist had maintained permanent accommodations at the Boston hotel on a continuing basis.

Goldfine's credibility, as well as that of Sherman Adams, suffered a further setback when the gift-giving businessman refused to answer a barrage of questions about his financial practices voiced by the Congressional subcommittee. He was cited for contempt of Congress and subsequently convicted of this charge.

Jubilant Democrats made much political hay out of the relatively minor indiscretions of Sherman Adams. The royal pastel mink coat of the Truman dynasty seemed to pale beside the relatively inexpensive vicuna coat of the Eisenhower dynasty. At press conferences, and later in his memoirs, the embattled Eisenhower expressed undying confidence in the integrity of his chief assistant. He conceded that Sherman Adams may have been "imprudent" but that "a gift is not necessarily a bribe. One is evil, the other is a tangible expression of friendship."

Eisenhower, the military man, seems not to have realized that when an official in public life accepts valuable presents from a businessman in private life, the recipient becomes in some degree the "bought man" of the giver. The beneficiary finds it embarrassing to show ingratitude by later denying a seemingly reasonable request by the benefactor. In his final news conference on this subject Eisenhower delivered what he called his last word on this disagreeable Adams-Goldfine affair. He declared, "I personally like Governor Adams. I admire his abilities. I respect him because of his personal and official integrity. I need him."

The need for Adams became increasingly less apparent to Eisenhower's Republican party. The returns in the Congressional elections in Maine in the autumn of 1958 revealed that the party in power was being hurt by the continued presence of the gift-receiver in the White House. Adams was either asked or forced to resign. In a bitter television address he denied all wrongdoing.

Eisenhower's letter accepting this resignation spoke in the most glowing terms of Adams' "brilliant" and "unselfish" work and gave assurances that the assistant had enjoyed throughout "my complete trust, confidence, and respect." Eisenhower's memoirs, published seven years later, shower the highest praise on the discredited Adams.

Loyalty to a faithful and efficient subordinate is a trait that high-ranking officers may carry over from their military life. General Grant, the only other West Pointer, reminds one of Eisenhower in his support of henchmen who had strayed from the straight and narrow path of virtue. Both Presidents accepted gifts of considerable value from private citizens, perhaps thinking that such benefactions were just rewards for having led the nation to victory in great wars. These two men evidently were not disposed to brand as bribes what suspicious citizens and seasoned politicians were inclined to look upon as a down payment for possible favors to come.

It is indeed ironical that while Sherman Adams was under heavy fire for exchanging or accepting gifts of relatively minor value, President Eisenhower came under considerable criticism in the press for accepting highly expensive presents for his farm at Gettysburg, Pennsylvania.

Most Presidents have been discreet enough not to have kept gifts of any real value, realizing that the giver may be seeking to pay in advance for favors to be sought later. To avoid giving offense, presents from a "king, prince, or foreign state" can be placed in museums, public buildings, or elsewhere. But there is a fine line between a gift and a down payment on a future favor. Eisenhower clearly allowed that line to be crossed, but so strong was his reputation for honesty that only his severest critics seriously believed that he was ever unduly influenced by these donations. Such benefactions never became a serious political issue, partly because they came from big business Republicans, whom Eisenhower's political philosophy already favored without the added inducement of bribery.

In 1955 one weekly magazine estimated that during the first three years of his first term the President had accepted gifts worth more than $40,000, most of them for livestock and equipment for his Gettysburg farm. About the same time came the gift of a tractor and cultivator from three farm cooperatives. The press stated that the current White House policy was not to refuse valuable gifts, but that no money would be accepted. Eyebrows were raised when a White House aide declared, despite the strict standards set for other federal officials, that "The office of the President is too big to be influenced by any gift."

After considerable comment in the press about gifts for the President, Eisenhower stated in a news conference on July 31, 1957 that because he was an elected official, "the conflict of interest law does not apply to me." A Democratic Senator from Oregon was not backward about criticizing this Republican President for ignoring the spirit of the conflict-of-interest law in having accepted a $4,000-tractor, a $1,000-bull, and thousands of dollars worth of other machinery and livestock for the Gettysburg farm. One estimate by a not too reliable journalist put the figure at $300,000.

Eisenhower defended himself in a news conference (August 7, 1957) by saying that most of these gifts had come from large organizations, had been put on the public record, and had been given for a specific purpose, including beautifying his Gettysburg retreat with bushes that perhaps one day would all become public property. (Indeed, in 1967, six years after leaving office, he deeded this farm to the federal government.) Eisenhower further declared that he never accepted a gift that appeared to be given for a selfish motive, or one from a corporation or business firm. He tried to keep his relations with individuals on a "friendly, decent basis."

Even so, the President was not as circumspect as many of his admirers wished. Perhaps the worst that can be said is that he was naive rather than dishonest. A newcomer to politics, he seems to have had a higher regard for the motives of his benefactors than the facts seemed to warrant.

Shortly before leaving office in 1961, Eisenhower wisely warned the nation of the growing power of the "military-industrial complex." Evidently he had learned something about how corporations secured lucrative defense contracts, often with huge cost overruns, from the Pentagon. He did not say so, but Congress was also involved in this "complex," as influential members steered the enormous appropriations toward their own districts or otherwise kept a finger in the defense pie. Such was the "military-industrial-Congressional complex."

CHAPTER **34**

John F. Kennedy
1961–1963

No responsibility of government is more fundamental than the responsibility of maintaining the highest standards of ethical behavior by those who conduct the public business.

John F. Kennedy, message to
Congress, April 27, 1961

John F. Kennedy emerged as the most famous of four sons born to Joseph P. Kennedy, a multimillionaire Bostonian of Irish Catholic descent. The father gained some fame and much notoriety as Ambassador to Great Britain, 1937–1940, during which service he showed a surprising amount of sympathy for the fast-rising Hitler. At the London Embassy, young John, then a Harvard student, gathered materials for a well-received book titled *Why England Slept* (1940).

Joining the U.S. Navy as a commissioned officer in World War II, young Kennedy did not display exceptional caution or skill when his fragile PT boat was cut in two by a swift Japanese destroyer. Yet he displayed real heroism, for which he was subsequently decorated, in shepherding the survivors ashore. With

becoming modesty, he made light of this achievement, yet he
appears never to have recovered completely from a back injury
suffered in the tragic sinking.

After six years in the national House of Representatives from
1947 to 1953, young Kennedy was elected to the United States
Senate in 1952, and served inconspicuously while partially recovering from his back injury. During this period he wrote a
Pulitzer-Prize-winning book, *Profiles in Courage,* which extolled
the willingness of heroic figures in public life to do what was right
in the face of angry public disapproval. This was the era when
Senator Joseph McCarthy of Wisconsin was hounding out of public office men who were allegedly tainted with the red badge of
Communism. Countless Americans became hysterically more
fearful of the supposed Communists under the bed than they
were of the Communists in the Kremlin.

During all this uproar the young profile in courage from
Massachusetts was reacting with a low profile to the vicious assaults on many loyal citizens by "low-blow Joe" McCarthy. For a
part of the time Kennedy had the excuse that he was recovering
from an operation on his injured back, but he made clear to
friends that it would be political suicide to condemn Mc-
Carthyism. In a private conversation he said, "Hell, half my voters
in Massachusetts look on McCarthy as a hero." The Irish Catholics of the Bay State had no love for atheistic Communism, and
Kennedy fully realized that he could best serve his people in Congress by being elected and re-elected.

No Catholic had ever been elected President of the United
States, though Al Smith had made a valiant try in 1928. A widespread fear persisted that the Pope was just waiting to bring influence to bear on the White House. Yet John F. Kennedy managed
to win the presidential nomination on the Democratic ticket in
1960, thanks in large part to clever campaigning and his father's
financial backing. The successful candidate made much of the
alleged missile gap in America's defenses against the Soviet
Union. He later said in a birthday speech (May 27, 1961) that
when he got into office he was most surprised to find that "things
were just as bad as we'd been saying they were." But this is the
usual course of politics.

Kennedy also made an asset out of his biggest handicap, his
religion. Using reverse psychology, he urged Americans to rise
above narrow-minded bigotry and show the world they could be

big enough to vote for a man born to a Catholic family. Why should good Americans be denied the White House forever simply because of their religion?

In this heated presidential campaign of 1960, much hinged on the so-called joint debates involving Richard M. Nixon and Kennedy, for which there were no official judges. In the first encounter Nixon, just having been released from a hospital, appeared thin, pale, and sickly. Kennedy seemed to be bursting with energy and memorized factual data. In the course of these staged clashes Kennedy wanted to know why the Eisenhower-Nixon administration was not doing something behind the scenes to overthrow Cuba's Castro. Preparations for the disastrous Bay of Pigs invasion were then well under way, and Nixon was taken aback because he then supposed, as he claims to have verified later, that Kennedy had been privately alerted to them. Thus trapped, Nixon felt obliged to deny that the Eisenhower administration had any intention of promoting an invasion of Cuba.

Kennedy triumphed at the polls in one of the most closely contested presidential elections in American history. Nixon and Kennedy each garnered over 34 million popular votes, but only 112,707 popular votes separated them. If Illinois and Texas had gone to Nixon, he would have won by a comfortable margin in the Electoral College. In his book, *Six Crises* (1962), Nixon claims that in three precincts in Texas and three in Illinois, in all of which the balloting went heavily for Kennedy, many more votes were recorded than there were names of voters on the official voting lists.

An official recount might or might not have turned up enough votes to elect Nixon; indeed, the chances were good that some Republican irregularities would also surface. Nixon claims in his *Six Crises* that he decided not to insist on a recount because it would cause delay, create confusion, increase bitterness, and blacken the good name of the United States abroad. When we remember the fanatical determination of Nixon to win and win big in 1972, with the help of the Watergate-related crimes, we are entitled to suspect that he did not demand a recount in 1960 because he had more to gain than to lose by such a course. In any event, the winning Kennedy could take little satisfaction in the ethics of some of his supporters in the victory of 1960.

The incoming Kennedy may not have known about the CIA scheme to support an invasion of Cuba by Cuban exiles, but he learned about it soon after he entered the White House. With considerable misgivings he half-heartedly endorsed the operation, but declared on April 12, 1961 that in no circumstances would the armed forces of the United States become *directly* involved. The abortive blow fell five days later. Some official Americans were ultimately sucked in, but this incredibly bungled invasion probably would not have succeeded anyhow. The invading contingent numbered a sparse 1,200 men and Fidel Castro commanded a militia force of some 250,000 men and women on the island.

Kennedy was mistaken if he reasoned that the absence of direct American forces would leave him in an ethically strong position in the eyes of the outside world. The invaders had been trained, armed, and equipped in Guatemala by official agents of the United States. By thus conniving at this coup, the United States, as represented by President Kennedy, was charged with having violated its own neutrality laws, as well as the charter of the United Nations and that of the Organization of American States. President Kennedy seemed to be willing to wound but reluctant to strike.

The American conscience was touched, as was that of the Kennedys, by the 1,100 or so surviving invaders rotting in Cuban jails. Castro demanded a ransom of $53 million in food and medical supplies as recompense for the damages and expenses involved in repulsing the attack. The money was raised by private sources in the United States, and ironically helped to undermine the embargo originally imposed on the island by the United States.

This bungled assault on Cuba appears to have had something to do with the fruitless attempt of the Soviets to emplace nuclear missiles on the island, well within reach of major American cities. In October 1962 Kennedy went to the very brink of a holocaust by forcing the Soviets to withdraw their lethal weapons. The Kremlin, taught a harsh lesson, next embarked upon an armament program that was to give Russia superiority in certain types of nuclear missiles. Such were some of the fruits of sponsoring half-heartedly the Bay of Pigs botch.

Kennedy's tentative support of the anti-Communist regime in South Vietnam, headed by the Catholic Ngo Dinh Diem, raises serious questions not only as to the President's judgment, but also as to a possible conflict between his religion and his constitutional responsibility. Some of these doubts relate to Kennedy's military competence and others to his alleged willingness to go out of his way to support fellow Catholics against Communists pouring down from North Vietnam.

The anti-Communist Truman administration had extended considerable financial support to the French and their loyalist supporters to fight the Vietnam rebels. After France had pulled out following the Geneva conference of 1954, the Eisenhower administration supplied substantial financial backing to the anti-Communist government of President Diem in South Vietnam, and finally went so far as to send in some 700 American military advisers to assist the resisting South Vietnamese.

President Kennedy, in what seems to have been a serious misjudgment, stepped up military aid to the point where there were about 16,000 American military men of various kinds in South Vietnam when he was shot in November 1963. This commitment was a fatal one because the President could not have withdrawn so large a body of troops under enemy fire without an intolerable loss of face for the United States in the eyes of its numerous treaty allies the world over.

When President Kennedy ran for the presidency in 1960, he repeatedly gave assurances that a Catholic could be trusted to govern the nation in the interests of the United States, not those of the Pope or the Catholic church. There was a large Catholic population in South Vietnam, partly because many of the faithful had been expelled from North Vietnam. President Diem, supported by Washington, was a Roman Catholic who had earlier spent some time abroad, mostly in the United States. While there he had lobbied persistently for American support, had met with the then Senator John F. Kennedy, and had won the enthusiastic backing of Cardinal Francis J. Spellman of the archdiocese of New York.

There can be little doubt that President Kennedy felt some concern for the hundreds of thousands of fellow Catholics in South Vietnam who faced possible liquidation by the victorious Communists. What part such sympathy played in his fatal step of committing 16,000 American men to the war cannot be determined. We do know that he became dissatisfied with the stern rule of President Diem, but that he evidently had no hand in the plot to overthrow him. Nor did he scheme to have Diem shot, as happened on November 1, 1963. Coincidentally, Kennedy was himself killed three weeks later.

We recall that the narrow Kennedy-Nixon electoral contest

of 1960 had resulted in many charges, some not altogether groundless, of vote-stealing and other species of fraud. For various reasons, Nixon did not demand a recount and Kennedy saw nothing to be gained and much to be lost in pushing a probe himself. Yet he did go so far in May 1961 as to recommend to Congress legislation designed to strengthen existing regulations against conflict of interest among officeholders.

Shortly thereafter Kennedy's Secretary of the Interior, Stewart Udall, indiscreetly involved himself in an affair that reflected unfavorably on the incumbent administration. Udall, who was a major figure in controlling the nation's natural resources, had asked a prominent executive of an oil company to support a fundraising dinner for Democrats. This businessman was to secure a contribution of $100 for each ticket from other businessmen in the oil and gas industry.

When a vigilant press exposed Udall's transgression, the indiscreet Secretary covered up as best he could by denying any wrongdoing, by claiming that his intentions had been misunderstood by President Kennedy, and by demanding that the solicitations bearing his name be quashed. For his part, the President diverted attention from the accused by mounting an attack on the existing methods of financing political candidacies. He rather unconvincingly remarked that no one should contribute to campaign funds in the expectation that his donation would do the donor "the slightest bit of good." Kennedy must have been fully aware that little campaign money would be wrung from these hardheaded businessmen if they did not expect that their contributions would do them some good, perhaps in the form of higher tariffs, government contracts, or other benefactions. Such donors have commonly hedged their bets by giving equally large sums to each of the two major parties.

The Kennedy administration was singed, though not badly burned, by its involvement with Billie Sol Estes, a prominent speculator from Pecos, Texas, who had visions of cornering the fertilizer market in his area. With credit based on nonexistent tanks of ammonia and other illegalities, he built a remarkable financial empire. But ugly cracks ultimately became glaring, and in April 1962 a federal grand jury indicted Estes on several counts of mail fraud, three counts of illegally transporting securities in interstate commerce, and one count of conspiracy.

Side effects of the Estes operation were soon felt in the Washington government, especially in the Department of Agriculture. A half-dozen or so officials in the lower echelons, having accepted monetary or other favors from Estes, resigned or were fired. Two separate investigations were launched by Congressional subcommittees that probed possible graft in government subsidy programs and in dealings with the Department of Agriculture. Demands arose for a non-partisan inquiry, not just investigations by the Democrats in Congress. There was even some agitation for the dismissal of Secretary of Agriculture Orville L. Freeman.

Freeman did not resign but he did defend himself. He noted that possibly only three employees of his department had received gifts from Estes, who seems not to have gained special treatment in return. The embattled Secretary Freeman was firm in his belief that the government had lost no money to the empire builder.

In public Kennedy staunchly defended the integrity of Secretary Freeman. He noted that his department had indicted Estes, and that if any members of the executive branch were implicated they would be promptly disciplined. Kennedy further declared that 76 FBI agents were working on the case. As could have been anticipated, the partisan Democratic committees absolved the Department of Agriculture of wrongdoing, criticizing it for laxness of supervision, but praising it for clearing house expeditiously as soon as the irregularities were exposed.

The case of Billie Sol Estes was small potatoes indeed compared with the strange case of the TFX fighter-bombers. This scandal involved the awarding by the Department of Defense to the General Dynamics Corporation of a contract to build 1,700 of these aircraft at the colossal cost of $6.5 billion. The job-giving construction would take place in Texas, with the primary subcontractor being located in the state of New York.

This announcement came on November 24, 1962, less than two years before the election of 1964, when President Kennedy presumably would be running for a renewed residence in the White House. New York then had the most electoral votes of any state, 45, and they had gone to Kennedy by much less than a landslide in 1960. Texas had 24 electoral votes, and it had squeezed into the Kennedy column by the margin of a few allegedly fraudulent ballots.

The plot seemingly thickened when Senator Jackson of the state of Washington entered the fray. He learned that the selection board of the Pentagon, consisting of prominent generals and admirals, had found that the proposal submitted by the Boeing Corporation of the state of Washington was technically better and also less expensive than that presented by General Dynamics. Boeing's state of Washington had only 9 electoral votes, and Kansas, where the construction on the Boeing job would take place, had only 8. Boeing could dangle only 17 electoral votes, as compared to 69 for Texas and New York. Senator Jackson evidently had this disparity in mind when he accused the civilian Secretary of Defense and the civilian secretaries of the Air Force and Navy of overruling the Pentagon's selection board and choosing "to buy the second best airplane at the higher price." Possibly relevant was the fact that Texas and New York had narrowly gone for Kennedy in 1960, whereas Washington and Kansas had fallen to Nixon. Additionally, anti-Kennedy feeling in Texas was growing.

A Congressional subcommittee probed into the awarding of the contract but could find no evidence of improper political pressures. President Kennedy clearly approved of the transaction, but the record does not show that he expressed a preference for one or the other of the prime contractors. Yet serious doubts were raised about the conduct of two officials in the Defense Department, as will be related.

Deputy Secretary of Defense Gilpatric was an attorney on leave from his law firm in New York City. Prior to coming to Washington, he had as a lawyer established numerous contacts with General Dynamics. Soon after the TFX contract had been awarded, this favored corporation chose Gilpatric's former law firm to be the ccmpany's counsel. Critics believed that this lawyer on leave should have disqualified himself from having had any part in the TFX decision. President Kennedy expressed the highest regard for his subordinate, who finally left Washington and rejoined his old firm. After he was gone the investigating Congressional subcommittee declared that Gilpatric had been "guilty of a flagrant conflict of interest" in the General Dynamics (TFX) decision.

A more serious embarrassment to the Kennedy administration in the TFX affair was Secretary of the Navy Fred Korth. Before coming to Washington, he had been president of a bank in Fort Worth, Texas, in which capacity he had approved a loan of $400,000 to General Dynamics. While Secretary of the Navy he had retained $160,000 of stock in the bank of which he had been head. During the TFX contract discussions, he had made 16 contacts with General Dynamics but only two with rival Boeing.

At first President Kennedy stood loyally behind Korth, but more evidence about the banker's conflict of interest kept surfacing, and his days as a Secretary in Washington were numbered. Kennedy omitted the usual regrets in his letter of acceptance, but conspicuously thanked Korth for what he had done to improve the Navy.

The Kennedy administration appears to have harbored no desire to have the TFX scandal made worse than it seemed to be. Word was spread that Korth had to resign because of his opposition to a nuclear-powered aircraft carrier. In a press conference Kennedy declared flatly but improbably that he had no evidence whatever that Korth had "acted improperly" in the TFX matter. On the morning of November 22, 1963, Kennedy spoke to the Fort Worth Chamber of Commerce, declaring that the TFX was "the best fighter system in the world," and promising that it would save the taxpayers a total of one billion dollars. Later that same day the President lay dead.

As for money-honesty, the millionaire Kennedy presents no problem. As for political honesty, he was more tender with indiscreet subordinates, notably Korth, than he should have been. It could be that he was trying to court a Texas that had gone for him in 1960 by, allegedly, only a handful of fraudulent votes.

As for moral honesty, more whispering circulated about Kennedy's unfaithfulness to his marriage vows than had tarnished any other incumbent. Where there was so much smoke there may have been some fire. One of the President's alleged paramours has written a book about her nocturnal trysts at the White House, but she may have been a rumor-monger more interested in writing a best seller than in recording facts. If all these tales are true, whether oral or printed, one is inclined to be more awed by Kennedy's virility than distressed by his immorality. In any event, such extracurricular activities, if they occurred, appear not to have interfered significantly with his presidential duties.

CHAPTER **35**

Lyndon Baines Johnson
1963–1969

I'm a compromiser and a maneuverer. I try to get something. That's the way our system works.

Lyndon B. Johnson, quoted in *The New York Times*, December 8, 1963

A born politician, Lyndon Johnson first saw the light of day in a farming community, deep in the heart of Texas, as the Taft-Bryan presidential campaign of 1908 was getting well under way. Coming up through the public schools, he graduated from the Southwest Texas State Teachers College, and for a short time served as a high school teacher in the city of Houston.

Johnson entered active political life through the back door when in 1932 he became secretary to Texas Congressman Sam Rayburn. Through Rayburn's good offices the young aspirant was appointed director in Texas of the National Youth Administration (1935).

An ambitious Johnson was elected to the national House of Representatives from 1937 to 1946, though defeated in his bold try for the Senate in 1941. Still retaining his seat in the House, he

served briefly as an officer in the U.S. Navy in the Pacific, whereupon he was called back to Congress in 1942. In 1948 he was
elected to the Senate after having won the Democratic primaries
by the margin of 87 votes, a turn of fortune that led to the name
"Landslide Lyndon." There were ugly rumors of ballot-box stuffing and other skulduggery, but the paper-thin count was allowed
to stand.

Now in his chosen element, the ambitious Johnson rose to
the position of Democratic whip in the Senate (1951) and then
floor leader. After 1954 he served as majority leader and admin-
istrator-in-chief of the "Johnson treatment," which was supposed
to mean seizing an opponent by the coat lapels, sticking one's face
into his, and arguing so vociferously that the victim had to surrender in self-defense. As an arm-twisting and flesh-pressing
wheeler-dealer who could make things move, Johnson was acknowledged to be without a peer as an achiever in Washington.
Though a Democrat, he deserves much credit for having shepherded President Eisenhower's Republican legislative program
through a Democratic Congress, and the tall and talented Texan
gained much praise for his bipartisan approach.

Failing to wrest the presidential nomination from John F.
Kennedy in 1960, Johnson humbly accepted the second-fiddle
vice presidential prize and campaigned strenuously for his former
rival. As the rear of his train pulled out of town, he would reportedly shout in his best hog-calling voice, "What has Dick Nixon
ever done for Culpepper?"—or whatever the town happened to
be. The Kennedy-Johnson ticket carried Johnson's Texas in 1960
by an extremely narrow (and controversial) margin, and the evidence more than suggests that Kennedy might well have lost if
Johnson had not loyally given his all for the common cause.

President Kennedy had come to the White House with a widely
heralded "New Frontier" program, designed to achieve sweeping
economic and social reforms. He was making discouraging progress with a balky Democratic Congress when assassinated in Dal-
las, Texas, November 22, 1963. Johnson seized the falling torch
with eager hands and in an impressive demonstration of leadership he rammed through Congress a series of measures, including a stalled tax-cut proposal, a farm program, the landmark Civil
Rights Act of 1964, and the funding for a losing billion-dollar
"War on Poverty."

After this impressive showing, Johnson was nominated for

the presidency in his own right in 1964. During the subsequent campaign he unveiled his "Great Society" program, involving economic reform, civil rights, and welfare measures that were to an impressive degree enacted by Congress. Johnson's Republican rival for the presidency, Senator Barry Goldwater, was so indiscreet as to suggest the use of tactical nuclear weapons to assist the relatively small contingent of American troops in Vietnam. Rival Democrats cried in alarm that Goldwater was scheming to provoke a nuclear war in which the living world would envy the dead. But President Johnson assured an audience in Akron, Ohio (October 21, 1964): "We're not about to send American boys nine or ten thousand miles away from home to do what Asian boys ought to be doing for themselves." If ever a campaign promise was broken, this one was.

Doubts as to Johnson's candor ("the credibility gap") deepened as a result of the Tonkin Gulf incident, August 2–4, 1964. Without the knowledge of Congress, ships of the U.S. Navy had been cooperating provocatively with those of the South Vietnamese in missions along the coast of North Vietnam. Two of these U.S. destroyers were reportedly fired upon by North Vietnamese torpedo boats in the Tonkin Gulf, without loss of life or significant damage to the American vessels. Despite subsequent investigations, what actually happened remains somewhat unclear.

Critics of Johnson then and later charged that he had deliberately provoked this Tonkin Gulf encounter so that he could make political hay out of the incident by seizing upon this excuse to fight back. Johnson was a great admirer of President Franklin Roosevelt, whom the Texan called his political "daddy," and we recall that Roosevelt had used the provocative *Greer* incident, September 4, 1941, to justify attacks on German U-boats.

Johnson falsely claimed, like Roosevelt after the *Greer* clash, that the United States had suffered an unprovoked attack in the Tonkin Gulf. He ordered a "limited" but devastating aerial assault (64 sorties) against nearby North Vietnamese naval bases, along about one hundred miles of the coast, all the while proclaiming that he sought "no wider war."

Johnson's two-fisted response to foreigners who dared fire upon intruding American destroyers no doubt struck a patriotic chord among countless American voters. Many of them trusted the President's assurances that he sought "no wider war," contrary to what Goldwater was supposed to be proposing. Johnson took full advantage of this rising war spirit to rush through Congress his fateful Tonkin Gulf resolution. Entangling though it was, it cleared the House of Representatives with no voting dissent, and the Senate with only two negative votes out of 90 cast.

The blank-check Tonkin Gulf resolution of August 7, 1964, clothed the President with power "to take all necessary measures to repel any armed attack against the forces of the United States and *to prevent further aggression.*" The words here italicized threw the door wide open, for the President was left free to recognize what he judged to be aggression. And he made the most of his opportunities.

Curiously indeed, and unknown to Congress, Johnson's underlings in Washington had already prepared a draft of this Tonkin Gulf resolution more than two months earlier, and these advisers had also chosen possible targets for the aerial strikes. This is contingency-planning with a vengeance.

It is difficult to avoid the suspicion that Johnson, a master wheeler-dealer, deliberately and for political purposes secretly provoked the Tonkin Gulf incident. It helped him in his bid for reelection, beyond a doubt, and it enabled him to railroad through Congress the entrapping Tonkin Gulf resolution. Many of the members who voted for it were not fully aware of what they were doing, and later regretted their action. But by that time the United States was knee-deep in the Vietnam War, and Congress recoiled from repealing the resolution when American boys were bleeding and dying in the jungles of Vietnam. Johnson was elected overwhelmingly in his own right in November 1964, and before the end of 1965 there were 184,000 American troops in Vietnam, the vanguard of more than a half-million to come.

Closer to home, suspicions also clung to Johnson's armed intervention in the Dominican Republic in April 1965. A bloody uprising by left-wing elements against the right-wing (and Washington-backed) government ultimately cost some 2,000 Dominican lives and jeopardized American citizens. The United States ambassador, supported by his eight subordinates, appealed for an armed intervention by Washington to protect hundreds of American lives. Four days after the eruption, Johnson helicoptered in several hundred American troops, adding to them later until they ultimately numbered about 25,000.

Grim-faced President Johnson had a difficult choice to make.

Not since 1933 and the days of Roosevelt's Good Neighbor policy had American troops profaned Latin-American soil, and Washington's permitting Latin Americans to have their own revolutions in their own way had become an unquestionable feature of Good Neighborism. But Johnson appeared on television to explain that he was not solely concerned about American lives but that he could not permit a Communist-dominated Dominican Republic to become another Caribbean cancer, in the fashion of Castro's Cuba.

Latin Americans could understand why Johnson would want to protect American lives, but they accused him of deception in dragging in the Communist bogey. Two principles were involved. Many Latin Americans claimed that the Communist influence was exaggerated, because the Department of State could name only few known Communists in the unhappy republic. Besides, a basic principle of Good Neighborism was that the independent republics of Latin America should be allowed to enjoy the right of revolution and to have any kind of government that they chose.

Fortunately for Johnson, the Organization of American States was persuaded to authorize a neutral Inter-American peace force, to which five Latin American nations ultimately sent at least token manpower. Command of the policing visitors was given to a Brazilian general, although the United States had by far the largest contingent. Under the calming auspices of the Organization of American States, new elections were held in June 1966. The moderately right-wing candidate defeated his moderately leftist opponent by a wide margin. Obviously the Dominicans were tired of bloodshed, and President Johnson escaped from this embarrassing entrapment in better shape than could have been predicted when the intervention first began.

As for Southeast Asia, there can be little doubt that President Johnson's decision to plunge deeper into the Vietnam War was motivated in part by a desire to attract votes from the "hawks," who naturally gave him strong vocal support. He was also worried, or professed to be, by the so-called Communist monolith, especially as exhibited by the takeover of China in 1949 and the incursion into Korea in 1950. Actually there had never been a monolith, especially not after the Soviet-Chinese split in the early 1960s. Yet both the Soviets and the Chinese sent enormous quantities of military supplies to the North Vietnamese who were battling Americans.

President Johnson and fellow hawks believed, or professed to believe, that unless the United States effectively halted Communism in Vietnam, the embattled Americans would ultimately be desperately defending their own beaches against Communist invaders. In view of the bitter antagonism between Communist Russia and Communist China, one can hardly believe that President Johnson's vigorous prosecution of the Vietnam War was really motivated by such exaggerated fears. But he undoubtedly remembered the taunting Republican battle cry against the Democrats, "Who lost China?"

The Vietcong guerrillas in South Vietnam, with much support from North Vietnam, seemed to be near collapse when, in January 1968, they launched their Tet holiday offensive against 30 key cities and towns. Although finally beaten off with bloody losses on both sides, the shadowy Vietcong guerrillas amply demonstrated that the war was far from won by the American intruders and their allies. Popular support in America for the futile fighting sagged dramatically, and criticism of Johnson's handling of the war rose frighteningly.

At this point politics reared its head in a startling way. President Johnson was generally assumed to be a candidate in 1968 for a second full term on the Democratic ticket. Yet on March 31, 1968, he appeared on television to announce dramatically that he would wind down the unpopular Vietnam War unilaterally, and that he definitely would not accept another nomination. In his memoirs he declared rather convincingly that he had made the decision to "abdicate" some months before his announcement, and that he had been concerned with the strain of office, his weariness, his ill health, and his short life expectancy. Ironically, he died on January 22, 1973, only four years and two days after the end of the four-year term for which a president is elected.

President Johnson's later explanations seem rather persuasive, but given his "credibility gap" many critics jumped to the conclusion that he had bowed out primarily because of fear that he could not win the Democratic nomination again, much less the election. The first real shocker had come in the early presidential primary held in New Hampshire in March 1968. Little-known Senator Eugene McCarthy, a leading "dove" regarding Vietnam, gleaned an incredible 42 percent of the Democratic vote to 49 percent for Johnson, and the senator won 20 of the 24 convention delegates. But the president had been a write-in candidate, and considering this handicap had attracted a much stronger plurality than the tally alone indicated. In fact, Johnson had deliberately refrained from entering a number of primaries he would not have ignored if he had been making serious plans to succeed himself.

Senator Robert F. Kennedy, the dead President's brother, now sprang forward. Enheartened by the questionable evidence from the New Hampshire polls of Johnson's unpopularity with the antiwar doves, Kennedy threw his hat into the ring of the ensuing Democratic primaries. His vigorous campaign was crowned with victory—and assassination—in the California primaries. Vice President Hubert Humphrey received the Democratic nomination in 1968, and then narrowly lost to Richard M. Nixon.

Despite Johnson's plausible explanation of the "abdication" in his autobiography, *The Vantage Point* (1971), doubts will still linger. If he had bowed out of the primary race *before* McCarthy's startling showing in New Hampshire, there would be little argument. But the timing of the withdrawal suggests that Johnson feared defeat if he ran again.

As for money-honesty, serious questions were raised during the presidency of Lyndon Johnson about his family fortune, for this President may have been the wealthiest man ever to occupy the White House in terms of then current dollars. His assets of about $14 million had been mainly acquired after he entered the Senate in 1948 and acquired national power. Centrally at issue was ownership of the radio-television station KTBC, which, as the only enterprise of its kind, enjoyed a monopoly in the city of Austin, Texas, with its 200,000 or so people. The activities of this lucrative enterprise were governed by the Federal Communications Commission (FCC), a branch of that same national government of which Senator Johnson was also an influential part.

After falling heir to the presidency, Johnson was advised by his aides that propriety required him to disassociate himself from a private enterprise controlled by an arm of the Washington government. A blind trust was therefore established to take care of these properties, but the trustee chosen by the Johnsons was an old friend whom the President saw frequently on social occasions. Doubts were created as well as allayed, and strong suspicions were voiced as to an improper conflict of interest.

In December 1963, the month after Kennedy's death, Johnson and KTBC were again in the news. The Federal Communications Commission again upheld the Johnson television monopoly, while denying an application for a competitive community service. In two press conferences in April 1964, the President was less than candid. On the first occasion he declared, "I have no interest in any television any place." He was hiding, of course, behind the blind trust. On the second occasion he insisted, "I don't have any interest in government-regulated industries of any kind and never have had." The television stock was actually in the name of Mrs. Johnson and his two daughters. Johnson cleverly employed indirection in such a fashion as to tell the truth while giving currency to a species of untruth.

During the summer of 1964, when Johnson was running for President, various newspapers and magazines publicized various unproved suspicions about this wealth. Nor were these critics willing to accept the President's own story that Mrs. "Lady Bird" Johnson was the creator of this fortune, and that Johnson, the master wheeler-dealer, had refrained from bringing pressure of any kind on the governmental agencies concerned.

After *Life* magazine had estimated the family fortune to be $14 million, Johnson vainly brought pressure on the publishers to have the article dropped or at least revised. Johnson promptly released an audit prepared by a well-known accounting firm, and it placed the Johnson family assets at $3.5 million. The wheeler-dealer evidently was at work somewhere, for his shrunken figure represented the pre-inflation market value some two decades earlier. Suspicions to the contrary notwithstanding, critics failed to turn up convincing evidence of direct and improper pressure upon government agencies.

The highly publicized Bobby Baker scandal had little direct relationship to President Johnson, and it proved far more devastating to the clandestine dealings of Baker than to the presidential aspirations of the talented Texan. Robert G. Baker was a clever but slippery young man whom Senator Johnson had managed to have selected as majority secretary of the United States Senate in 1955. Apparently Johnson developed a fatherly affection for him.

In 1957 a Maryland insurance salesman, Donald B. Reynolds, sold Lyndon Johnson a $100,000 life insurance policy. Subsequently Bobby Baker, whom Reynolds had taken into his firm as vice president, suggested (or claimed he did) that Reynolds make a gift to Senator Johnson of a high-fidelity stereophonic phonograph in which Mrs. Johnson had shown an interest. Senator Johnson later testified that the gift, worth $584.75 had come from Bobby Baker. Indeed, the two families had exchanged gifts before, and Johnson could well afford to buy the set for his wife.

Yet the Bobby Baker affair was used by the Republicans to pin charges of corruption on President Johnson, who had been only a Senator when the gift of the stereo was made, and obviously in no position to bestow presidential favors. In 1966, while Johnson was President, a grand jury indicted Baker on nine counts of fraud, conspiracy to defraud the government, and evasion of income taxes. None of these charges related to Senator Johnson's connection with this underling. In 1967 Baker was convicted on seven of the counts and sentenced to prison.

At the Republican national convention in San Francisco, where Goldwater was nominated, the keynote orator drew a laugh when he declared that no matter how carefully one sweeps a stereo set under the White House rug, the bulge still shows. The truth is that the Bobby Baker scandal touched President Johnson only lightly and indirectly, and its relationship to Senator, not President, Johnson fell far short of being a major scandal.

In 1964, on the eve of Johnson's bid for election in his own right, a sex scandal shocked the nation. Walter Jenkins, the White House chief of staff, was arrested in the men's room of a YMCA building, one block from the White House, on a charge involving homosexuality. President Johnson was then in New York, and his agents in Washington made a determined effort to keep the story out of the newspapers. They succeeded only temporarily.

At first blush, the Jenkins scandal seemed to be extremely damaging to Johnson's prospects for reelection. For one thing, homosexual government officials were judged to be especially vulnerable to blackmailers, domestic or foreign, who could supposedly pressure them into revealing state secrets. President Johnson countered criticism by accepting the resignation of the overworked Jenkins, and then, after Jenkins was hospitalized, arranging for a hasty investigation by the FBI. Not surprisingly, Johnson's sleuths found that there had been no leakage of state secrets. Fighting back, the President privately threatened to dig up evidence of homosexuality among prominent Republicans, for he had access to the confidential files of the FBI. Whatever the reasons, the Jenkins scandal gradually faded into the background, and President Johnson overwhelmed Senator Barry

Goldwater on election day. A popular pro-Johnson campaign slogan had been "All the Way with LBJ!" An off-color paraphrase by Republicans went, "Either Way with LBJ!"

Ironically, few people believed that Johnson was a homosexual, but the Washington whispering gallery remained convinced that he was less than a completely faithful husband.

CHAPTER 36

Richard M. Nixon
1969–1974

In all my years of public life, I have never obstructed justice. People have got to know whether or not their President is a crook. Well, I'm not a crook; I earned everything I've got.

Richard Nixon, speech, 1973

Richard M. Nixon, born in southern California in 1913, graduated from the nearby Whittier College and later the Duke University School of Law. After practicing law in his home state and working for the Office of Price Administration in Washington, Nixon joined the Navy in 1943 as a junior officer and served in the Pacific theater. After being twice elected to the national House of Representatives, he won a seat in the United States Senate in 1950 by defeating Helen Gahagan Douglas in a campaign that grossly over-stressed her left-wing leanings. Though victorious, Nixon earned for himself the lasting title of "Tricky Dick."

As a Republican, Nixon was elected vice president of the United States in 1952 and again in 1956, although he came close to being thrown off the ticket in 1952 when word leaked out that he had been benefiting in his professional life from a secret "slush fund" of some $18,000, provided over a two-year period by a group of wealthy California business men. This under-the-table financing was more a case of impropriety than criminality, and, as previously noted, a frightened Nixon appeared on television and rode out the storm with his melodramatic Checkers speech.

In 1960 Nixon was nominated by the Republicans as their candidate to succeed President Eisenhower, but he lost the ensuing election by an extremely narrow and questionable margin. Hitting the comeback trail in 1962, he ran for the governorship of California but was soundly rebuffed. After moving to New York City to practice law, he was nominated for President on the Republican ticket and narrowly defeated Democrat Hubert Humphrey in 1968.

Both candidates had committed themselves to waging the Vietnam War until the enemy would accept an "honorable peace," and this happy outcome was taken to mean an American victory. Nixon had declared publicly that he knew how to "end the war" and "win the peace," if elected. But he declined to reveal details, so he patriotically explained, for fear of jeopardizing the peace negotiations with North Vietnam then stalemated in Paris.

As President, Nixon managed to withdraw the American fighting men gradually from Vietnam, but he did not bring "peace with honor," as he claimed. He took slightly more than four years to accomplish this alleged feat, thus achieving the distinction of presiding over the longest major foreign war in the nation's history.

In 1972, twelve days before Nixon's bid for reelection, Secretary of State Kissinger returned from the Paris negotiations to proclaim that peace was "at hand." Skeptical Democrats replied that if this boon was at hand, it should have come some four years sooner, thus sparing thousands of American casualties. But Nixon forthrightly declared that he would approve the proposed accord "only when the agreement is right." With peace seemingly in the bag, he won an overwhelming victory over Senator George McGovern, the Democratic nominee.

During the month after the election, the fighting on both sides in Vietnam escalated, and Nixon launched a furious bombing of North Vietnam in what was cynically called the "Christmas blitz." The cost to the Americans in bombers and human lives was considerable, but this sacrifice seemed to be the only way to in-

duce the North Vietnamese to release some 500 American prisoners of war and come to the peace table seeking peace.

Evidently this blistering bombing had the desired effect, because North Vietnam reluctantly agreed to cease-fire arrangements in January 1973, about three months after peace had been
declared to be at hand. By the terms of the agreement, the United
States would withdraw its remaining 27,000 troops, but would be
allowed to supply South Vietnam with replacements for worn-out
weapons. Prisoners of war on both sides would be freed, including about 560 known Americans. The beleaguered South Vietnam government would be allowed to remain under the despotic
President Thieu, supported by the United States. Ominously, the
North Vietnamese still occupied a substantial part of South Vietnam, and were allowed to retain there some 145,000 troops, probably to spearhead the new overwhelming offensive that ultimately
prevailed in 1975.

Nixon evidently labored under the common delusion that
the United States had won all of its wars in the past, and he
desperately did not want to go down in history—way down—as
the President who had presided over the nation's first lost war.
Accordingly, he hailed the lopsided cease-fire terms as "peace
with honor." He evidently meant that the nation had secured
peace without having to be chased out of Vietnam in disgrace.
Critics, both in the United States and in Canada, cried out that
Tricky Dick was simply up to his old tricks of pulling wool over
peoples' eyes.

The truth is that peace, whether with or without honor, did
not come to Vietnam then or the years following. The cease-fire
was daily violated from the time of its signing, and at least 50,000
Vietnamese were reportedly killed during the first year of the
"peace with honor." Nixon evidently sent President Thieu a reassuring letter on White House stationery promising to come to
the aid of South Vietnam, presumably with aerial and naval
forces, if the North Vietnamese should attack again.

We recall that as far back as April 29, 1970, without consulting Congress, Nixon had ordered American troops to strike at
Communist supply bases and staging areas in neighboring Cambodia. This incursion made military sense, and evidently came
within the purview of the Tonkin Gulf resolution, which Congress did not repeal until June 1971. The "doves" in the United
States, especially the aroused college students, resorted to arson

and riots, and the police and armed forces retaliated. The worst incident involved the deliberate shooting and killing of four students at Kent State University by the National Guard, May 4, 1970. Nixon promised that the Cambodian incursion would be limited to the border area and that soon the American troops would be withdrawn, as they were after some two months.

About three years later, in July 1973, the American people were shocked to learn that, unknown to them, the Nixon administration had already secretly conducted some 3,500 bombing raids against North Vietnamese positions in neighboring Cambodia. These forays had started in March 1969, and had continued for 14 months prior to the incursion by American troops in 1970. Evidently the menaced Cambodian government had proved cooperative. Also Nixon had privately notified a few hawkish leaders of Congress, as though the concession would take care of all the formalities.

To many Americans, Tricky Dick seemed to be running true to form in the secretive bombing of Cambodia. All the while that many tons of explosives were being dropped, American officials, including President Nixon, were avowing that Cambodian neutrality was being respected. Sensitive Americans wondered what kind of representative government they had when they were supporting a private war that they knew nothing about and probably would have opposed if informed of its existence.

Congress finally rose in its wrath and, using the power of appropriations, forced Nixon to put an end to the aerial bombing of Cambodia, which by 1973 was being carried out with no pretense of concealment. The President had obviously stretched his warmaking powers unacceptably, but he rather speciously contended that the crushing of the Communists in Cambodia was in support of the Vietnam cease-fire, which the United States had committed itself to uphold. In the end Congress literally compelled Nixon to terminate the bombing of Cambodia after a six-week delay. Thereafter he was to seek Congressional approval of any future bombings in that unfortunate country.

Nixon did not have long to enjoy his smashing reelection triumph of 1972. It became indelibly besmirched by the Watergate-connected scandals, growing out of a bungled Republican burglary (June 1972) of the Democratic national headquarters in Washington, located in the Watergate apartment-office complex. Five men were arrested inside the building with their electronic "bugging" equipment and were subsequently sentenced to prison. They were being employed by CREEP—the acronym for the Committee for the Re-election of the President. These professional fund-raisers managed to amass tens of millions of dollars, often by secretive, unethical, or unlawful means. The personal attorney of the President, Herbert W. Kalmbach, promised a diplomat a better assignment in return for a contribution of $100,000. Nixon himself kept an anxious eye on CREEP, for he preferred to raise too much money rather than just enough. He well remembered his painfully narrow loss to Kennedy in 1960.

Among other activities, CREEP put the pressure on giant corporations or officials of these corporations, many of which either did business for the government or hoped that they would. A score or so of such benefactors had made unlawful contributions in the range of $100,000, and subsequently were assessed relatively light fines for their felonious purchase of future favors. Republican agents also engaged in a campaign of "dirty tricks," including unethical espionage, sabotage, and faked documents, all designed to undercut Democratic candidates in the campaign of 1972. Of course, in this particular area the Democrats did not have completely clean hands. Yet the head Republican "trickster" pleaded guilty and served a short prison term because he had worked with 28 agents in 12 states. They had planted "stink bombs" and had faked a letter in which a United States senator accused two colleagues of sexual misconduct. One Republican "trickster" forged an official telegram that falsely implicated former President Kennedy in the plot to murder the South Vietnamese Prime Minister Ngo Dinh Diem in 1963.

The bungled Watergate burglary proved to be but the tip of the iceberg in the slimy sea of corruption known as Nixon's Washington. A number of prominent White House officials and advisers were compelled to resign or serve time in prison or both. Many were implicated in a criminal obstruction of justice by bungled cover-ups or the payment of hush money. By 1974, 29 individuals had been indicted, had pleaded guilty, or had been convicted of Watergate-related crimes. Among those found guilty of illegal acts, some not related to Watergate, were Nixon's White House chief of staff, his chief domestic adviser, two men chosen to be Attorney General, three White House counselors, Nixon's personal attorney, the chairman of his campaign finance organization, his deputy campaign manager, and his appointments secretary.

Also involved in the Watergate scandals was the improper use by the Nixon administration of the Federal Bureau of Investigation and the Central Intelligence Agency. Additionally, the Internal Revenue Service was employed by Nixon or his aides to audit or otherwise harass political opponents or other persons who had incurred the disfavor or wrath of the Nixon administration. A White House "enemies list" turned up, including innocent citizens who were to be vengefully hounded in various ways, including audits of income taxes, by officials of the government that they had elected to protect their interests. Again the question was asked: Is the President an employee and servant of the people or their master?

Secretly invoking national security, Nixon had authorized a "plumbers' unit" to stop leaks of classified information. A prime offender was Dr. Daniel Ellsberg, and the "plumbers" resorted to a fruitless but sensational burglary of the office and files of his psychiatrist. Altogether Nixon ordered that the telephones of 17 government employees be tapped, all without a court order.

In May 1973, a prominent Senate committee began a televised probe that headlined a former White House aide, John Dean. He testified at length on the involvement of the President or his aides in the cover-up of the Watergate break-in, including the authorization of "hush money." This testimony directly implicated the President in the serious crime of obstructing justice. The possibility of confirming this charge became a probability when the Senate committee, to its surprise, learned from a White House witness that Nixon had installed tape recorders in his official quarters. He evidently had preserved all conversations, whether in person or on the telephone, without informing the other party as to the presence of the "bugging devices."

To preserve for posterity the frank comments of callers or visitors at the White House without their knowledge or consent is not a federal crime, although some states have passed legislation designed to curb this practice. The claim was made that President Johnson had done so, and had recommended the practice to Nixon. In fact, there are occasions when the president may find it useful to check his memory against what he or his caller had actually said. But the Senate committee was eager to examine the tapes for confirmation of Dean's testimony as to President Nixon's part in the serious crime of obstructing justice by the Watergate cover-up.

Nixon would have saved himself much agony if he had

burned all of the White House tapes as soon as their existence was known. But he flatly refused to turn them over to the Senate committee, taking refuge behind such shelters as "executive privilege" (confidentiality) and the constitutional separation of powers between the executive and legislative branches. His unwillingness to lay bare the evidence seemed to countless American citizens as proof that there was evidence on the tapes (as indeed there was) of his having been involved in the crime of obstructing justice in pressing for the Watergate cover-up.

In several televised reports or appeals to the nation Nixon did not tell the complete truth. In fact, he lied. Forced to yield the tapes, he made a dramatic plea on television, April 29, 1974, before a pile of delusive folders. He declared that the relevant tapes were all there and that they would further prove him innocent of wrongdoing. In fact, they were not all there and they did not prove him innocent of the most damning charges.

The issue of handing over all the tapes finally reached the Supreme Court, with its considerable number of Nixon appointees. The justices ruled unanimously, on July 24, 1974, that the President had no right, under executive privilege, to hold back from the special prosecutor those portions of the 64 tapes that presumably involved relevant criminal activity. Nixon was forced to knuckle under.

Concurrently the House Judiciary Committee pressed ahead with its articles of impeachment for "high crimes and misdemeanors." Late in July 1974 it passed its first article of indictment, charging obstruction of "the administration of justice," including Watergate-related crimes. The vote was 27 to 11, with all of the Democrats and about half of the Republicans supporting impeachment. Only one article of impeachment was needed for action by the full House, although two others were later added accusing Nixon of having abused the powers of his office and of having been guilty of contempt of Congress by ignoring lawful subpoenas for relevant tapes and other evidence. Informed observers were absolutely certain that the first article of impeachment, at least, would be approved by the House, leaving to the Senate the disagreeable task of finding Nixon guilty or not guilty of impeachable offenses.

Seeking to cushion the impact of imminent disclosures, Nixon made public three subpoenaed tapes of conversations with a chief aide shortly after the Watergate break-in. One conversation evidently had the President giving orders to the Central Intelligence Agency, six days after the burglary, to hold back an investigation of Watergate-related crimes by the Federal Bureau of Investigation. Blocking a criminal investigation was in itself a blatant obstruction of justice, and Nixon, as the phrase went, was seemingly left with a "smoking pistol" in his hand. Leaders of his own Republican party came to him and told him bluntly that he had no chance of escaping removal by vote of the Senate. If convicted, he would lose his normal retirement benefits; if he resigned, they reportedly would amount to more than $150,000 a year.

In a dramatic farewell address on television, August 8, 1974, Nixon admitted having made some "judgments" that "were wrong," but insisted that he had always had the best interests of the nation at heart. Artfully ignoring his imminent conviction by the Senate, he declared that he was resigning because he had lost his "political base in Congress" so essential to carrying out his duties as President. Tricky Dick to the end, he acted as though the United States enjoyed a parliamentary form of government like Great Britain.

In subsequent months Nixon claimed, in writing and on television, that the President is above the law, and that when he commits a supposed crime in the national interest, it is not a crime, and that he should be commended, not crucified. Lincoln, he pointed out, had been enough of a statesman to rise above the Constitution and override the law of the land, confronted as he was by the terribly divisive Civil War. Nixon pointed out that he himself had been President during the Vietnam War, and that there had been serious internal disorders and massive demonstrations. He did not add that the internal convulsion during his presidency was only remotely comparable to Lincoln's.

There was undoubtedly partisanship in the House proceedings against Nixon. The Democratic majority on the investigating committee solidly backed the impeachment charges, interpreting Nixon's conduct as constituting high crimes and misdemeanors. Actually, high crimes and misdemeanors are whatever a majority of the House of Representatives judges them to be. But some Republicans, recognizing that their support for the slippery Nixon would do them no good with the voters, reluctantly supported the impeachment proceedings. A number of Nixon's subordinates, including his two chief White House aides and his

Attorney General, served terms in prison while the chief conspir-ator enjoyed the freedom of his palatial California home.

In retirement, Nixon continued to insist that as President he had broken no laws, for the President is always above the law. Democrats in general did not agree, but many Republicans sin-cerely believed that their hero had been railroaded out of office.

The House Judiciary Committee, heavily loaded with Demo-crats filled with righteous indignation, had evidently been out to get Nixon's scalp. The Republicans had generally defended their harassed leader with vigor. Yet part of a minority committee re-port, signed by 10 of the 17 Republican members, denied that Nixon had been maliciously "hounded from office." These good Republicans pointed out that it was Nixon who had "impeded the FBI's investigation of the Watergate affair by wrongfully attempt-ing to implicate the Central Intelligence Agency"; that he had concealed the "terrible import" of this transgression from his own counsel; and that a unanimous decision of the Supreme Court (including Nixon appointees) had forced Nixon to turn over the incriminating evidence.

Only the House Judiciary Committee approved the charges to be brought against Nixon, for the full House never voted to impeach him. If it had done so, the Senate would have assumed the duty of convicting or acquitting him of "high crimes and misdemeanors." This sidetracking of the actual trial was probably all for the best, because unseemly partisanship would inevitably have entered into the final decision.

As for crime and the courts, often overlooked was the deci-sive action of the State Supreme Court of the State of New York, Appellate Division, on July 8, 1976, in a 4 to 1 decision. At issue was the uncontested and permanent disbarment of Nixon as a lawyer in the State of New York—the most severe penalty that this court could impose. Nixon had twice tried to resign from the New York bar, without admitting any misconduct, but these at-tempts to cut loose were blocked by the New York City Bar Asso-ciation, whose rules prohibited a resignation by a defendant under investigation by its grievance committee. In its resounding opinion upholding disbarment the court indicated that its deci-sion was sustained by five specifications presented by the prose-cution and published in *The New York Times* (July 9, 1976) but not in the proceedings of the court.

"Mr. Nixon improperly obstructed an investigation by the

Federal Bureau of Investigation into the unlawful entry into the headquarters of the Democratic National Committee in Washington on June 17, 1972.

"He improperly approved the surreptitious payment of money to E. Howard Hunt, who was indicted in connection with the break-in.

"He improperly concealed and encouraged others to conceal evidence relating to unlawful activities of members of his staff and the Committee to Re-Elect the President.

"He improperly engaged in conduct that interfered with the legal defense of Mr. Ellsberg, who was on trial in Los Angeles on charges arising from the publication of the Pentagon Papers in 1971.

"He improperly attempted to obstruct an investigation by the Justice Department into the unlawful entry into the offices of Dr. Lewis Fielding, a Beverly Hills, Calif. psychiatrist who had treated Mr. Ellsberg."

Nor should it be forgotten that in 1974 a grand jury named Nixon as an unindicted conspirator in the Watergate cover-up. Neither this body nor the New York Supreme Court regarded the President as above the law, although he believed, or at least argued, otherwise.

Critics of Nixon charged that he was a greedy man, and this acquisitive trait probably had evolved from the straitened circumstances in which he had been reared. During the course of the various probes, the following circumstances were revealed:

On April 3, 1974, the Internal Revenue Service announced that Nixon owed $432,787 in back taxes, plus another $33,000 in interest penalties. Nixon had made a deductible gift of what were reputed to be his vice presidential papers. Many of them were of little worth, especially the numerous refusals to accept speaking engagements. Yet a hand-picked appraiser had advised so large an income tax deduction that he was prosecuted and convicted, as was one other tax consultant.

The federal government, largely for purposes of presidential security, had built improvements at Nixon's homes in Florida and California, altogether worth $17 million, according to a House committee. Yet Nixon evidently made no real effort to reimburse the federal government properly when he sold all these holdings at an inflated figure. He probably concluded that these expensive security arrangements were a well-earned part of his job. A more scrupulous ex-president, like George Washington, probably would have returned these windfalls to the government when he sold the properties.

Defenders of Nixon claimed that Lyndon Johnson and John Kennedy had bugged White House conversations (which was no crime), and had overstepped the bounds of propriety in using the FBI and the CIA to harass honest citizens who were also taxpayers. But the "you're another argument" does not get us far. Nixon's predecessors had sinned, if indeed they had sinned, on a relatively small scale, and more important, they had not been caught in blatantly interfering with the course of justice. The Nixon administration was so riddled with wrongdoing as to threaten the democratic form of government itself. The scandals of the Grant and Harding administrations pale into insignificance when compared with those of the Nixon era.

The Supreme Court of the State of New York evidently did not believe that Richard Nixon of the New York bar was above the law. The culprit must have felt a considerable sense of relief when his successor, President Ford, after about a month in office (September 8, 1974) pardoned Nixon for all the crimes ("offenses") against the United States that he "may have committed or taken part in" during his presidency. An ex-president still under fire could hardly have asked for more. One wonders what the thoughts must have been of the men who were still in jail for having loyally carried out the policies or orders of their chief.

CHAPTER 37

Gerald R. Ford
1974–1977

I do believe, with all my heart and mind and spirit, that I, not as President but as
a humble servant of God, will receive justice without mercy if I fail to show mercy.

> Gerald R. Ford, on pardon of
> Richard M. Nixon,
> September 8, 1974

President Ford was unique in being the first Chief Executive to come to the White House after an "appointment" to the vice presidency under the new Twenty-fifth Amendment of 1967. The incumbent vice president, Spiro Agnew, had been forced to resign after being accused of taking bribes or "kickbacks" from Maryland contractors while governor of Maryland and also as vice president of the United States.

Not many citizens had thought seriously of Ford as presidential timber before he became the first non-elected vice president. A football star at the University of Michigan, he was widely but unfairly stereotyped by political foes as just another "dumb football jock." He had also graduated from the Yale University Law School, and had become a twelve-term Congressman from Grand

Rapids, Michigan. As the Republican House minority leader, he had received much partisan training in obstructing Democratic programs. Even after the damning Watergate evidence had been revealed, he at first continued to defend Nixon's innocence in appearances before the public. Yet his reputation for honesty and integrity remained high.

For what it is worth, Nixon informs us in his memoirs that Ford was his fourth choice for vice president, ranking behind Nelson Rockefeller, Ronald Reagan, and John Connally, but Nixon concluded that Congressman Gerald R. Ford would most easily be confirmed by Congress without causing serious internal dissension within the Republican party. The country wanted no more Watergate scandals, and Ford's nomination triggered a meticulous Congressional probe of the nominee's private life. Jerry Ford emerged as "Mr. Clean."

At the outset of his administration, Ford addressed Congress, in which he had many friends and where he commanded much respect as a person. He asked for a "good marriage" rather than a prolonged "honeymoon," but actually got neither. The Congress was heavily Democratic, and partisanship repeatedly reared its bloated face. What honeymoon there was ended after about a month, when President Ford granted his predecessor a "full, free, and absolute pardon" for "all offenses against the United States which he, Richard Nixon, has committed or may have committed or taken part in" during his presidency. In view of the public suspicion that much dirt remained to be uncovered, this blanket forgiving of yet undiscovered sins seemed to many to be going much too far.

President Ford resolutely appeared on television to explain the reasons for a step that he had reason to believe would prove highly objectionable to millions of anti-Nixonites. First, many months and perhaps years would have to pass before Nixon could get a fair trial in the courts of the United States. After the nation had long been convulsed by angry passions and after free institutions had been undermined, "the courts might well hold that Richard Nixon had been denied due process," and the prolonged national convulsion would have been in vain. Ford's conscience told him that mercy was in order, and that the very health of the country and its free institutions required that current and prospective passions be allowed to cool. Finally, Ford declared, "Richard Nixon and his loved ones have suffered enough and will continue to suffer, no matter what I do" or what the American people do.

Nixon promptly accepted the all-inclusive pardon but was careful not to confess that he had committed any crimes. Mistakes, indecision, poor judgment, yes, but crimes, no. And all this had occurred in line of duty while he was doing what he thought was best for the country. President Ford himself explained that mere acceptance of the pardon was "tantamount to an admission of guilt."

President Ford evidently expected considerable dissent from those Democrats who longed to lodge Nixon in jail, especially those people who had changed the song, "Hail to the Chief" to "Jail to the Chief." But Ford was not braced for the frightening uproar that followed. A host of citizens leaped to the conclusion that Ford was merely carrying out a "buddy deal" in which Nixon had promised to make Ford the vice president and then resign. Thereupon Ford would issue a blanket pardon as a part of the deal. To a nation of people who were partly descended from horse-traders, this seemed to be an entirely believable explanation.

All uproars ultimately die down, and this one was no exception. Ford appeared voluntarily before a Congressional committee to deny that the pardon had been secretly pre-arranged. Technically, he may have been right, but the existence of an unwritten and unspoken understanding remained within the realm of possibility.

After all, Ford was going to be handed the presidency, which was the richest single reward that an American politician could bestow upon an ambitious member of Congress. Nixon may have been clever enough not to bring up the subject of pardons and thus compromise his successor, who was a man of honor. Neither man could have been so ignorant of the Constitution of the United States as not to know that the chief executive was clothed with extensive pardoning power. Under these circumstances, Ford may have believed that in taking the high office he was assuming a moral obligation to reciprocate with the one favor that Nixon needed most and one that his successor was empowered to give him. A written agreement, or even an oral one, was not really needed.

Thus the chief culprit, living in kingly retirement, went completely free, except for the bearable burden of shame and dishonor. At the same time, a considerable number of Nixon's aides and close associates languished in jail for having carried out his illegal orders or otherwise giving him support. The public clamor had died down to some degree by the time Ford ran for reelection in his own right, but those who felt that Nixon had got off too easily were able to vent their frustration at the polls in 1976. The popular vote for Jimmy Carter was 51 percent to 48 for Ford. The loser told the press that, in his judgment, the decision to pardon Nixon cost him enough votes to account for the victor's triumph. This explanation seems plausible, although we shall never know for certain.

Early in 1975, the North Vietnamese launched their long-expected drive southward, driving their South Vietnamese foes in panic before them. True to Nixon's long-term commitment, President Ford honorably urged the sending of more military supplies, but this attempt further to salvage America's honor came too late. In April 1975, the last American officials were frantically helicoptered out of Saigon. President Ford, feeling a strong responsibility for the pro-American Vietnamese who had incurred the wrath of the North Vietnamese, arranged to admit some 140,000 refugees to the United States.

Ford's great contribution as President was to restore credibility and respectability to the Republican party, which came near to being permanently engulfed by the scandals that had proliferated during the stewardship of President Richard M. Nixon. Nominated in his own right for the presidency in 1976, Ford fell into a trap of his own making in one of his three joint "debates" with Jimmy Carter. Reference was made in the second contest to the Soviet satellite nations in Eastern Europe, including Poland and Czechoslovakia, and Ford proclaimed emphatically, "There is no Soviet domination of Eastern Europe, and there never will be under a Ford administration."

The truth is that the Soviet Union dominated its satellites in Eastern Europe, as all the world knows. Ford could not have been guilty of a mere slip of the tongue, for he resolutely defended his position, partly with mistaken judgments. He had recently visited Poland and Rumania, and apparently what he had been permitted to see confirmed his appraisal.

An alert Jimmy Carter was quick to take advantage of his opponent's blunder. He responded by saying, "And I would like to see Mr. Ford convince the Polish-Americans and the Czech-

Americans and the Hungarian-Americans in this country that those countries don't live under the domination and supervision of the Soviet Union behind the iron curtain."

Ford's offending of hundreds of thousands of American voters who had ethnic ties behind the iron curtain may in itself have been enough of a blunder to cost him election. After all, he lost the popular vote by only a two percent margin. He tells us in his autobiography, *A Time to Heal,* that he had meant to say, "Although the Soviet Union dominated Polish territory by stationing troops there, it didn't dominate the heart, soul and spirit of the Polish people."

Doubts will still remain as to the credibility of Ford's explanation. At the time he made the blunder, he seemed to be in possession of all his faculties, and may have spoken out of ignorance, thus confirming the stereotype of a "dumb football player."

Probably Gerald R. Ford will never be judged one of the great Presidents. Never elected to that high office, he served only about two and one-half years. His most spectacular and popular feat was to rescue from Cambodian clutches 39 American seamen from the *Mayaguez,* at a cost of 41 American service men. More important, he restored respectability to a Republican party that was careening down the road to the Federalist-Whig cemetery. This, in itself, was no mean achievement.

CHAPTER 38

James Earl Carter
1977–1981

I don't intend to break a single promise. I'm giving you my word of honor.

Jimmy Carter, speech in campaign
of 1976

A virtual unknown nationally, Jimmy Carter of Plains, Georgia, managed to work his way up into the White House in 1977. Ranking high among his personal assets were a gracious manner, a soft-spoken Southern accent, a winning smile, and a born-again Baptist Christianity. Among his limited political assets were experience as a one-term governor of Georgia and a prolonged campaign for the Democratic presidential nomination. Out on the stump he gave voice to numerous and repeated assurances as to needed changes and reforms. These hope-giving projections into the future were later referred to by critics, chiefly Republicans, as hard and fast "promises." When fulfillment did not come, as disturbingly often it did not, Carter was branded a liar, although he had earnestly promised not to lie to the voters.

Veteran politicians well know that "promises" dangled in party platforms and political speeches are aspirations rather than iron-clad pledges. The hope is that they can be carried out, provided that conditions are favorable and that Congress is cooperative. Often it is not, as Carter soon discovered to his sorrow. In 1980 the White House compiled a list of 660 Carter promises, indicating that the President had already kept many and was working hard on the remainder. The Republican scorecard for Carter was much less favorable.

Some of Carter's "promises" clashed with one another, and on occasion he was forced to settle for the lesser evil. He arrived at the White House pledged to paring down the burgeoning bureaucracy, yet he introduced two monstrous new ones with tens of thousands of employees and billion-dollar budgets, namely the Department of Energy (DOE) and the Department of Education.

Carter came to the Oval Office committed to reducing both inflation and unemployment, and he conquered neither. Yet he signed a new minimum wage law that not only tended to increase monetary inflation but eliminated low-paying jobs which had been something of a boon to ill-educated blacks. Organized labor was pleased but the blacks, who had heavily supported Carter in 1976, were repelled.

As a faithful, born-again Baptist, Carter honored one promise that he had made before being elected, and that was to issue a pardon to the ten thousand or so draft evaders of the Vietnam War. President Ford had stubbornly refused to take this humane step. Carter also fought doggedly and successfully for the "giveaway" Panama Canal treaties; he evidently regarded the original acquisition of the canal zone under Teddy Roosevelt as a grievous wrong that needed to be righted. Actually Colombia had been wronged and Panama benefited, notably in the early decades.

Carter's Christian desire to uphold human rights abroad led him at the outset into some curious inconsistencies. At the beginning he openly condemned Castro's Cuba and Idi Amin's Uganda, while abruptly cutting foreign aid payments to dictatorial Uruguay, Argentina, and Ethiopia. But he conspicuously failed to take similar punitive action against dictator-ridden South Korea and the Philippines. In short, the good dictators were those that supported American policies, and the bad dictators were those who did not. Critics were quick to respond that this kind of selectivity did not befit a really righteous Baptist.

Carter's official family caused him much embarrassment by alleged misconduct. A prominent member of the White House staff was accused of misbehavior while off the job, including the sniffing of illegal cocaine. But Carter rode out his minor storm, and the alleged offender was cleared of wrongdoing. Burt Lance, Carter's personal friend from Georgia, had been named the powerful Director of the Office of Management and Budget, and this former banker soon became an object of suspicion for his freewheeling, off-the-cuff banking practices in Georgia. When Lance was forced to resign, Carter accepted the resignation of this close personal friend with great regret.

Lance and two codefendants were vigorously prosecuted on charges of improper banking practices that were even alleged to have involved the Carter peanut business. After lengthy litigation, Lance was found not guilty on some of the charges. On six other counts, the jury was deadlocked and the judge finally dismissed the indictments in June 1980 as unlikely to bring convictions. Sloppiness in banking procedures is not to be applauded, but it is not in itself a prison offense. In any event, the alleged crimes committed by underlings in the Carter administration or in Georgia were as nothing when compared with those of the Watergate-cursed Nixon regime.

President Carter was roundly criticized for his lack of effective leadership, and on balance his record of achievement was less than impressive. But the basic problem, as Franklin Roosevelt learned to his dismay, was not so much the President's lack of leadership as the absence of followership in Congress. Roosevelt had become keenly aware of this great truth in trying to lead an isolationist Congress against the dictators in the late 1930s.

One of the oldest continuing scandals in Washington is the log-rolling practice among members of Congress of voting reciprocally for the costly and often unnecessary dam and water-power projects in their respective districts. At the outset President Carter met this problem head on, but backed down substantially when he discovered that if he expected Congress to approve his pet projects he would have to go easy on theirs.

The problem is that the Chief Executives are generally professional politicians, or they soon become such; otherwise they are retired as ex-presidents. We must never forget that the president is nominated by a political party and owes allegiance to it. Most dedicated politicians will stoop to some form of deception, major or minor, to achieve their ends.

The present study is concerned primarily with the President's honesty and his avoidance of unseemly deception, not with his bad judgment or bad luck. Carter had been fully warned in advance that if he permitted the deposed Shah of Iran to enter the United States, American hostages in Iran might be seized. But the President was a humane man, and the Washington government had heavily backed the Shah's repressive regime. America's credibility with its numerous allies would be weakened if the United States turned its back on the Shah in his hour of need.

The seizure of some 50 American hostages in Iran late in 1979 triggered a mood of "stand behind the President," and Carter's ranking shot up in the polls. Word went out from the White House that the President was much too busy with the Iran crisis to go out on the campaign trail for re-election, much less meet his opponents in debate. But news quickly leaked out that he was spending many hours in the Oval Office politicking on the telephone. Evidently he was milking the Middle East crisis for all it was worth politically, and although this procedure was what any clever politician would have done, it was to some degree uncandid, especially for a born-again Baptist.

In the summer of 1980, on the eve of Carter's renomination for President, the "Billygate" affair burst into the headlines, thus greatly embarrassing the incumbent. The uproar involved Jimmy Carter's bibulous brother, Billy, whose alcoholism and eccentric conduct has caused him, in his own words, to be regarded as "a buffoon, a boob, or a wacko."

Billy had made an expense-paid trip to Libya as early as 1978, and had been honored with some gifts and a reciprocal visit from a Libyan delegation the next year. Then the news leaked out, and was confirmed by Billy himself before a Senate subcommittee in 1980, that he had received $220,000 as an initial payment on a "loan" of $500,000 from the Libyan government, all part of a private business deal that involved Libyan oil. Obviously Billy was trading on the Carter name to advance his private fortunes, and no less obviously the Libyans were hoping to exert backstairs influence on the White House. Belatedly, Billy was permitted by the Carter administration to register as an agent of a foreign government, as required to do by federal law. Prosecution for violation of this statute had been uncommon.

Other presidents have been burdened by bothersome brothers, notably Presidents Lyndon Johnson and Richard Nixon. But as this investigation ground forward, it became clear that President Carter, though not involved monetarily, had tried through his boorish brother to induce the Libyan government to persuade the Iranians to release the 50 or so American hostages. As matters stood, the United States then had no ambassador in Libya.

President Carter volunteered to appear in person before Congressional investigators, something Nixon had declined to do. He also spoke at length with seeming candor at a televised press conference of one hour. His greatest error was to have become indiscreetly involved with his irresponsible brother in trying to induce Libya to intervene in the desperate deadlock over American hostages in Iran. Yet other presidents had used unofficial agents and advisers, notably President Wilson's Colonel House. Carter had on occasion employed his sister and had sent his wife abroad to represent him in his so-called "Mom and Pop" presidency. One should also note that this alleged scandal did not involve seriously or conspicuously a member of the Chief Executive's official family.

At the worst, President Carter was indiscreet in hoping to bring pressure to bear on the Libyan government through his unpredictable brother. But such was the extent of the President's eagerness to effect the release of the American hostages in Iran. Billy Carter was examined at length under oath by a Senate subcommittee, and he appears to have used all of the large Libyan advance to discharge debts, including income tax liabilities. No evidence was forthcoming that the President himself had pocketed a penny of Billy's Libyan loan, or had ever intended to do so. Other influential Americans had been courted by the oil-rich Libyans. But the sensation-seeking press, including Republican newspapers, continued to bracket Carter's "Billygate" with Nixon's "Watergate." Significantly, the so-called scandal seems to have done little to prevent Jimmy Carter's overwhelming renomination by the Democrats in 1980.

Yet Carter, the Democratic incumbent, was defeated for re-election in November 1980 by a landslide vote for the Republican nominee, Ronald Reagan. On the eve of the balloting, the pollsters had anticipated a relatively close race. The eleventh-hour stampede to Reagan seems to have resulted primarily from alarm over the sickly state of the economy, with its feverish inflation and unemployment. Another fatal drawback was President Carter's failure to secure the release of the American hostages in Iran sooner, rather than on the same day Ronald Reagan was sworn in as the new President, on January 20, 1981.

CHAPTER **39**

Summary and Conclusions

Most of the presidents have been men of integrity, although on occasion a few have wandered conspicuously from the straight and narrow path of righteousness into the bypaths of deception, usually in pursuit of what they conceived to be the national interest. President Polk, a master prevaricator, seized and kept the priceless Mexican cession, which in turn contributed to bringing on the Civil War and ultimately the flood of illegal Mexican immigrants. Oftentimes the presidents, although not one-termer Polk, have conceived of the national interest as being in part their re-election.

Franklin Roosevelt resorted to considerable deception of the American people, confronted as he was with an extremely vocal isolationist minority. His policies enabled the United States to enter and win the war to curb the dictators, at least temporarily, and his most faithful supporters claim that this interventionist course was in the national interest.

Most presidents have been elevated to the highest office by their political party, and politics is traditionally dirty business. Many of the incumbents have played politics to pull wool over the eyes of the voters and secure the endorsement of a re-election. The election year candidate often plays to the galleries, whatever the issue. George Washington did not govern with one eye on the ballot box, but organized national parties were yet unknown when he first took office, and he did not want the presidency in the first place.

Bull-headed "Old Grover" Cleveland operated on the principle of "politics be damned," which in the long term may be the best politics, though not in the eyes of professional politicians. Although defeated for re-election in the Electoral College in 1888, Cleveland was sufficiently esteemed to win a popular plurality in three consecutive presidential elections. Inflexible political courage is such a rarity that many Americans greatly admire it on those rather rare occasions when they see it.

Most presidents have perceived that the donor of a gift of great value often expects a hard-to-refuse favor in return. President Eisenhower, though probably not seduced, graciously accepted gifts of considerable monetary value for his Gettysburg farm. Most of these may have been expressions of gratitude to a beloved war hero who had led the Allied armies to victory in 1945. Yet there were partisan critics who felt that the exalted occupant of the White House should be above the slightest suspicion.

A great majority of the presidents appear to have been money-honest, despite the fact that high salaries and handsome pensions are a relatively recent icing on the cake. Harry S. Truman rejoiced that he had family land near Independence (Missouri) that he could use to fall back on. Richard M. Nixon, who was often described by critics as a greedy man, tried unsuccessfully to gain some $330,000 through unacceptable income tax deductions, and he directly benefited from large-scale government improvements on his private properties. His presidential pension benefits amounted to more than $150,000 annually.

Following the coming of air transportation and the placing of airplanes and helicopters at the disposal of the White House, millions of dollars of the taxpayers' money have been spent on the transportation of family, friends, associates, and even dogs. Much money has also been expended on presidential trips involving campaign appearances, and some effort has been made to limit this kind of extravagance. But in general all such outlays are widely regarded as perquisites of the office and not in the same category with outright graft.

Obviously, the incumbent president can be more candid and predisposed to do what is right, rather than what is politically expedient, if he does not crave the accolade of reelection. How often we hear that the president cannot propose needed legislation and the Congress cannot act on it because the timing involves an election year. Members of the House are elected or re-elected for two-year terms, even in the year of the presidential election, when "presidential paralysis" sets in. From this point of view there is something to be said for a single six-year term for the President, without the possibility of re-election. One term of four years is generally judged not long enough for the incumbent to redeem his "platform promises" and his personal promises.

The constitution of the Southern Confederacy in 1861 provided for a six-year term for president, without the possibility of re-election. This reference to bygone days is helpful only in revealing Confederate recognition of election year paralysis for the chief executive, but that is about all. The Confederacy lasted only four years.

The chief objection to the six-year incumbency is that the person elected may turn out to be intolerably incompetent, prematurely senile, or even mentally deranged. Yet one advantage of reelecting a six-year incumbent is that for six years he can govern in the interests of the nation rather than in those of his party or himself. He will also have had six precious years of on-the-job training and there would be less effective pressure on him (or her) to resort to deceptions and other wiles designed to render the incumbent party more electable.

In retrospect, the overwhelming number of American presidents have been men of integrity as far as money-honesty is concerned. Virtually none of them has been deemed guilty of any large-scale attempt to filch funds from the Treasury to fatten his own bank accounts. Most of the black marks have been inflicted by untrustworthy subordinates or by the incumbent's playing politics in what are conceived to be, often erroneously, the best interests of himself, his party, or even his nation.

A careful observer must conclude that the American electorate does not generally applaud devious or otherwise dishonest dealings on the part of their chief executive, his appointees or his associates. But partisanship aside, most potential voters usually do not go overboard in their manifestations of displeasure. This is a remarkable phenomenon.

When President Nixon was forced out of the White House

rather than face removal by the Senate on impeachment charges, he could claim an immense body of loyal Republican backers. These partisans, unwilling to face damning realities, counter-charged that the impeachment move was "all politics" and that Nixon had really done nothing that his more recent predecessors had not done with impunity. This defense turned out to be par-tially true, yet these previous presidential sinners had been lucky enough to avoid the same kind of exposure during their occu-pancy of the White House.

At other times the Republicans have enjoyed better luck. They renominated Lincoln in 1864, although during the ongoing Civil War their candidate had overridden the Constitution and flouted personal liberties in order to restore the Union. After considerable uncertainty "old Abe" finally won re-election over a Democratic general, George B. McClellan, whom he had earlier relieved of his command.

The Republicans were even more fortunate in riding out the scandals spawned during the era of the inept President Grant. Despite the blackened White House, this naive war hero was triumphantly re-elected in 1872, and came close to being formally nominated in 1880 for a third non-consecutive term.

Luck was still riding with the Republicans when they nomi-nated and elected Calvin Coolidge in 1924, thus seeking to restore respectability to a party that had been scalded by Teapot Dome and other scandals of the graft-blighted Harding administration. Despite all the hammering on Teapot Dome, Coolidge was re-soundingly elected. A cynic would be tempted to conclude that there have been times when stealing under the government's aegis was profitable financially and acceptable politically, at least to many people.

President Polk, as earlier observed, slyly provoked war with Mexico and then grabbed about half of that nation's territory, thus providing a noteworthy example of how nothing succeeds like success. President Harry S. Truman, himself a dabbler in history, rated Polk as one of the greatest of all the Presidents. Professional historians do not give Polk such high marks.

President Franklin Roosevelt, as we have noted, repeatedly deceived the American people in striving to shape events for their own good, or what he deemed their good, notably in getting aid to Great Britain to fight off Hitler. He was overwhelmingly elected four consecutive times and died in the harness. Critics branded him a "gay deceiver" who tried to "do good by stealth" by saying in effect that "father knows best."

Clearly an immense segment of the population of voting age does not particularly care if the president is less than candid or even dishonest. Otherwise these citizens would manifest their displeasure at the polling booth or by not voting. Many of them reason—if they reason at all—that crookedness is inevitable in politics; that platform promises are made to be broken; and that all true politicians, including congressmen and presidents, engage in some form of deception, chiseling, or graft, usually on an inconspicuous scale. Such irregularities are commonly regarded as an inevitable part of political life. But one aspect of the Nixon uproar that especially caught the public eye was the uncovering of an "enemies list," as though the government was the prosecutor rather than the protector of the people.

Dishonesty can come in various forms and guises. President Polk, for example, supported the Democratic platform of 1844 which declared that America's claim to the Oregon territory was "clear and unquestionable." As a matter of fact, the title was not unquestionable. Polk also proclaimed that Mexico had forced a war on the United States, when in reality the reverse was the case. Many, if not most, Americans evidently believed him, or wanted to, partly because it was "patriotic" to do so.

Dishonesty regarding money matters—money-honesty—is generally objectionable, possibly because the workaday American can relate to dollars more readily than to deception. President Nixon was not forced out of office primarily because of his personal financial dealings, but, as we have seen, many of his critics were especially shocked to learn how much he owed the government in back taxes and how much his private real estate holdings had increased in value, largely as a result of improvements at the government's expense.

When Nixon was about to resign in 1974, he chose as his successor, Gerald R. Ford, a long-term member of the House of Representatives. Congressional investigators, as obligated to do by the new Twenty-fifth Amendment to the Constitution, undertook an incredibly careful examination of the nominee's public and private life to make sure that there was no taint of scandal. They came up with nothing, so Ford was elevated to the White House.

After he had been in office about a month the new President

himself created a gigantic new scandal by issuing a pardon to Nixon for all crimes that he had committed, known or unknown, as President. Ford had solid reasons for doing what he did, but the anti-Nixon zealots were outraged by what appeared to be a pre-arranged deal. Ford denied these charges, but suspicions lingered and in 1976 they certainly contributed to his narrow defeat for election in his own right.

Jubilant Republicans welcomed the pardon of Nixon; vengeful Democrats deplored it. The conclusion is inescapable that a large body of the American people are rather indifferent to wrongdoing in the White House, especially if it involves the titular leader of their own party. Yet "eternal vigilance" is the price, as Thomas Jefferson once observed, that must be paid for liberty.

Bibliography

A bibliography is herewith appended, rather than the conventional thicket of footnotes or backnotes. The basic reason is that practically all of the major presidential scandals here dealt with were, by definition, public property and consequently were aired in the newspaper press. My task has been to put together in one book on a comparative basis the falls from grace, if any, of all the presidents. In addition to what is here listed I have made use of the classic multivolume histories of the United States, including Leonard D. White's four volume *Administrative History*. Of particular value was C. Vann Woodward, ed., *Responses of the Presidents to Charges of Misconduct* (N.Y., 1974), prepared for the House Committee on the Judiciary that was investigating President Nixon. These selections are listed without derogation of other meritorious works. A much fuller but older listing appears in Thomas A. Bailey, *Presidential Greatness* (1966).

Chapter 1. George Washington, 1789–1797

James T. Flexner, *George Washington* (4 vols., 1965–1972); D. S. Freeman, *George Washington* (7 vols., 1948–1957); Forrest McDonald, *The Presidency of George Washington* (1974).

Chapter 2. John Adams, 1797–1801

Gilbert Chinard, *Honest John Adams* (1933); S. G. Kurtz, *The Presidency of John Adams* (1957); Page Smith, *John*

Adams (2 vols., 1962); RALPH A. BROWN, *The Presidency of John Adams* (1975).

Chapter 3.   Thomas Jefferson, 1801–1809

DUMAS MALONE, *Jefferson and His Times* (5 vols., 1948–1974); M. D. PETERSON, *Thomas Jefferson and the New Nation: A Biography* (1970); FORREST MCDONALD, *The Presidency of Thomas Jefferson* (1976).

Chapter 4.   James Madison, 1809–1817

IRVING BRENT, *The Life of James Madison* (6 vols., 1948–1961) and *The Fourth President* (1970).

Chapter 5.   James Monroe, 1817–1825

WILLIAM P. CRESSON, *James Monroe* (1946); ARTHUR STYRON, *The Last of the Cocked Hats* (1945).

Chapter 6.   John Quincy Adams, 1825–1829

SAMUEL F. BEMIS, *John Quincy Adams and the Foundations of American Foreign Policy* (1949) and *John Quincy Adams and the Union* (1956).

Chapter 7.   Andrew Jackson, 1829–1837

JOHN S. BASSETT, *The Life of Andrew Jackson* (2 vols., 1928); MARQUIS JAMES, *The Life of Andrew Jackson* (2 vols., 1938).

Chapter 8.   Martin Van Buren, 1837–1841

J. C. CURTIS, *The Fox at Bay* (1970); R. V. REMINI, *Martin Van Buren and the Making of the Democratic Party* (1959).

Chapter 9.   William Henry Harrison, 1841

FREEMAN CLEAVES, *Old Tippecanoe* (1939); DOROTHY GOEBEL, *William Henry Harrison* (1926).

John Tyler, 1841–1845

OLIVER P. CHITWOOD, *John Tyler,* (1939); R. J. MORGAN, *A Whig Embattled: The Presidency Under John Tyler* (1954); ROBERT SEAGER, *And Tyler Too* (1963).

Chapter 10. James Knox Polk, 1845–1849

E. I. MCCORMAC, *James K. Polk: A Political Biography* (1922); CHARLES A. MCCOY, *Polk and the Presidency* (1960); CHARLES G. SELLERS, *James K. Polk* (2 vols., 1957–1966).

Chapter 11. Zachary Taylor, 1849–1850

BRAINERD DYER, *Zachary Taylor* (1946); HOLMAN HAMIL-
TON, *Zachary Taylor* (1966).

Chapter 12. Millard Fillmore, 1850–1853

W. E. GRIFFIS, *Millard Fillmore* (1915); ROBERT J. RAYBACK,
Millard Fillmore (1959).

Chapter 13. Franklin Pierce, 1853–1857

ROY F. NICHOLS, *Franklin Pierce: Young Hickory of the Granite Hills* (1958).

Chapter 14. James Buchanan, 1857–1861

PHILIP S. KLEIN, *President James Buchanan* (1962); ELBERT
B. SMITH, *The Presidency of James Buchanan* (1975).

Chapter 15. Abraham Lincoln, 1861–1865

RICHARD N. CURRENT, *The Lincoln Nobody Knows* (1958);
J. C. RANDALL, *Lincoln the President* (4 vols., 1945–1955);
BENJAMIN P. THOMAS, *Abraham Lincoln* (1952).

Chapter 16. Andrew Johnson, 1865–1869

E. L. MCKITRICK, *Andrew Johnson and Reconstruction*
(1960); *Andrew Johnson, A Profile* (1969); ALBERT CASTEL,
The Presidency of Andrew Johnson (1979).

Chapter 17. Ulysses Simpson Grant, 1869–1877

BRUCE CATTON, *U.S. Grant and the American Military Tradition* (1954); W. B. HESSELTINE, *Ulysses S. Grant, Politician*
(1935).

Chapter 18. Rutherford Birchard Hayes, 1877–1881

HARRY BARNARD, *Rutherford B. Hayes and His America*
(1954); H. J. ECKENRODE, *Rutherford B. Hayes: Statesman of
Reunion* (1930).

Chapter 19. James A. Garfield, 1881

R. G. CALDWELL, *James A. Garfield, Party Chieftain* (1931);
ALLAN PESKIN, *Garfield* (1978); T. C. SMITH, *The Life and
Letters of James Abram Garfield* (2 vols., 1925).

Chapter 20. Chester Alan Arthur, 1881–1885

G. F. HOWE, *Chester A. Arthur* (1934); T. C. REEVES, *Gentleman Boss* (1975).

Chapter 21. Grover Cleveland, 1885–1889

H. S. MERRILL, *Bourbon Leader: Grover Cleveland and the Democratic Party* (1957); ALLAN NEVINS, *Grover Cleveland: A Study in Courage* (1932).

Chapter 22. Benjamin Harrison, 1889–1893

HARRY J. SIEVERS, *Benjamin Harrison* (3 vols., 1952–1968).

Chapter 23. Grover Cleveland, 1893–1897

See Chapter 21.

Chapter 24. William McKinley, 1897–1901

MARGARET LEECH, *In the Days of McKinley* (1959); H. W. MORGAN, *William McKinley and His America* (1963).

Chapter 25. Theodore Roosevelt, 1901–1909

W. H. HARBAUGH, *The Life and Times of Theodore Roosevelt* (1961); EDMUND MORRIS, *The Rise of Theodore Roosevelt* (1979); HENRY F. PRINGLE, *Theodore Roosevelt: A Biography* (1931).

Chapter 26. William Howard Taft, 1909–1913

P. E. COLETTA, *The Presidency of William Howard Taft* (1973); HENRY F. PRINGLE, *The Life and Times of William Howard Taft* (2 vols., 1939).

Chapter 27. Woodrow Wilson, 1913–1921

R. S. BAKER, *Woodrow Wilson: Life and Letters* (8 vols., 1927–1939); ARTHUR LINK, *Wilson* (5 vols., 1947–1965).

Chapter 28. Warren G. Harding, 1921–1923

R. K. MURRAY, *The Harding Era* (1969); ANDREW SINCLAIR, *The Available Man* (1969); EUGENE P. TRANI AND DAVID L. WILSON, *The Presidency of Warren G. Harding* (1977).

Chapter 29. Calvin Coolidge, 1923–1929

CLAUDE M. FUESS, *Calvin Coolidge* (1940); DONALD R. McCOY, *Calvin Coolidge* (1967).

Chapter 30. Herbert Clark Hoover, 1929–1933

E. E. ROBINSON AND V. D. BORNET, *Herbert Hoover* (1975); HERBERT HOOVER, *Memoirs* (3 vols., 1951–1952).

Chapter 31. Franklin Delano Roosevelt, 1933–1945

J. M. BURNS, *Roosevelt: The Lion and the Fox* (1956) and *Roosevelt the Soldier of Freedom* (1970); FRANK FREIDEL, *Franklin D. Roosevelt* (4 vols., 1952–1973); A. M. SCHLESINGER, JR., *The Age of Roosevelt* (3 vols., 1957–1960).

Chapter 32. Harry S. Truman, 1945–1953

R. J. DONOVAN, *Conflict and Crisis: The Presidency of Harry S. Truman* (1977); HARRY S. TRUMAN, *Year of Decisions* (1955) and *Years of Trial and Hope* (1956).

Chapter 33. Dwight David Eisenhower, 1953–1961

D. D. EISENHOWER, *Mandate for Change, 1953–1956* (1963) and *Waging Peace, 1956–1961* (1965); ELMO RICHARDSON, *The Presidency of Dwight D. Eisenhower* (1979).

Chapter 34. John F. Kennedy, 1961–1963

ARTHUR M. SCHLESINGER, JR., *A Thousand Days* (1965); R. J. WATTON, *Cold War and Counter-Revolution: The Foreign Policy of John F. Kennedy* (1972).

Chapter 35. Lyndon Baines Johnson, 1963–1969

ERIC GOLDMAN, *The Tragedy of Lyndon Johnson* (1969); L. B. JOHNSON, *The Vantage Point* (1971).

Chapter 36. Richard M. Nixon, 1969–1974

R. M. NIXON, *RN: The Memoirs of Richard Nixon* (1978); GARY WILLS, *Nixon Agonistes: The Crisis of the Self-Made Man* (1970).

Chapter 37. Gerald R. Ford, 1974–1977

G. R. FORD, *A Time to Heal* (1979); CLARK MOLLENHOFF, *The Man Who Pardoned Nixon* (1976).

Chapter 38. James Earl Carter, 1977–1981

J. E. CARTER, *Why Not the Best?* (1975); DAVID KUCHARSKY, *The Man from Plains* (1976); CLARK R. MOLLENHOFF, *The President Who Failed* (1980).

Index

X

Y